AMERICAN FLAVOR

AMERICAN FLAVOR

ANDREW CARMELLINI
AND GWEN HYMAN

PHOTOGRAPHY BY QUENTIN BACON

An Imprint of HarperCollinsPublishers

All photographs by Quentin Bacon except for the following:
pages 91, 221, 293 by Michael Chan; pages 51, 69, 201 by Suet Yee Chong.

Designed by Suet Yee Chong

Library of Congress Cataloging-in-Publication Data has been applied for.

ISBN 978-0-06-196329-2

12 13 14 15 ID/QG 10 9 8 7 6 5 4 3 2

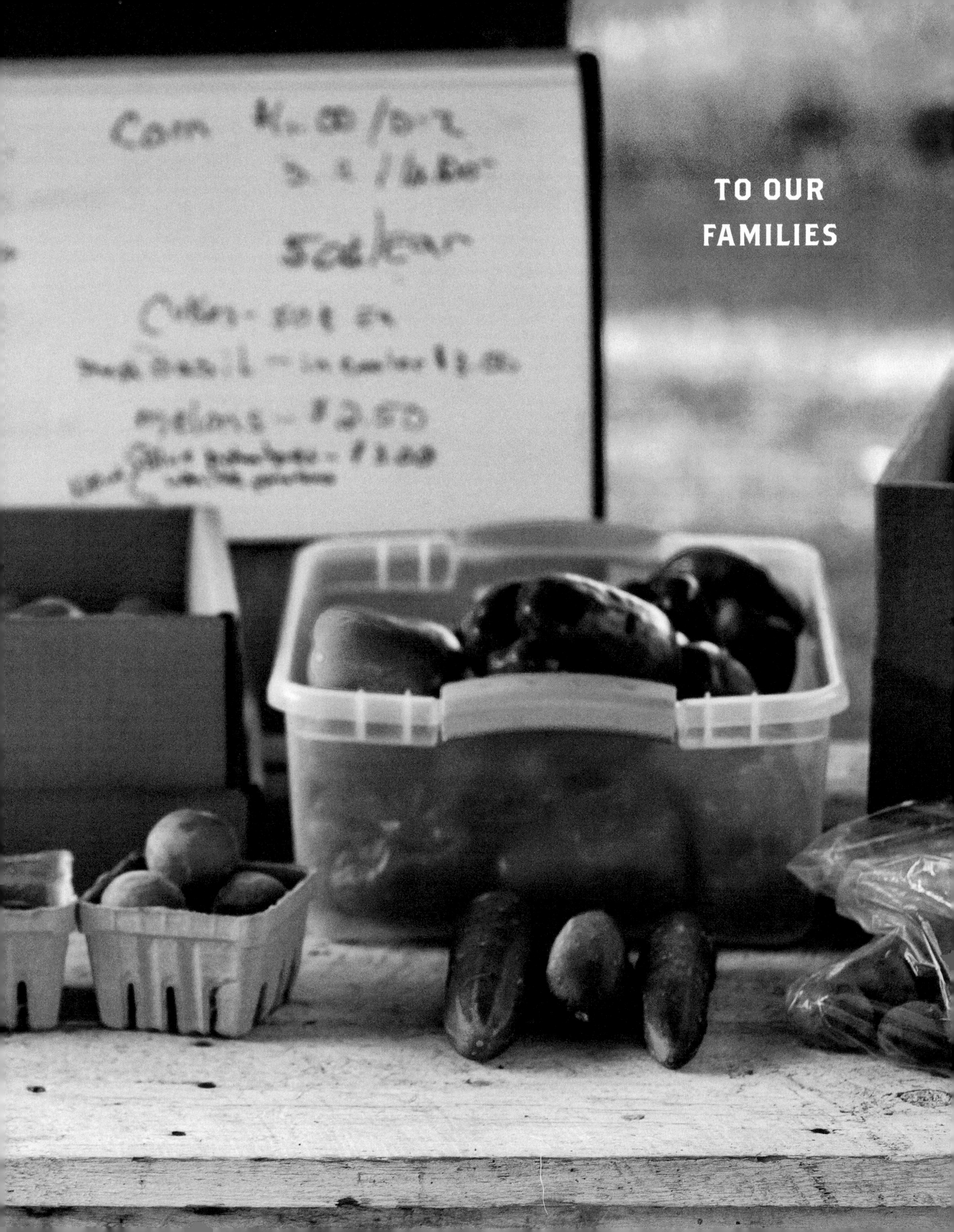

TO OUR FAMILIES

CONTENTS

WHERE THEREIS
LOVE THERE
IS LIFE
NIE
AL GUESTS:

ACKNOWLEDGMENTS

We'd like to thank . . .

Dan Halpern, fearless editor

Libby Edelson, intrepid associate editor

Kim Witherspoon, our amazing agent

Quentin Bacon, photog extraordinaire

Emily Iguchi, official sous-chef for *American Flavor*

Karen DeMasco and Kierin Baldwin, who brought the dessert ideas to life

Anthony Coffee, Julie Farias, Matt Greco, Dean Nole, and Michael Oliver, who generously passed along their family recipes

Andrew's business partners, Luke Ostrom and Josh Pickard

Margaret Marshall, Kevin Berg, John Mitchell, and Michael Fuchs, financial angels behind The Dutch

Partners at Locanda Verde: Robert De Niro, Ira Drukier, Richard Born, and Ken Friedman

Fishs Eddy for donating some of the great plates and tabletop stuff you see in this book

All the hardworking staff of Locanda Verde and the Dutch.

. . . and, of course, all of our intrepid volunteer recipe testers, whose help was so important in taking these recipes from chef-world to the real world:

    Kate Atherley and Norman Wilner

    Amy, Michael Jr., and Vincent Bandwen

    Margaret Bertin

    Margo Bertin

    Amy Blitz

    Paolo Burzese

    Victoria Carmellini

    Brad Cook

Joanne Cuffaro

Michael Derbecker and Abigail Lee

Ken Dewey and Devorah Miller

Hillary Eklund

Dorene Finer

Lisa Foley

Michal Freedhoff

Andrea Freeman

Katherine Gleason

Emma Marie Graves

Peggy Grodinsky

Claire Gunning

Beth Haviland

Samantha Heller

Joanna Holzman

Michelle Horowitz

Bryna and Gerry Hyman

Karen Hyman

Jim Lewis

Sean McGlade and Terry Fegan

Cindy Megesi

Heather Messal

Darren and Hannah Mieskowski

Amir Moosavi

Mike Moreal

Mark Moreal

Jeff Morris

Alana Richman

Adrienne and Vince Scalera

Martha Schulman

Kelly and Maura Shay

Catherine Siemann and Martin Woess

Sylvia Spader

Carol Swedlow

Laura Swedlow

Becky Varner

Carolyn Varner

Peter Waisberg

Isabella Wojcik

INTRODUCTION: STORIES FROM THE ROAD

WHEN I THINK ABOUT AMERICAN FOOD, I THINK about the road. Ever since I was a kid, I've spent a lot of time driving across the country, and that's how I learned firsthand about regional American cooking.

I'm a Midwesterner born and raised, but my dad's a Florida boy: he grew up fishing in the Miami canals, hanging out on the beach, not wearing shoes much. When he was seventeen, he moved north to Ohio to work with his uncles in the terrazzo business. After he met my mom, he decided to stay in Ohio for good—but he never got used to those flat, gray, icy Ohio winters. Every chance he got, he'd head back down south, and when I was lucky, I got to go with him. Nothing stopped him: not bad driving weather, or work, or major life events. One of my first memories is driving home from Miami with my dad and my Uncle Jimmy in my dad's yellow Pontiac Tempest—and finding a new baby in the house when we got there. My brother had been born while we were heading south.

My mom sometimes flew down to meet us in Miami, but she didn't really like to do the road trip. I can't blame her. Those trips were everything you'd expect from a two-day drive with two boys in the car, and then some: my brother and me fighting, my dad yelling at both of us, too much food in the car, not enough washing of bodies or changing of clothes. So most of the time, it was just the guys.

I loved being on the road. I used to try to stay awake, no matter how tired I was, to watch the Rust Belt winter turn into green southern endless summer. We would leave Cleveland really late at night; by the time the sun came up, we'd be in the foothills of Appalachia. Our first stop was always at a pancake house in Beckley, West Virginia. Even though we were only a couple of hundred miles away from Cleveland, that pancake house felt really foreign to me, because it served two things I could never get back home: buckwheat pancakes and fried mush. That's basically sweetened polenta, made into patties and then fried. When it's ready, you drizzle it with maple syrup and maybe some crumbled sausage meat. It was pretty much the best road food ever.

After Beckley, we'd drive straight over the Appalachian Mountains till we hit a particular rest stop in the North Carolina Piedmont. We almost never stayed in hotels: why pay for a room, my dad would say, when you can sleep in the car for free? So we'd pull off the road and sleep right there in the car, our feet hanging out the open windows. (This was back in the day when you could do stuff like that without getting your throat slit by a crazed rest-stop maniac—or at least before we knew we should be worried about crazed rest-stop maniacs.)

We'd cook on the side of the road, too. My dad had a Coleman gas-fired stove he'd haul down to Florida with us, and in the mornings we'd eat "rest-stop fry-up." That was an open-faced sandwich, just ham and eggs and bread, with maybe some coffee (I know, I know—but it didn't exactly stunt my growth, or my brother's, either). Breakfast, like most activities, usually included what my mom would call "tussling" between me and my brother, which made my dad upset; or we wouldn't clean up our mess in the back seat or on the picnic table, which also made my dad upset; or we wouldn't be ready to go when he wanted to hit the road, and that, too, made my dad upset. Once he got so mad, he threw a can of Coke at my brother. Vince ducked, and the Coke hit this big burly West Virginia trucker in the head. They almost went Swing City. It was exciting, the road.

When we got down into South Carolina, we'd hit another restaurant for dinner. By then we were into Southern cooking for real: it was all Alabama slaw, rice and gravy, country-fried steak. The weather would get warmer; we'd make our way down I75 or I95; the land would flatten out; when it got so a bump in the road counted as a hill, we were in Florida. We'd cross the Suwannee River, and then we'd stop for citrus at Boudrias Groves in Fort Pierce. We'd tried every citrus place on the road to Miami, and this one had the best stuff: grapefruits and oranges and red oranges too, and red orange juice, which was like drinking paradise. We always brought a case of fruit and a couple gallons of orange juice down to Miami, because even though it was just down the way, there was no way you could get citrus like this in the city.

We ate plenty of very local citrus in Miami, though. My grandmother's place in Little River had a double lot, and it was full of mango trees and grapefruit trees and orange trees and Cuban banana trees and sour orange trees, even a sapodilla tree. For breakfast I'd eat ripe grapefruit right off the tree, sprinkled with sugar, and after dinner, I'd have caramelized fresh-picked bananas with sugar and ice cream and a little bit of rum (my Italian family didn't exactly believe in the no-drinking-till-you're-twenty-one thing). If I was really lucky, my aunt or my grandma would make a sour orange meringue pie.

There was always fresh fish at my grandma's place, too, even though we didn't catch much of it ourselves: we didn't have the touch. We'd spend hours fishing from a bridge or off the beach; the guys on either side of us would be reeling in yellowtail snappers, and all we'd catch were sunfish. At the end of a long day of fishing, my aunt would go down to the docks and buy fish right off the boats. She'd cook up Southern feasts with my grandma just about every night when we were in Miami. My grandma's kitchen was the best joint around.

But even though the food at my grandma's place rocked, my favorite thing to do in Miami was to go out to a fancy restaurant for dinner. We'd go to Clifford's on Route 1, which was real '70s Miami fabulous: plush blue curtains, flocked velvet wallpaper, prime rib. I had stone crabs for the first time at another fancy high-'70s joint in the city, and it blew my mind. You didn't get anything like that back in Ohio, that was for sure. For me, Miami was the gastronomic Promised Land, the epicenter of culinary cool.

The ride home was rough—I hated leaving behind the sunshine and heading back into the sad, gray Ohio weather. My dad would give us a treat right near the end: in southern Ohio, we'd always stop either at the Clifton Mill, an American Inn with American Inn Fare, or at the Golden Lamb, in Lebanon, Ohio, another

Olde American Inne (really old: there was a sign say-ing Mark Twain had spent a night there). These days, the Golden Lamb has a gift shop attached to it, sell-ing Christmas ornaments and overpriced souvenirs, but back then it was *the* fancy place to have dinner. The men were in suits and ties; the women wore high heels and had their hair done. There was deep-pile carpeting, classical music, and wait staff in formal wear. My dad was a sharp dresser, and usually he was pretty strict about appropriate clothing—we always went to church in jackets and ties, we dressed up for family parties, and we cleaned up when we went out to eat. But we'd walk into the dining room at the Golden Lamb in our sweatshirts and jeans and tennis shoes after twenty-four straight hours on the road without showers or toothbrushes or pretty much any of the basics of personal hygiene. We were stinky. We were gross. People edged away. It was the best.

. . .

I LOVED EATING IN RESTAURANTS, BUT I LOVED cooking at home, too. By the time I was eight years old, I'd blown through my mom's copy of Betty Crocker and I was ready to take it to the next culinary level—but what can you do when you're an eight-year-old budding chef in Cleveland in 1979? Well, if you're really lucky, your grandma gives you a copy of *La Méthode,* the culinary bible by the great French chef Jacques Pépin. *La Méthode* is an amazing book: they just don't make 'em like this anymore. For example, my buddy Jacques shows you how to make fish that look like mushrooms, and cucumbers that look like turtles, and apples that look like swans. And the level of detail is something else. Want to make rabbit with prunes? Jacques starts by showing you how to skin the rabbit.

This was a window onto a world well beyond Betty Crocker Ghost Cakes. I'd never seen anything like it, and I was completely hooked. I worked my way through *La Méthode* and Pépin's next book, *La Tech-nique.* I didn't make everything in the books (and I didn't skin any rabbits), but I tried everything that I could possibly make in my mother's kitchen with a rea-sonable chance of not burning the house down. Peach Melba, for example. And Pommes Anna. Not every-thing worked: *oeufs à la neige*—floating islands—was an embarrassment that was luckily not documented in photography, and pâté was a disaster my family may never recover from.

But that was my fault, not Chef's. As far as I was con-cerned, Jacques Pépin was a rock star.

One day, my mom spotted an ad in the food section of the paper: Jacques Pépin was going to be doing a book signing at my local supermarket. Crazy! My mom drove me down there, and I marched into the super-market with my copies of La Méthode and La Technique under my arm, so excited I could barely talk. Jacques Pépin! Here! At Rini's Supermarket! As far as I was concerned, it was going to be like meeting Eddie Van Halen.

. . . And there he was, sitting all alone under the fluorescent lights of the produce section with a stack of books. South Cleveland housewives maneuvered their brimming shopping carts around him, trying not to look. After all, he wasn't giving out free samples. It must have been pretty surprising for the guy when this kid rolled up with copies of his books held out like offerings, tripping over his own words. I like to think he was happy to see me.

I asked the great man what it would take for me to be a great chef. He told me that either I had to go to school or I had to apprentice myself to a really accomplished chef. And he signed my copy of La Méthode.

I still have that book—it's gone everywhere with me. The inside cover reads: Sept 8 1986: to Andrew: best wishes and best of luck in your career.

Your career. What a great phrase.

. . .

I LANDED MY FIRST KITCHEN JOB WHEN I WAS a freshman in high school. I have to admit that at that point, my motivation was not entirely culinary. I was fixated on getting a car, and on driving around town with a girl in that car, and on parking with a girl in that car—and I couldn't do any of those things without the cash to acquire a car. So when I saw a posting for a weekend and after-school job at a place called The Party Joint, I called them up and told them all about how I was a seriously good cook.

The Party Joint was the kind of place that did business luncheons, weddings, and big family events. It was run by an Irish family: a husband and wife who spent all of their time screaming and yelling at each other in the kitchen, while their daughters—who were a little bit of ahead of me in high school—worked in the front. Then there was Dieter the chef, an ancient old-school German guy with slicked-back hair and a habit of smoking and drinking cooking wine while he worked the stoves.

I did everything: washed pots, ran the dishwasher, did party setup, carved steamship rounds—legs of beef—and moved cases of beer upstairs and downstairs. But the actual cooking part of the job was pretty limited. I opened up cartons of pre-peeled, pre-sliced potatoes and put them in the deep-fryer. I opened up packages of ham, put the hams on trays, dumped pre-made pineapple glaze from the bag over them, and stuck the trays in the oven. I shredded carrots for the pre-made salad. I took desserts out of boxes and put them on little white doilies. The chef did the big jobs. For example, he took the precooked turkey out of the bag and put it in the oven, to get that nice roast-turkey glaze on it.

But that was OK with me. I wasn't really there to cook. I was there to make money. Plus, this was an all-the-beer-you-can-drink kind of job. As an after-school gig, you really couldn't beat that.

And anyway, good food or not, the place was pretty busy. Weddings were our most popular events. We hosted weddings for a wide variety of south Cleveland ethnic groups—we had Italians, Irish, Poles, Hungarians, *and* Serbs. Whatever the background, the basic setup was always the same: There was a carving station with the meat-from-a-bag the chef had roasted up; on the buffet, there were iceberg salads with shredded carrots, and a big tray of the potatoes from the carton, and carrots glazed with something sweet, along with the formerly-in-the-bag ham with pineapple glaze. Then there was the ethnic stylizing: an Italian wedding included ravioli; Irish weddings got corned beef and cabbage; the Poles ate pierogies. The Slavs and Hungarians had some kind of goulash-type item. Because weddings are all about tradition!

Another big tradition in our part of town was the wedding fight. On average, one out of three weddings at the Party Joint included a significant physical altercation. One side of the family would fight the other side; or some drunken brother-in-law would get up and insult the bride, maybe question her chastity, in front of a large group of her brothers and uncles; or somebody would dance with the wrong person's girlfriend. Nobody "took it outside." This was the Midwest—it was cold outside. Instead, they fought on the dance floor, which was warmer, more conveniently located, and offered better access to booze and to furniture that could be used in an aggressive manner.

Nobody minded. It kept things interesting. The owners enjoyed fights, their own and other people's. Sometimes we placed bets.

The Party Joint was a great first job, offering me excellent experience in a wide range of skills—package opening, beer hauling, beer drinking—but by the time I was a sophomore, I was ready for new challenges. I moved on to a local Italian restaurant, where my beer-drinking skills served as a solid basis for more advanced workplace indulgences. Also, I started doing some actual cooking, with ingredients that did not come pre-prepared, in bags. That's when I realized that I could cook for four hundred people a night without breaking too much of a sweat—and that the cooking part was almost as much fun as the girls-and-beer part.

ON THE NEXT PAGE, CLOCKWISE FROM TOP LEFT: MAKING TERRINE IN FRANCE; IN TORINO, ITALY; ON THE BEACH IN MIAMI, 1976; MY FIRST ROAD TRIP; SIDE OF THE ROAD, INDIANA; DEEP-SEA FISHING IN FLORIDA; GARDENING WITH MOM; DAD WITH HIS CATCH OF THE DAY, BACK IN THE DAY; MOM'S OLD-SCHOOL BARBEQUE SAUCE.
ON PAGE 7, TOP ROW, LEFT TO RIGHT: THE CREW AT ARPEGO, 1995; IN THE BAR-ARMAGNAC REGION, FRANCE. MIDDLE ROW: IN BORDEAUX; IN THE BACKYARD WITH MOM; IN GRANDMA'S GARDEN. BOTTOM ROW, LEFT TO RIGHT: ON THE ROAD IN POTTER, NEBRASKA; IN THE PYRENEES, 1996.

GRILL

BARBECUE WINE SAUCE

1 sm. onion, finely chopped
1 clove garlic, crushed
1 cup red wine
1/2 cup water
1/2 olive oil
1/4 cup red wine vinegar
1 tsp. Worcestershire sauce

1/2 tsp. chilli sauce
1 tsp. sugar
2 tsps. french mustard
1 tsp. salt
1 tsp. paprika pepper
1/4 tsp. Tabasco sauce

Place all ingredients in saucepan & bring to the boil. Simmer for 5 minutes strain & cool Use to marinate & baste meat

From Barbecue Cookbook By: Eliz Sewell

CRITTER GITTER
PONCE INLET, FL.

IT IS OUR COUNTRY
SEE AMERICA FIRST
WMAQ 67
IT IS BEAUTIFUL
"THE MOONLIGHTS FAIR TONIGHT ALONG THE WABASH"
TERRE HAUTE, INDIANA

. . .

LATER ON THAT YEAR, MY ENGLISH TEACHER—we'll call her Mrs. Jones—gave us an assignment: write an essay on your future career. Most kids wrote about the usual stuff, but that wasn't really an option for me: I was going either to Berklee School of Music or to cooking school. I was smart enough to figure I probably shouldn't write an essay for Mrs. Jones on wanting to be a session guitarist in L.A. who partied with rock stars. So instead, I wrote about wanting to be a chef and restaurateur. Once I got started, I took the assignment pretty seriously: I detailed my past experience and my future goals; I wrote about my plans for cooking school; I talked about wanting to open my own restaurant someday; I even worked in Chef Pépin's advice. I was pretty proud. It was the most work I'd put into an English assignment since I'd done that thing on Metallica and "The Rime of the Ancient Mariner" in middle school.

Mrs. Jones gave me a C.

Now, a C wasn't a bad grade for me in English class, since mostly I spent English class thinking up ways to disrupt the proceedings and in this way get out of English class. But on this assignment, it hurt. So I took my mom's advice, and I went to talk to the teacher. I gave this little speech I'd gone over in my head about how I'd really put a lot of effort into this paper, and I didn't understand why I'd done so badly, and could she maybe read it again?

Mrs. Jones just looked at me. "I asked you to write a paper on a career," she said. "What you wrote about is just a job." Then she handed my paper right back to me.

. . .

WRITING THAT PAPER WASN'T A TOTAL WASTE, though: Mrs. Jones's response was very motivational. I wanted to prove to her in a big way that she was wrong. To do it, I needed to start getting serious about cooking. That meant taking Chef Pépin's advice. Part 1: apprentice myself to a great chef.

Sounds pretty straightforward, right?

Sure. Cleveland in the 1980s was just full of great chefs.

I didn't think it was possible, but my mom, who was also pretty unhappy about Mrs. Jones's grading system, decided to get motivated right along with me. She did some research, she talked to friends of friends, and somehow she did the undoable: she found a great chef in my hometown.

ME AND MY FRIEND JEN, 1988

Chez François, a fancy joint on the shore of Lake Erie, is still one of the best restaurants in the area. It's run by the chef, John D'Amico, and his restaurateur partner, Matt Mars. And it's not exactly a stuffy old-school place. The food is classic French, but John's always updating his game: in the slow winter season, he and Matt travel and eat everywhere, so whatever's going on in the food world is going on at Chez François.

Matt and John both love learning everything they can about food and cooking, and they're really generous about sharing that experience, too. They took on this kid from Seven Hills whose professional experience was limited to red sauce and pre-cooked roasts and put him right in the middle of the action in the kitchen. Chez François was pretty far away from my house, so rather than leaving me to figure out how to manage the commute, John and his wife even put me up at their house on weekends. I would spend all day Saturday and Sunday in the kitchen, learning firsthand about the kind of cooking I'd only seen in Jacques Pépin's book: stuffed puff pastries with Saint-André cheese; lobster thermidor; sole meunière . . . It was a whole different culinary universe, about as far as it was possible to get from The Party Joint.

And it wasn't all about high white hats and refinement. John was the first real chef I'd seen in action—and he was completely bad-ass. He didn't have a huge kitchen full of highly trained cooks: he did almost everything himself. For example, he'd be butchering sole, and he'd turn around—knife still in hand—and start making mayonnaise. He'd toss some egg yolks and mustard and vinegar and water into a KitchenAid and turn it on. When you make mayonnaise, you need to add the oil slowly to the other ingredients as they're mixing. But that took too much time, so John figured out a way to rig up the olive oil and grapeseed oil bottles next to the whisk attachment at exactly the right angle. He'd poke a hole in each bottle, and he'd just let them pour out slowly as the mayo mixed; then he'd go right back to his fish butchering. And all this was going on while he was making buttercream in another mixer—and checking on meat in the oven—and signing for deliveries from purveyors—and making sure that I wasn't completely destroying whatever it was I was working on. The man was a machine.

There weren't a lot of girls around at Chez François, but the kitchen drink was a French ale called Trois Monts, which came in 750-ml bottles, so that made up for a lot. The bar down the street let me drink with the cooks, no questions asked, and I think I still hold the high score on Defender there. Along the way I learned a lot about food, and I graduated from the John D'Amico school of Banging It Out. That was the real beginning of my life as a chef.

. . .

SO THERE I WAS, DRIVING CROSS-COUNTRY from Toronto to Vancouver in a ten-year-old gold Volvo with a couple of bikes on the roof, two weeks before I was scheduled to start work in New York.

There was, obviously, a girl involved.

I had just got back to the States after a year in Italy, and I had less than zero money. I should have headed straight back to New York, but I wanted some time to chill out, to play guitar, to take life easy. And New York in the summer? Working all day in a kitchen without air conditioning? That wasn't my idea of a smooth re-entry to American life.

Plus I wanted to make some real money, and that wasn't going to happen in a kitchen.

So I told my chef I'd start in September, and I headed home to Cleveland. And two months later, there I was: working in my friend's dad's furniture factory or sitting around my parents' house, bored out of my mind, waiting for it to be time for me to go back to the city and start my life again.

I spent a lot of time talking to my friend Mitchell, who was back home in Toronto, trying to put some money together himself so *he* could go to New York to start his life as a food writer. Or a food impresario. Or a food something. Whatever. He'd figure it out when he got there.

My life was so boring that summer that I figured even the Greyhound bus across the border was more interesting than watching my dad try to blow up the groundhog in our backyard or studying the fine points of Cleveland's basic TV service, so I went up

to see Mitchell a couple of times. He had a roommate, and it turned out this roommate was a girl, and also kind of cute. She was a vegetarian who got around town on her bike and wore flouncy miniskirts and taught swimming lessons. She was helping to direct a play that Mitchell and I went to see: something about outer-space creatures and time travel and a live rock band. It wasn't really exactly clear to me what was going on, but I think I said it was a great piece of theater.

One long, boring, cricket-filled night back in Cleveland, I called Mitchell, and the roommate picked up the phone. I said, "Hey, what's going on?" and she said, "Mitchell and I decided we're going to drive cross-country to get me to grad school in Vancouver in a couple of weeks." I packed my clothes in my guitar case and I got on a Greyhound bus. I'm a specialist in road trips. I figured they might need help.

Since every road trip has to have a goal beyond getting from here to there, we made ours the search for the Great American Breakfast. It is, after all, the holy grail of road food: perfectly fluffy eggs, a pile of pancakes-from-scratch so high you can't see over it, the freshest fresh-squeezed orange juice. Legend has it there's even good diner coffee out there, at that Shangri-La of greasy spoons where the food is killer and the truckers are friendly. Isn't that what every American who hits the road is really after? A perfect version of the most important meal of the day?

This kind of quest was a lot harder back in the day, before you could go online and, in approximately two and a half seconds, find out what a hundred million people thought about some breakfast joint in Ashton, Idaho. There were no breakfast blogs, no 1000 Days

Cookin' good

Andrew Carmellini (front) prepares sausage in the newly remodeled kitchen at Cleveland's P.M. restaurant in Valley View. Part of an $800,000 expansion project, kitchen improvements include a 40-gallon steam kettle dedicated exclusively to P.M.'s special-recipe marinara sauce; a state of the art pasta cooker and ultramodern computer-controlled oven hoods. The Granger Road eatery serves about 5,000 guests each week. A second Cleveland's P.M. is under development by owner Pete Maisano in the Flats.

of Breakfast stunt sites, no Chowhound reports. We had somebody's dog-eared copy of Jane and Michael Stern's *Roadfood,* handed down from culinary seeker to hungry cross-country driver. We had some clippings and photocopies of articles: "Breakfast in America: the Best 10"; "Restaurants of Northern Wyoming." Mostly the articles told us to go to the Four Seasons for the Sunday buffet. Any Four Seasons, really.

That wasn't exactly what we were after. So we used the force. We'd see a great old neon sign—a cowboy and a stack of pancakes, maybe, looming out of the Badlands; or "Moe's Home Cooking" in red letters on a pole a hundred feet above the grasslands—and Mitchell would say, "That's it for sure," and Gwen would say, "This one's gotta be the one," and I would pull us off the road. Or we'd ask the guy sleeping behind the desk at the Bates-esque motel we'd stayed at the night before, or the guy at the gas station, or the woman buying sodas ahead of us, who seemed to be pretty discerning from the way she didn't look at the Pepsi

or the Mountain Dew for even one second. "She's getting *root beer,*" I would whisper to Gwen and Mitchell. "She'll definitely know."

We learned one really important lesson, driving cross-country: never trust the locals.

"Go to Sally's Place on Route 5!" the woman with the root beer would say with total authority and a lot of enthusiasm. "It's the best there is! People drive *miles* for Sally's flapjacks! Miles!" She would take us there herself, she said, introduce us around, help us order—only she'd just eaten.

And so we would get in the gold Volvo and pull out onto Route 5, and there would be Sally's, in some broken-down prefab by the side of the road, with a bunch of trucks parked out front, and a blonde with a beehive hairdo hustling coffee at the tables by the window. (Two things we believed: truck drivers know where to eat, and beehive hairdos are the sign of the

375°

Cinnamon - Apple Coffee Cake

1 cup minus 1 tbsp. whole wheat flour
1 ½ tsp. baking powder
¼ tsp. salt
1 ½ tsp. cinnamon
½ cup raw sugar
1 egg
milk
½ cup safflower oil
1 apple, peeled and th...

Mix dry ingredients. Break egg into measuring cup, beat lightly and add milk to measure ½ cup. Using a knife or ... cut oil into dry mixture until well blended. Reserve 2 TBSP. Add egg mixture. Stir only till moistened. Spread batter into 8" oiled square pan. Put apple slices
20-25 min.

real deal. I mean: Flo, right? Kiss my grits? Can't go wrong!)

So we'd walk into the joint, Gwen and Mitchell and I, and you know that thing in old movies where you hear the sound of a record scratching and everything just—stops!—? Well, that's how it would be. Every single time. You could pretty much hear some old-timer with three teeth and suspicious stains on his overalls drawling, "Strangers in town, huh?"

These places always looked OK: Formica booths, a long counter, a pass-through window to the kitchen or an open griddle, waitresses in uniforms straight out of 1952. And the menus, long or short, always looked right, too: either there were a hundred things to choose from, East Coast–style, or the place would specialize. That meant twelve kinds of pancakes or seven egg dishes or whatever, plus sides. Our waitress would bang thick ceramic coffee mugs down in front of us, and she'd bark, "WhatcanIgetchoo?" in that national diner-waitress accent, Brooklyn crossed with Nashville. And we'd think, *Hey, this is gonna be . . . OK! Maybe even . . . great!* And we'd put our elbows on the Formica tabletop and wait for excellence, American-style.

And then it would appear, along with our watery coffee and our Tang-flavored orange juice: pure disappointment, American-flavored.

We tried the diner in Wyoming next to the general store that sold cattle dewormer; we tried the cafe in Kansas where all the locals, dressed in their Sunday best, watched us walk through the restaurant in our cutoffs and third-day road shirts; we tried the truck stop in Paw Paw, Michigan, where there was a trucker in every booth, every one eating a meal the size of my head at warp speed. No matter where we went, the breakfast was always the same. Pre-made waffle mix. Dehydrated milk. Eggs that came in cartons. It was like there was one big central kitchen, somewhere underneath the desert in Utah maybe, that shipped out breakfast to every diner in the country. By the time we got to Vancouver, I'd finally given up: the Great American Breakfast was a myth. It didn't exist. It was like the City of Gold, or Atlantis. Just a story to keep you going, because otherwise, how would you get up and get yourself to eat the most important meal of the day on the road every day? You would just skip it completely and go right to lunch, is what you would do.

Funny thing, though. When we finally got to Vancouver, at the end of the long and winding road of sad, sorry American breakfasts, we landed one morning at a little local place called Sophie's Cosmic Cafe, on West 4th Avenue, in a clutch of funky stores and restaurants on the edge of the Kitsilano neighborhood. It was a weekday morning, but there were crowds of hungry people outside. OK, they were locals—but there were an awful lot of them. We figured maybe we'd give the trust-the-people thing one more try. Inside there were red leatherette booths; the walls were covered with record albums from the '50s, vintage lunch boxes, stuffed animals even; the place smelled good. Of course, we knew that design meant nothing. We did not trust. We did not, even, hope. We waited. But when our order came to the table, we knew we'd stumbled, finally, on the Promised Land of morning food. There it all was: fluffy pancakes with fresh blueberries; actual egg-colored omelettes with fresh veggies and homemade sausage; flaky biscuits; rich dark coffee . . . We sat looking at each other across the table. There were no words. We had found the Great American Breakfast, and it was in Canada.

In the years since, Gwen and I have kept looking, and every once in a while we've found some pretty great versions of that roadfood Holy Grail. There was Juan in a Million in Austin, where the Great American Breakfast included tortillas and hot sauce; there was Mrs. Olsen's Coffee Hut in Oxnard, California; there was Walker Brothers outside Chicago; and the awesome Hominy Grill in Charleston, South

Carolina. We've heard one of the best breakfasts in the country can be found at the Huckleberry Cafe in Los Angeles. But I wouldn't know. In a week in L.A., we never once managed to beat the traffic and get to the place before it started serving sprout sandwiches for lunch.

. . .

WHEN I GOT BACK TO NEW YORK AFTER MY road trip to Vancouver, I moved into employee housing owned by the Italian restaurant where I had landed a job. The place was like a cross between a dorm room and a hostel, with a little bit of flophouse thrown in: one big room with three beds, of varying sizes and origins, and some mismatched dressers and desks tossed around, apparently randomly. The bathroom had last been cleaned in 1979. The kitchen had nothing in it.

It was, in other words, exactly the kind of lousy housing situation you expect when you're a poor cook in New York City—except that it was located in one of the fanciest buildings on Central Park South, which, back in the day, was pretty damn fancy.

We had a doorman—a team of doormen. We could mail letters by putting them in special vacuum tubes next to the elevator on our floor. Ladies in fur coats paraded through the lobby; men in expensive suits came in and out, calling for cabs. There was a rumor that Christie Brinkley lived on the other side of the building, that you could look right into her apartment from our place, that you could probably even see her naked. I spent some quality time looking, but I never saw her. I figure she probably had a park view.

The restaurant owned a handful of these places, studio apartments scattered through the building. They used them to house Italian cooks who were in the country on temporary visas, and American cooks like me who were too cheap to pay rent for a place of their own. I guess the restaurant figured it was a good deal: they paid us almost nothing, and since we lived right on site, we could be at work any time they needed us. The Italian restaurant operated on the old-school European model: none of this cushy American day-shift-night-shift business. You worked all morning, starting at seven or so; you took a couple of hours off for "free time," which usually meant sleeping; then you worked from three or four till the restaurant closed. After that, you cleaned. You ate all your meals at the restaurant, and you were off on Sundays, when the place was closed, and you were grateful that you didn't work seven days a week. That's how they did it in the old country, and that's how they did it on Central Park South.

Nobody complained. There were only two Americans in the kitchen, counting me; everybody else was Italian. You might say the Italians weren't here to learn about serious Italian cooking—if that's what they had wanted, they probably would have just stayed home. No, these guys—mostly kids from small towns in the middle of nowhere—were here to party. After service, they'd rush back upstairs to shower; they'd get all dressed up, and they'd spray themselves with cologne, and then they'd go out and spend every penny they made at the restaurant. They liked high-end places, quality joints: for example, they were very fond of Flashdancers, a gentlemen's establishment that was widely advertised on the tops of New York City cabs and on flyers handed out on street corners. And the boys didn't just sit back and watch the strippers: they dated them. My roommate Gianni went out for quite a while with a nice girl named Cathy Cantaloupes.

* * *

A YEAR INTO MY RESIDENCY ON CENTRAL Park South, the owner of the Italian restaurant offered me a sous chef gig. But I decided I'd had enough of the old-country system and the flophouse and the late nights with Cathy Cantaloupes and her friends. I was ready to take on new challenges, to explore a wider range of cuisines, to pay my own rent.

The American food movement had definitely begun by that point, but if you wanted to be a chef back then, you still had to develop a pretty strong French accent, so to speak. *Larousse* was the bible; the lingua franca of the kitchen was French; the only way to be trained was "classically," which meant *nouvelle*. So I decided I wanted to work in the best French-based kitchen I could find.

I landed in the kitchens of Lespinasse—the most interesting new restaurant in town at the time. Lespinasse wasn't strictly French: it was stricter, because the chef was Swiss. Gray Kunz's kitchen was as disciplined as the military. He believed in making every single thing from scratch, every day: stocks, bases, everything. In most kitchens, leftovers from the night before become the basis for sauces and pickles and so forth the next day; at Lespinasse, we threw everything away at the end of service every night. It meant we made the freshest, most super-perfect food you can imagine—but it also meant that every day was like the first day at a new restaurant.

The kitchen at the Italian restaurant during service was the rough equivalent of a rave attended by some of the skinnier, more hungover members of the Hell's Angels. Service at Lespinasse, on the other hand, was like a ballet run by a drill sergeant. The kitchen was spotless, all night long, even in the roughest parts of service; every plate went out looking perfect. And at the end of every night, when we were so tired we could barely stand, we would clean our stations. That didn't just mean wiping down the stoves and cleaning the cutting boards. It meant polishing the stoves with brass polish and rubbing out the dirt in the cracks and crevices with toothbrushes. Chef Kunz would stand behind us, hands clasped behind his back, inspecting. Nobody went home till the stoves gleamed.

But even though I was totaled every night in a whole new way, it was worth it, because Gray Kunz was doing the most exciting food in New York. He combined classic French cooking with ingredients from India and Thailand and China and Japan: we were using fish sauce, different kinds of curry paste, spices I'd never heard of before. The cooks came from all over, too—not just from Europe but from India, Asia, and across the U.S. They brought their own traditions, and Gray put their flavors and approaches to work in his menu. It was a brand-new way of thinking about food and cooking.

I'd never really come across serious cooking outside of the Italian and French traditions—even the "New American" chefs were really just cooking French food with American ingredients—so what Gray was doing blew my mind. I started learning as much as I could about food cultures from all over. I went to every corner of New York City in search of new flavors: Flushing for Chinese food, Woodside for Thai food, Brighton Beach for Russian food, and so on and so forth. And while I was learning the food, I was learning the city in a whole new way, too.

. . .

BUT THE BASIS OF GRAY'S COOKING WAS STILL French, and after four years working with him, I decided I wanted to go to the source. It had always seemed to me that before you messed around with cassoulet or bouillabaisse or foie gras terrine, you needed to visit the places these things come from, to learn about them in their native environment. Learning about these food traditions in America definitely isn't the same thing: when you cook French food in the U.S., you are, no matter what, making food in translation. And if you're using American ingredients, you're also making food that's in some way American. There's nothing wrong with that: it's what innovative American cooking is all about. (That's why I don't buy it when French and Italian restaurateurs insist that only this or that American restaurant has "authentic" French or Italian food, and all the rest are faking it. I mean: if you want the real thing? Get on a plane.)

But before you can break the rules in a way that makes sense, you need to learn them. So I wanted to go to France to see how these dishes I'd been studying since way back when I first started reading Jacques Pépin actually worked in their natural habitat. I wanted to learn about ingredients and folkways: I wanted to forage for mushrooms, to visit cheese-makers and winemakers, to see how things grew and how people treated them close to home.

It was tough for an American to get into a French kitchen back then, and even tougher when that American wanted to work with the really big chefs: the Ducasses, the Gérards, the Girardets, and so on. Since Americans couldn't work in European restaurants without a work visa, the usual way of doing that was through what's called a *stage*. It's basically slave labor: a kind of mini-apprenticeship, where you work for free in return for experience, knowledge, cultural exchange. But just because you were offering yourself up as a kitchen slave didn't mean that anybody wanted to take you. Back then, American cooks had a pretty sad reputation in Europe. The old-country chefs thought we were culinarily backward, that we didn't know how to work, that we were lazy or stupid or untrained. And they had a point: back in the day, most European cooks started working full-time when they were twelve years old or so, and they basically didn't see daylight again until they'd won their first Michelin star. In the States, on the other hand, we wasted time on going to high school, dating girls, and other stupid stuff you obviously didn't need.

The only way for an American cook to land a stage in a French kitchen back then was to work some pretty serious connections, and I didn't have any of those. Basically, I had nothing but a fax machine, and all it kept spitting out was rejection. So finally I just decided to buy a ticket, get myself across the ocean, and see what would happen. I flew to London, because it was cheaper than Paris, and I couch-surfed, and I hoped. And after a couple of months: a miracle. A friend of a friend of a friend had a connection. I landed a sort of kind of promise of maybe a stage at L'Arpège in Paris, with Alain Passard.

I figured I wanted to know something about the food before I showed up at the kitchen door and tried to get my stage going, so I had lunch at L'Arpège, incognito, with my friends Colin and Renée the day I got to Paris. We were just about the only table in the dining room for the early seating. We were having a good time: the food was great; the room was amazing; the wine wasn't bad, either. And then, just as we were getting to the end of the second course, Alain Passard himself came barreling out of the kitchen. He steamed right up to our table, and he clapped his chest, and he took a huge breath, and he puffed his eyes out like a crazed fish, and he announced, at the top of his lungs, *"Je sens les saisons."* *I smell the seasons.* Then he turned around and went back to the kitchen.

I started my stage the next day.

When I turned up at eight o'clock in the morning, the chef de cuisine heard one syllable of my American-inflected French and sent me downstairs to the pastry kitchen. Now, I'd never worked pastry before, so I knew I would learn something. But the pastry kitchen at Arpège was in the basement of this building that's got to date from the 16th century. The ceiling was about six and a half feet high, which put it about three inches above my head, and there was exactly zero ventilation. And there were pots bubbling and bread ovens going eighteen hours a day down there, so the kitchen felt a lot like that part in Dante where the sinners are bobbing in a boiling river of blood.

Don't get me wrong: it was worth the suffering. The food and the techniques I was learning were amazing. Every day, I made *pain de miche*—bread that rises in bowls in the wine cellar—and little baguette rolls, and tarts, and puff pastry, and all kinds of crazy-classical stuff, things I'd never even seen in the U.S.

But there was always drama—every day, much, much drama.

The pastry chef was a young guy who talked very fast in a seriously dense Parisian accent. My French was good, but this kid sounded like he was trying to eat fish around a mouthful of marbles: everything came out like "Pourquoi ffdfsfdkjljlk commeça eh?" He'd started working in the kitchen when he was about ten years old, so even though he lived in one of the most cosmopolitan cities in the world, he was really provincial: he'd never been anywhere or done anything, he'd never read anything but cookbooks, and he had some very small ideas about the world. (And I guess he hadn't had the chance to do too much learning about basic hygiene, either: even at eight o'clock in the morning, he smelled bad.)

One of the many things the pastry chef didn't like was foreigners. This was a problem, since his pastry staff consisted of me and three Japanese stages. The pastry chef had no clue how to deal with this situation, so most of the time, he just yelled at us. In the beginning he yelled at us all equally, but after a while, he decided I wasn't a complete idiot, even if I was an American, especially after he figured out that I actually did speak French (even if I never could understand a word he said). As a result, I got yelled at a little bit less than the Japanese guys, and I sometimes got out of doing the seriously bad jobs.

For example, the most famous dessert at L'Arpège was the *tomate douze saveurs:* tomato with twelve flavors. The idea was to treat a tomato like a fruit: it was stuffed with pineapple and licorice and all kinds of different fruits and nuts, and then cooked in caramel. The dish was pretty bad-ass, but cooking it was just a pain in the ass. First you stuffed the tomatoes; then you made the caramel in a special spot, a narrow corner with a stove one-burner-wide stuffed into it. Then you put the tomatoes in the pan of hot caramel and *arrosed* the tomatoes with the caramel, constantly spooning the caramel over the top as they cooked. This was very, very, very boring, especially since the stove was so narrow that you could only do four tomatoes at a time. Four tomatoes take about twenty minutes to cook—and every night, we needed about thirty tomatoes for service.

All of that was bad, but what made tomato prep the worst job in the kitchen was the fact that the dish had to be made in the middle of the afternoon—during the one break the cooks got all day. So while everybody else was going for coffee or running home to their apartments or taking naps in the park or whatever, one poor slob would have to stay behind and spend his break spooning caramel over tomatoes in the hottest corner of the kitchen. It wasn't anybody's regular job. Instead, the pastry chef would assign it to the person he hated the most that day.

So one afternoon, while the rest of us were out enjoying the daylight, the most-hated Japanese kid of the day was back in the kitchen, using a metal spoon to endlessly spoon caramel from a shallow pot over the tops of the tomatoes. The spoon made a sound as it hit the pot: *tictictictictictictic* over and over–you'd switch hands–*tictictictictictictic*–repetitive, constant, almost trance-inducing. The ovens had been on all day, and the kitchen was hot and still and quiet, everybody else outside breathing air, no sound at all but that *tictictictictictictictic*. And as I said, this was the world's most boring job. So I guess the kid fell right into some kind of stupor as he was spooning. His hand just slipped all the way into the hot caramel, like sliding your hand into a glove.

We were hanging out in the park around the corner from the restaurant when he came running towards us screaming, with the skin falling off his hand.

Turns out I was next in line for being hated that day, so I had to pick up duties where he left off. I was very careful.

Given our crazy schedules, it really should have been no surprise to anybody that a cook had fallen asleep on the job. All of the cooks worked lunch and dinner, five days a week, from eight a.m. until one o'clock in the morning, with barely any kind of break at all. And at the end of the night, after we served the last dessert, we all sat down with tubs of vinegar water and wiped down every plate in the kitchen. By the time we were done, the subways had stopped running. This was fine if you were a Parisian kid with a motorcycle. It

was a lot less fine if you were an American kid without a motorcycle who lived way over on the other side of town. Sometimes I'd get a lift partway home on the back of somebody's bike; sometimes, if I was really tired, I'd spend money I didn't have on a very expensive cab ride. Most nights, after I put away my rag and my vinegar water, I walked the forty-five cold, dark minutes home.

The restaurant was closed on Saturdays, so on Friday nights, after the last plate was wiped down, we'd all go out to a club together. The French cooks liked this place called Le Bus. We'd fill up a couple of tables, and everybody would drink vodka and dance to Euro songs and *party party party*. Sometimes Passard himself would show up. At six a.m. or so we'd all go home to bed. Twenty-four hours later, we'd be back at the restaurant again.

That was it. That was our whole life. It was insane.

I kept up the pace for about three months: I spent my days in the pastry dungeon, getting yelled at in garbled French, and my nights trekking through the cold or partying with the cooks. But being American, I guess I just didn't have the training for that kind of life, and after a while, I got sick. And it was April, and I don't care what the movie says: April in Paris sucks. The weather was terrible, and I was tired and chilled and coughing all the time, and I was working like a dog, and I was short on money, since I was working for free. So I finally decided to get the hell out of Paris before I turned into a character in one of those really depressing operas.

My buddy Adam was in Paris at the time, and he said he was going south. Sounded good to me: I heard they had sun there. Paris hadn't seen the sun in months. A week later, I was in Nice, because Nice sounded nice.

And Nice *was* nice—at least when it came to work. (Living conditions were another story. Let's just say my dream of the French Riviera didn't include a view of the train tracks, or drunken Australian backpackers, or bugs.) A friend of a friend of a friend hooked me up with this little bistro, a real old-school family place: the staff consisted of two brothers running the kitchen with their dad and two other family members who worked the front of the house. The bistro was just about the opposite of L'Arpège. It wasn't fancy, and it wasn't expensive; nobody screamed; nobody had to ladle hot caramel over tomatoes for hours on end; nobody smelled the seasons. The food was super-simple

regional dishes: steak au poivre, pommes Niçoise, grilled fish fresh from the docks. In the morning we'd go to the markets and pick out the nicest produce for stuffed vegetables. I made terrines with the dad: duck pâtés, foie gras, all that stuff. Everything we cooked was straightforward and really good, and everyone who ate it appreciated it, and everyone was happy to be there. It was my dream French experience, the storybook cooking gig.

But after a month and a half I was, well, bored.

I thought I'd go back to fancy cooking, so I tried getting a stage at Ducasse in Monaco, but the chef de cuisine wouldn't even let me into his office. "No stages," he said, and then amended his statement: "No Americans." It was the same everywhere. Not a lot of love. I mean, these were the guys who gave us the Statue of Liberty, right? And now they wouldn't even let me chop their onions.

So I tried Switzerland instead, since I'd already learned at Lespinasse that Swiss-French chefs were more French than the French. A friend of mine from New York, a great Swiss cook named Franc, was working at Girardet. Fredy Girardet was doing some of the most interesting cooking anywhere back then; everybody was talking about the crazy-beautiful food he was making. I really, really, really wanted to get into that kitchen. So I took the train up there with the express purpose of finagling my way in.

Franc was working when I got there. He brought me into the kitchen, and then he went over to the desk where Girardet was working, and he said, trying not to cringe, "Chef, my friend here has come all the way from New York to work with you. He used to work for your protégé in New York, and he's a great guy, a great cook, and he wants to stage here for free for the rest of the summer."

Girardet didn't even turn around to look at me. He didn't even glance up from his paperwork. He just said, "No Americans."

Finally, I gave up. I wasn't learning a lot in the restaurants I could get into; I was tired of busting my ass for free six days a week; and I was just a little bit sick of being the abused American. So I packed up my knives and I rented a car and I went exploring.

I decided that I'd just start driving, that I'd never get on a freeway ever, and that whatever happened, happened. I didn't stay in any more fleabag hotels: instead, I bought a guide to the *gîtes de France* system, and I did farm stays or took rooms in people's houses wherever I went. *Gîtes de France* is a kind of bed-and-breakfast system out in the countryside, and it's pretty cool: you get to have breakfast and dinner with people on their farms, and you see what they're growing and what they're cooking for themselves. It was much more educational than snipping herbs in the basement of some one-star restaurant.

I would talk to my hosts about what I was doing, and they'd always know about something I should see or somebody I should talk to. "Oh, yeah," a farmer would tell me, for example, "you need to go to this town and see this guy and he'll take you to a foie gras farm." So I'd get in the car, and I'd go find the town, and I'd ask around until I found the guy, and I'd tell him about the people who sent me, and that's how I got to stuff foie gras geese and make fresh foie gras. Other times I'd just be going down the road and I'd see a sign saying, for example, "BUY LOCAL CHEESE HERE," so I'd stop and buy some cheese. I'd start talking to the owner of the shop, and I'd end up spending the afternoon in some ancient tiny cheese cave, learning to make some special regional cheese with a guy wearing an apron and a big porn mustache. Once I was traveling with another cook, and we stopped at this Bas-Armagnac producer outside of Eauze. The guy closed down his stand so he could show us around the farm, let us see how he pressed the grapes, took us out to the vineyard. Then he made us lunch.

I covered about 3,000 kilometers, sometimes by myself, sometimes traveling with another cook, or a friend of a friend, or somebody I met on the road. I went to almost every region in the south of the country, from the Atlantic to the Mediterranean, and I tasted and hunted and helped make everything from black truffles in Provence to hazelnut oil in the Dordogne Valley to goat cheese outside Figeac. I met artisans and producers and winemakers who'd spent their whole lives perfecting their craft. And people were incredibly cool. When I started asking questions, they were always surprised. They'd say, "No one's interested in that kind of thing anymore; no one cares about the old ways." And then they'd teach me all about what they did. That's how I really learned about French food: meandering down the road till I found something interesting. No more pastry dungeons for me. I wandered around, meeting people and tasting things and making stuff, until I ran out of money. Then it was time to go home.

. . .

AT THE END OF MY TRIP, I FOUND MYSELF IN the south again, right at the Spanish border. I remem-

" GNOCCHI "

Prepare (allowing about 4½ hours)

Meanwhile, wash, pare and cook covered in boiling, salted water to cover.
   3 medium-size (about 1 LB)
   potatoes, cut in quarters
cook about 20 min. or until tender when pierced with a fork (or strainer) Drain. To dry potatoes, shake pan over low heat.
Scald with boiling water, potato masher food mill or ricer. Mash or rice potatoes; keep hot.
   Measure into a bowl
   1¾ cups sifted flour. Make a
well in center of flour. Add mashed potatoes. (The mashed potatoes should be added when they are very hot, add one egg yolk. Mix well to make a soft elastic dough. Turn dough onto a lightly floured surface and knead. Break off small pieces of dough and use palm of hand to roll pieces to pencil thickness. Cut into pieces about ⅜ in. long. Curl each "finger" and pulling one piece of dough toward you. Gnocchi may also be shaped by pressing each piece lightly with a floured fork.
   Bring to boiling in a saucepan.
   3 qts. water
Gradually add the Gnocchi (cook about one half the Gnocchi at one time) Boil rapidly uncovered about 8 to 10 minutes, or until Gnocchi are tender and come to the surface. Test tenderness by pressing a piece against side of pan with fork or spoon. Drain by pouring into a colander or large sieve.
Mix Gnocchi with 2 cups Tomato Meat Sauce and grated parmesan cheese or Romano cheese. Top with remaining sauce. Serve immediately. About
   6 servings
(I hope these recipes will be helpful)
(for you and easy to make, any)
(question please call me)
   with Love Fernande

bered that there was this restaurant in Spain that a chef I knew had been talking up. The chef claimed the Spaniard was doing incredible stuff. He said, "If you get down that way, you've definitely got to go see this guy." So even though I was seriously running out of cash, I made a reservation for lunch. I figured I'd have some really good paella.

The restaurant was a very traditional-Spanish-looking place, in a beautiful little area at the end of a dirt road, right on the Mediterranean. Inside, it was all heavy beams and dark furniture. Turns out I was literally the only table for lunch that day, so I got the best seat in the house, right by an open archway overlooking the water. Nobody gave me a menu. I figured: yup, paella. And then the food started to arrive. And twenty-seven courses later, my mind was completely blown.

So I asked to see the chef.

The waiter walked me to the kitchen, and the sliding glass doors whooshed open, and the first thing I noticed—well, the second thing, after the sculpture of the bull's head coming through the pass—was that there were no ovens.

The chef came up and shook my hand. I introduced myself—in French, since my Spanish was not up to a discussion of what I had just eaten—and I told him how amazing my meal had been: all those courses full of things I'd never seen before—tuna marrow, crazy sea creatures—and combinations I'd never imagined—porcini with truffles and pine nuts? And even though I'd sworn off staging in Europe, I asked, I had to ask: "Could I stage here? Could I work for you for free?"

The chef shook his head. "I have too many stages already," he said, "but why don't you get a little education on what we're doing here? Come back for lunch tomorrow."

I laughed. "I can't even afford the gas to get back to France," I told him.

"Come as my guest, come for lunch," he insisted.

So I slept in the car, in the parking lot of the restaurant. In the morning, I got up and took a swim in the ocean, and I put on my clothes from the day before, and then I went inside to have lunch.

The chef had set up a table for two inside the kitchen. Turns out, the table for two was for me and him. He made lunch—thirty courses—and he brought every course to the table himself. And as he cooked and we ate, he told me his philosophy: he'd been making traditional Spanish food since he was nineteen, he said, and he'd been eating in France his whole professional life, but those old cuisines were starting to get very boring for him. Everywhere he went, it was the same food, the same flavors, the same ingredients. He wanted to figure out a way, he said, "to challenge cuisine." His goal, he said, was to do "something new." He was working on figuring out *something*—he wasn't sure what it was yet—that was uniquely Catalan and completely different at the same time. He didn't know how he was going to do it, but he was working on it.

It was 1995. The chef's name, of course, was Ferran Adrià.

· · ·

BACK IN NEW YORK, MY NEXT GIG WAS NOT EXactly Adrià-style. In 1986, my grandma had shown me a picture in *USA Today* of a natty-looking, well-dressed gent holding what looked like a box of potatoes. She pointed at the picture. "Those are white truffles," she said. "They cost a thousand dollars a pound. Look—he's got a whole box! And the newspaper says their restaurant is the best. You should go to New York," announced my grandma. "You should cook with these Italians."

My grandma was a smart lady, and I always did what she told me to. So when those particular Italians came calling, I couldn't say no, right?

The gig was a sous-chef position at the new version of their famous French restaurant. After years on the Upper East Side, the restaurant was moving: a sultan had bought a luxury hotel in midtown, the Italians' French restaurant was his favorite place to eat in New York, and he wanted it in his new hotel. Sounded good to me: a solid position, a résumé builder, French cooking for Italian owners in one of the most famous restaurants in town. I had no idea, really, what I was getting into.

For starters, since I'd never worked an opening in New York, I was clueless about what the phrase "the restaurant is moving" really meant. The owner, a legendary restaurateur, told me we'd be open "right away," that construction was "almost all the way finished." I thought I'd be organizing the kitchen, helping to hire staff, buying equipment, doing menu development and so forth. Probably I also thought the Earth was flat and that the Tooth Fairy and the Easter Bunny were real. When I showed up on my first day, knives and whites ready, the kitchen was

a big gaping hole in which some construction dudes sat, having a cigarette.

So for the first six months of my great new gig, I showed up at work at 9 a.m., in a suit and tie, as per house rules. I spent my time sitting in an upstairs office in the hotel, inventing jobs for myself like an underemployed temp. I organized paperwork; I moved boxes (in my suit); I sifted through letters. There were lots of letters: just about everybody you'd ever heard of had eaten at the restaurant, and it seemed like they all wanted to write to the owner to thank him. There were letters from Henry Kissinger, thanking him for dinner at the owner's place; there were letters from Ronald Reagan. The day I found a letter headed "From the Office of Frank Zappa" was a good day.

After a while, even the owner got restless. So he came up with a plan: while we're waiting to open, let's do a world tour, rock-band-style! Fifteen cities in thirty-five days! Europe! Asia! Taking the food to the fans around the globe! There were sponsorships; there were partnerships; there were t-shirts. What could go wrong?

Well, we never made it to Asia.

The World Tour worked like this: We would land, for example, in London or Paris. We'd clear Customs (I was never sure how we managed that, given all the stuff we were bringing with us—we must have been violating at least six importing rules per country), and then we'd pile into cars and head to the hotel where we were cooking. The owner being who he was, this was not the Motel 6. In London, it was the Lanesborough; in Paris, the Plaza Athenée. Good to be the king, right?

I didn't get to spend much time hanging out in luxe hotel rooms, though. The morning after we arrived, the chef and I would get up at 7 a.m. or so to prep and cook a lunch for the local press. As soon as that was done—the desserts sent out, the owner and his boys shaking hands and air-kissing in the dining room—we'd start getting prepped for the main event: dinner for somewhere in the neighborhood of two hundred. It was amazing to me how much weight the French restaurant's name carried: we were big in London, in Paris, in Munich, everywhere. Every dinner was completely sold out. The menu was always the same: lobster salad, foie gras with cherries, bass paupiettes, beef tenderloin with cocotte vegetables and red wine sauce, and soufflé. It was old-school all the way, European classics for the Euros. You've heard of taking coals to Newcastle? This was taking continental to the Continent.

Back in New York, the restaurant was finally ready. A famous designer had turned the staid space into a luxe velvet-covered neon-and-crystal madhouse—perfect for a big, big, big opening party. Everybody was talking about it: chefs and restaurant people, socialites, celebrities, journalists, activists, lunatics. Even the homeless guy who hung out in front of the restaurant was angling for a ticket. There were a lot of details to take care of, some a big deal, others less so. For example, there was lots of concern about how we were going to make sure that the rented elephants were not going to step on I. M. Pei, but not so much concern about the five thousand PETA activists who threatened to protest. The owner dealt with that one personally: he screamed down the phone, "Show up! Show up! I can use the press: I'll call CNN myself!" Then he slammed down the receiver.

There were a thousand people at the party. The elephants made the scene. So did I. M. Pei. The protesters didn't. I don't remember if the homeless guy got a ticket.

The kitchen in the new restaurant was a big open space, a few wide steps up from the main dining room. The plan was for waiters to circulate with food and wine, but as far as I could tell, all one thousand guests decided they wanted to hang out in the kitchen with us. Bill Cosby came into the kitchen and did his best impression of being a chef. Chuck Mangione played "Happy Birthday" on his horn. Martha Stewart ate stuffed pig's feet with her fingers, right off the line. It was crazy; it was chaotic; it was intense. It was a hell of a party.

That party set the tone for what was maybe the biggest see-and-be-seen restaurant of the day. Everybody showed up in our dining room: chefs from all over the world, actors, rock stars, celebrities, royalty, billionaires—everybody from Donald Trump to Walter Cronkite to Joan Rivers. Everybody you'd ever heard of settled into the high velvet chairs in

that crazy circus-circus space. (Usually we took good care of everybody, but sometimes there were personal issues. Once, Wolfgang Puck was eating in the dining room. The chef set the pan of foie gras we were cooking for him on fire, on purpose, yelling, "I hate him!")

It was a high-maintenance crowd: even the less famous regulars had crazy demands. For example, we had a customer who would show up at least once a week for lunch, always with a table full of New York movers and shakers. He would settle in, order some wine for the table, and then walk into the kitchen and hand us a can of tuna fish. "Open it and put it on a plate with some salad and serve it to me," he would direct us. So we did. We charged him thirty dollars a pop as a can-opening fee.

One Sunday afternoon, when the restaurant was closed, there was a knocking on the front door. We ignored it, figuring it was some lost hotel guest, but the knocking got louder, more rhythmic, and we started hearing muffled yells. Finally, the chef headed out front to see what was going on. He came running back asking for the keys to the door, yelling, "Rolling Stone man is outside! Rolling Stone man is outside!" When I followed him up to the front, sure enough: Keith Richards and Ron Wood were knocking on the glass doors, yelling, "We're the Rolling Stones! Perhaps we could get a martini?"

Then there was the cast of characters on staff. There were all the stock players for a flashy New York restaurant opening: the out-of-his mind screaming chef; the womanizing maitre d'; the oversexed pastry chef; the drug-dealing stewards; the gun-wielding sauce cook; the French butcher who drank too much kitchen wine; the waiter who would slit your throat for an extra three bucks. It's too bad this was before reality TV. It would have been a huge hit.

. . .

THE CRAZINESS AT THE FRENCH RESTAURANT was interesting at first, but after a while, I got a little tired of drama. I started thinking that maybe it was time I took over a kitchen of my own. And I got the feeling I wasn't the only one who was spending time on this idea. One day, the chef and I were in a cab, going from an event uptown to a charity dinner downtown. As we drove through the city, the chef decided to give me a culinary geography lesson. "Andrew," he said, very gravely and out of nowhere, "you have to be very careful. New York is like the jungle. In every jungle there are many lions. And the lions like to piss, and you can't go where the lions piss, because it's their territory. Uptown, Daniel, he's the lion. And in midtown, Sirio, he is the lion." As we moved through the city's neighborhoods, he went on and on, listing the lions in every part of town. As we hit Tribeca, he finished his lesson: "Downtown, Drew is the lion downtown."

"So, Chef," I said, finally, "what you're saying is if I want to open up a restaurant, I shouldn't do it in New York?"

The chef, serious, nodded. "Maybe it's better that you get out of New York. There are too many lions."

. . .

WHEN I FINALLY DID DECIDE IT WAS TIME TO leave the French restaurant, two years in, the owner and the chef didn't take it very well. It didn't help that I was going to work for a chef who had once been the chef at the French restaurant, and who had definitely not yet been forgiven for leaving and succeeding elsewhere. So when I tried to do the right thing, giving two months' notice, what I got was two months solid of the silent treatment. No one on the management team would say a word to me; no one would even look me in the eye. I was instant persona non grata. On the last day, the chef finally spoke to me. "Bon continuation," he said. *Have a nice life.* That was it.

About three weeks after I'd left, my doctor's office assistant called about an appointment. I'd forgotten to give them my new work number, so the call went to the manager's office at the French restaurant. The owner picked up the phone.

"I'd like to confirm an appointment for Andrew Carmellini for tomorrow," said the doctor's assistant.

Said the owner: "Andrew Carmellini? He died three weeks ago." And he slammed down the phone.

. . .

WHEN I THINK BACK ON IT, I HAVE NO IDEA WHY Daniel Boulud decided to hire me as opening chef de cuisine for Café Boulud. I mean, he was making a huge move: turning the four-star Restaurant Daniel into the Upper East Side version of a luxe café while he was also busy opening a new, super-ambitious Restaurant Daniel in another space. And here I was, a twenty-seven-year-old American kid who'd never been the chef of a restaurant in his life—and never worked a day for Daniel, either—walking into his kitchen and taking over.

Daniel's chef de cuisine at Restaurant Daniel was Alex Lee, who was probably the best, most respected cook in New York at the time. When we started the changeover, Alex and I worked in the kitchen together. I was sweating bullets about it all, but Alex was great. The reception from the rest of the crew, on the other hand, was not exactly warm: it was many variations on "who the hell do you think you are?" It was clear that I had a lot to prove.

For the first three months, Café Boulud ran with Alex's menus and the Restaurant Daniel crew. But then the new place opened, and overnight, Alex was gone, along with pretty much the entire team. And there I was: I had this eight-million-dollar, *New York Times* three-star restaurant in my hands, and Daniel, crazy trusting man that he was, basically said, "OK, here you go. It's yours."

That first year was a big lesson for me. Chefs are control freaks by nature: we want to make sure everything is perfect, and we have a hard time trusting other people to achieve that perfection for us. But you can't do everything yourself if you want to succeed. You have to build a crew you believe in, and you have to teach them to work the way you want them to, and you have to prove to them that you're somebody worth working for. It took me a while to learn all that, so things were a little shaky at the beginning. I think I slept about three hours a night for that first year. I'd take one day off a week, and I'd usually go in for dinner service even on that one day, just to make sure things were OK.

But in the end, those six years at Café Boulud were amazing. Suddenly people were paying attention to what I was doing. I won a whole bunch of awards: James Beard Rising Star, James Beard Best Chef New York City, *Food and Wine* Magazine Best New Chef . . . and I finally had a great chef mentor in Daniel, who taught me and supported me and trusted me, even when I didn't trust myself yet. He was incredibly generous to me, too: when Gwen and I got married, he threw a big party for us at Restaurant Daniel, and then he sent us on our honeymoon.

Another reason those years were amazing was our customer base: we had the best customers in town. People who were willing to take culinary risks, to eat outside of their comfort zone, were a big deal back then. Now that eating in restaurants has become more or less a sport in New York City, a chef can open up just about anywhere in the five boroughs and count on excited, receptive, food-savvy customers who want to try new things, but this was back in the culinary dark ages, before you could find porcini mushrooms in the East Village, and waaay before people raised chickens in their backyards in Brooklyn. If you were a young chef anywhere in the country and you wanted to really be able to do whatever you wanted to do in the kitchen, the Upper East Side of Manhattan was the best place to be. Our customers were very well traveled, and they ate out a lot—sometimes every night of the week. They got bored fast, and they were always interested in trying new things.

So about a year in, when I had my crew together and I was a little less stressed about being in charge, we started to really play around with the food. If a customer came in and said, "Just tell the chef to cook for

Cherry Braid   (2 cakes)

2½ to 3 cups unsifted flour
¼ cup sugar
1 tsp. salt
1 pkg. yeast
¼ cup milk
¼ cup (½ stick) margarine
1 egg (room temperature)

In a large bowl thoroughly mix
¾ cup flour, ¼ cup sugar, salt and
undissolved yeast.

Combine ¾ cup milk and 2 T. margarine
in a saucepan. Heat over low heat until
liquid is warm. (Marg. does not need to melt)
Gradually add to dry ingredients and beat 2
minutes at medium speed of electric mixer,
scraping bowl. ~~Stir in enough additional~~
~~flour to make a soft dough.~~ Add egg
and ¼ cup flour or enough to make a thick
batter. Beat at high speed 2 minutes, scraping
bowl occasionally. Stir in enough additional
flour to make a soft dough. Turn out onto
lightly floured board. Knead until smooth
_____ _____ in over, about 1 hr.

Punch dough down, turn out onto lightly
floured board. Divide in half, Roll out to
14×8" rectangle. Place on greased baking
sheets. Spread filling down center of each
Slit dough at 1 inch intervals along
each side of filling. Braid strips over
filling Cover let rise in warm place
free from draft, until double 1 hr.
Bake at (350°) about 20 minutes
or until done.
Remove from baking sheets and cool on
wire racks.

me," we would do six savory courses, with different dishes for each diner at each course. We tried not to repeat ingredients—not only in the same menu, but for different menus, over time, for the same diner. We used ingredients from all over. In the summertime, I'd do wild and foraged menus: we'd cook with cattails from Massachusetts and wild asparagus from Virginia, mushrooms from Oregon, all kinds of stuff that showed up at our back door. Sometimes the customers brought ingredients in, too: somebody would go hunting, for example, and they'd come in with a moose or a brace of doves. We'd cook it and serve it on the fly. It was real ego cooking, and it was fun.

We had one customer who would roll up in his Ferrari with a couple of boy-toys about once a week. He loved food, and he was up for any kind of culinary adventure. He told us, "I don't ever want to order: I always want to have a menu." So we went nuts cooking for him. He might say to me, at the end of dinner one week, "Next time, let's do a menu only of Mexican food," so we'd pull out the books and start researching dishes, get on the phone and fly stuff in, all the right chiles and spices and vegetables and everything, and we'd get all this crazy stuff together and make the most authentic, delicious Mexican food we could possibly make. And we'd all learn a lot by doing it, too. And at the end of that meal, he'd say, "Next time, let's do something Alsatian," and we'd start all over again.

We had another regular customer who really started to throw down. This was the kind of guy who only wants to drink vintage Cristal and '61 Pétrus—the kind of guy who comes in with a couple of buddies and six or seven extremely high-end escorts and spends money like his wallet's on fire. We were never sure where the cash came from, but no question he liked to spend it: I once saw him tip a waiter five grand. After he'd been in a few times, this customer said to me, "You cook whatever you want to do, charge whatever you want to charge. Just give me four hours' worth of really interesting food every time I'm here." For a chef who's out to prove something, those are pretty sweet words. I promised him he'd never have the same dish twice. We started a database on the computer especially for his menus. He'd come in once a month, sometimes more, and he never said no to anything we made. He was pretty much the greatest customer of all time.

And he liked to have a good time. He held his Christmas party at the restaurant: he bought out the whole place, and he invited about a hundred guests, plus twenty escorts or so, for decoration. The house wine that night was '61 Pétrus. He brought in a dance troupe from Canada for a show—in the dining room—requiring five costume changes and a snow machine. And for the after-party, he rented half a club just for his friends, along with more entertainment, including a lesbian elf act. He invited all of us to go along: he left two limos at the club for the restaurant staff.

The world's greatest customer rang in the new millennium with dinner for twelve. He came into the kitchen, gave me a hug, said, "Happy friggin' New Year's, A.C.," and handed me a special titanium case holding six bottles of Cristal. "Where's your sous-chef?" he asked me. He introduced the sous-chef to one of his escorts. "Happy New Year, man," he said. I didn't see my sous-chef for a while after that.

Even on regular nights, our customer could get out of hand. Once he was seated next to the wife of a famous NASCAR driver. Around midnight, she came up to me and said, "Umm, I really love your restaurant, but the next time I come here, maybe there won't be a gentleman doing cocaine off the breasts of a nice-looking woman in the women's bathroom?"

But all good things must come to an end. One day, the best customer of all time disappeared. The story goes that the feds were coming down on him for something or other. Our customer got advance word that the heat was on, so one morning, he told his girlfriend he was taking the dog out for a walk, gave her a kiss, tied the dog to a tree near their place, got in a cab, went to the airport, and flew away to someplace where the word "extradition" doesn't translate.

There were other strange nights uptown.

One classic evening, the place was full, a Who's Who of New York society, not a reservation to be had. In walked a music producer who was a regular of ours, with a guest. When the maitre d' came up to his table, the producer, who was a friendly kind of guy, said to him, "Hey, do you know this guy?" pointing to his guest. "This is Chuck D!" The maitre d' came back and asked me, "Do you know who this guy is? I guess he's a rapper or something." I was pretty excited: famous people in the restaurant don't usually faze me, but Chuck D? I mean, come on!

We took a look at the cameras in the kitchen, but they were black-and-white, with a pretty fuzzy picture. And it was a crazy-busy night, so I didn't have a chance to go out into the dining room and shake the man's hand.

Meanwhile, Chuck D was out there making the rounds. He went up to Woody Allen and patted him on the back; he went over to say hi to Tommy Hilfiger, and Tommy Hilfiger stood up and shook his hand. He even wandered over to a famous socialite's table to say hello. Then he sat back down at the music producer's table, and he ordered three bottles of Cristal: one for Woody Allen's table, one for Tommy Hilfiger's table, one for the famous socialite's table. Nice, right?

So dinner went on; everyone was drinking their Cristal, table-hopping, turning the place into this little neighborhood club. It was packed with people. And at some point, Chuck D got up and went to the bathroom, and then he went outside for a smoke. In the meantime, the music producer asked for his check. When he got a look at it, he started turning purple: "This is $2,700!" he yelled. "I didn't spend $2,700 tonight!"

"Well, no, sir," the waiter told him. "Your guest did, buying those bottles for all those other people."

The music producer said, "Well, I'm not paying for it. Where the hell is this guy?"

"Oh, he's out having a smoke," said the waiter. "I'll get him for you, sir." So out the waiter went to tell Chuck D the producer was looking for him. And guess what? No Chuck D!

Turns out, Chuck D was not Chuck D at all: he was just some guy who hustled the music producer at the bar at the Carlyle. And when he took off from Café Boulud, he went down to Scores (that high-end gentlemen's establishment where Cathy Cantaloupes used to work), and he pulled the same Chuck D trick with a couple of business guys there. He ratcheted up a $100,000 tab on bottles for everyone in the room and lap-dances in the VIP room, and then he disappeared before the check showed up. We read all about it the next day on Page Six.

. . .

AFTER SIX YEARS AT CAFÉ BOULUD, IT WAS definitely time to move on. I'd been doing high-end French cooking for a long time, and I just wasn't feeling it anymore. And I was seeing that in my customers, too: a lot of my regulars, people who ate at the restaurant three or four times a week, were starting to say to me, "You know, we appreciate the fancy creations and the foamy sauces and everything, but what we really love is your ravioli." I hadn't cooked Italian full-time since I'd left the Italian restaurant all those years back, and I love Italian food and Italian cooking—not only because it's my roots, and not only because of all the time I've spent in Italy, but because it's so soul-satisfying and interesting and versatile and flavor-strong, all at the same time. So maybe, I thought, it was time for me to try cooking Italian in my own kitchen.

So how was I supposed to do that, exactly?

I knew the basics, of course: if you're a chef who wants to open a restaurant, you go out and raise some money, and then you find a space, and then you build a restaurant, and hopefully they will come. But I had no practical experience in actually doing any of this, and it's not the kind of stuff they teach you in cooking school: how to negotiate a lease, how to ask someone to be an investor, how to set up a company.

Since I had nobody to tell me how to make this work, I just did my best: I teamed up with a friend in the business, and I raised a little bit of money, and I started to look for a space (a process which is a huge superhustle in New York, land of shady landlords and strange deals). But a year later, I was not much further along than I had been when I started.

I was getting really frustrated when—lo and behold!—a restaurant angel appeared in the form of a fat, bald man bearing tales of putting together a huge, ambitious restaurant company with the backing of a guy from out of town—a guy with family money who'd already had some success elsewhere, and who wanted, the fat man said, to build the best restaurants in the world here, with my help. Starting with an Italian restaurant. Everything, the fat man said, would be up to me: the concept, the menu, all that. They just wanted to help me achieve greatness.

You know what they say about things that seem too good to be true?

Well, hell, yeah.

But I wanted to believe. So I signed on the dotted line.

I was foolish from the get-go on this one: I didn't have the right lawyer, and as they say, my paper wasn't correct. So it wasn't the best deal to begin with. And then we started working together on planning the first restaurant in our new American company—and two weeks in, I knew that I'd made a huge mistake.

It wasn't a total loss. I'd come into this thing wanting to learn about the business end of restaurateuring. You know how they say learning what *not* to do is more valuable, sometimes, than the other way round?

Yeah.

But I was determined to make it work, so when we finally got the place finished, I brought in all the best people I'd worked with in the past. We all busted our asses, and we managed to fill our dining room with great customers, and we even landed a three-star *New York Times* review and a Michelin star.

But about a year in, I parted ways with the fat bald man and his friends.

And then came the year of the hustle.

I formed a company with Luke Ostrom, then my chef de cuisine, and we set out to open a restaurant together. Our idea was pretty simple: we would do a pasta joint, something small and manageable that we could fund ourselves. No crazy egomaniacs, no designers, no huge crews—just a little restaurant of our own. So we raised some money, and we started looking at spaces, and thinking about menus, and batting names back and forth.

It was a pretty good plan.

But then Vegas came calling.

The offer came right out of the blue. One day we were thinking about twenty seats in the East Village; the next day we were planning a 7,000-square-foot kitchen serving a 14,000-square-foot "Carmellini restaurant," a diner, a couple of nightclubs, and room service for a hotel. And these investors were really something special: they knew we wanted to open up a place in New York, and they offered to fund it while this Vegas thing was getting built. Before we knew it, we were flying out for meetings with design teams, talking to managers and money people, working on six different menus at the same time for a project ten times bigger than anything we'd ever done.

And then another Vegas deal popped up—opening a couple of years down the line, outside the time frame of the non-compete, whatever we wanted to do, crazy budget.

And just when we were getting ready to sign on for that other casino deal, an art dealer who happened to be an old customer of ours called us up. He introduced us to these New York developers who, along with a major player in the hip-hop world, were putting together a hotel project in west Chelsea. And two weeks later, we found ourselves on the major player's jet, talking business with him on the way to his concert in Buffalo.

It was crazy. In one year, we'd gone from having no restaurant, no jobs, and no money to three seven-figure deals staring us in the face—one already inked. And we were still working out of my living room, just me and Luke, in jeans and t-shirts.

And then October 2009 rolled around.

By the time the dust from the financial crash had settled, all the debt providers in both Vegas projects and in the New York project had pulled their funding. There we were, still sitting in my living room in jeans and t-shirts, Luke and I, and suddenly we weren't about to be ridiculously successful. Instead what we were, basically, was screwed.

But we must have done something really good in a past life, because it was just then that De Niro came calling.

I'd known Bob for years—ever since the Café Boulud days, when he'd been a customer. He had a new restaurant at the Greenwich, this beautiful hotel he'd built in Tribeca, and the place wasn't doing so well. He wanted to make a change. So our buddy Ken Friedman set up a meeting, and we sat down with Bob and his partners, and two weeks later, we had a deal. Our friend Josh Pickard came in to run the front of the house, and Locanda Verde was born: an Italian restaurant in my own American style.

We've been lucky. I still want to kiss every customer who walks in the front door.

*   *   *

A YEAR INTO THE LIFE OF LOCANDA, LUKE and Josh and I started thinking about doing something new, a different kind of project: an American restaurant. Ever since the days when I was cooking French food, I've wanted to do a real New York restaurant. I wanted to explore what it really meant to be an American chef. I'm Italian-Polish-American, and a lot of my cooks are Mexican-American, Korean-American, Japanese-American . . . from all kinds of different backgrounds, and from all different parts of the country, too. To me, all of these food traditions were American cooking—and so was the Russian food I ate in Brighton Beach, the Indian food I ate in Queens, the West Indian food I ate in Brooklyn, the breakfast I ate in Chicago, the fish we ate in Miami, the peaches-and-cream custard we ate outside the racetrack. I wanted to see what happened when you brought all of these influences and flavors together in one place.

So what's the first step to figuring out what American cooking is all about right now? That's right: road trip!

We went coast to coast, eating American wherever and however we could find it. We hit hot dog stands and molecular gastronomy temples in Chicago; gumbo shacks and New Cajun fine dining in Louisiana; tamale dives and fried-chicken eateries in Mississippi; rib joints in Memphis; pulled-pork palaces in North Carolina. We visited taco joints in California and paid homage at churches of barbecued sausage in central Texas. We ate Korean in L.A., did dim sum in San Francisco, downed fried clams in Massachusetts, feasted on smoked fish in Michigan. For dessert, we had ice cream in Ohio and shave ice in Hawaii. And then we hit every single neighborhood in New York City.

We ate some great food, and we met some great people. Just like the artisans I met in Europe, the small-town barbecuers and tamale-makers of America were really happy to share their food with us and to show us what they did. Really, in all our traveling, we only ran into one problem.

Nashville.

I grew up listening to country music with my dad—I was pretty sure Dolly Parton was my girlfriend when I was little. There isn't exactly a lot of great country music in New York, so I was psyched when we got to Music City. Instead of going to three or four places for dinner, the way we usually did, Luke and I decided to do some music tasting instead. We hit something like nine bars that night—all live music, every new place a little bit better than the pretty damn good

place before. And every bar was different: the first one was playing countrybilly, the next one was all about old country songs, and so on. I was happy as a clam. At about one in the morning, we washed up in a bar with a band playing some newer country stuff. The joint was completely packed. It was a tough-looking crowd, a lot of bikers, but that wasn't so different from some of the other places we'd been. So we did what we did in every other bar: we grabbed a couple of beers and just stood back and listened to music.

A while after we got there, the band started playing "You Never Even Call Me by My Name," by David Allan Coe. Soon every single person in the whole bar was singing along—and that's a lot of people. Now, I know the words to the song (*you don't need to call me darlin', darlin'* . . .) but I'm not really a sing-along kind of guy. And Luke? He's enjoying himself, but he's not a country music dude. He's from Ithaca. But that's OK; we were just having a good time, listening to the music.

Then, right after the line "Even though you're on my fightin' side," the singer threw his hand up, and the band suddenly stopped playing. The singer waited for silence, and then he hollered, "There's a couple boys here that don't know the words to this song!"

Everybody started looking around. I guess it didn't take them too long to figure out that that the two guys in Adidas tennis shoes and skinny jeans and black t-shirts were the boys he was talking about. Then it was audience participation time. This one biker guy—about 5 foot 3 and 350 pounds, give or take—yelled, "They look like a couple Euros!" Another biker dude had something to say about New

Jersey. And then somebody else contributed a word about our possible sexual orientation.

Luke and I looked at each other, and we put down our beers, and we ran for our lives.

Just for the record: everybody's welcome at The Dutch, regardless of race, creed, color, orientation, or hairstyle. Including Euros. And people from New Jersey. And even, if they behave themselves, short fat bikers from Tennessee.

And why The Dutch? What's American about a name like The Dutch? Well, everything—even though my mom in Ohio thinks the waiters are going to wear wooden shoes, and my friend in California thinks it's somehow about people on dates splitting their checks. Somebody asked me, "Is that a drug term?" Somebody else said it might be a sexual position.

For us, The Dutch is a place that's all about New York, with a little bit of swagger. It's the Dutch history of the city, and of Soho in particular. It's a place to hang out—a casual, easygoing kind of place, where anybody would want to stop by for a bite to eat. It's a place where we serve up great food, but we don't take ourselves too seriously: we want everybody who walks in the door to have a great time. It's a place, in other words, where you can get some true American flavor.

SOUPS AND SALADS

BORSCHT LIKE MOM USED TO MAKE

CHILLED YOUNG CARROT SOUP WITH GINGER

TOMATO-CHILE-MANGO GAZPACHO

COCONUT-CURRY BUTTERNUT SQUASH SOUP
WITH LEMONGRASS AND CILANTRO YOGURT

CREAM OF MUSHROOM SOUP

GOOD OLD GOULASH

CHICKEN POZOLE

ITALIAN WEDDING SOUP WITH CHICKEN
MEATBALLS AND SAGE CROSTONE

MIDWEST WHITEFISH CHOWDER

LENTIL SOUP WITH BACON, APPLE, AND
MUSTARD

TOFU STEW WITH MISO AND SHIITAKE

SOUP DORIA

GARDEN SALAD WITH GRANDMA'S DRESSING

MOM'S FLORIDA AVOCADO AND ORANGE SALAD

SPICY SUMMER MELON SALAD

TOMATO SALAD WITH BUTTERMILK DRESSING

ENDIVE, APPLE, AND FARMHOUSE CHEDDAR
SALAD WITH COUNTRY HAM AND WHEAT BEER
DRESSING

GAZPACHO SALAD

BULGUR SALAD

TUNA POKE

BORSCHT LIKE MOM USED TO MAKE

When I was a kid, my mom, whose family is Polish, used to make a great cold summertime borscht. It's actually super-easy. The key is the beets themselves: they come out of the ground in the summer (as opposed to out of the cellar, which is what happens with hot wintertime borschts), so they're sweet-tasting and tender inside, and they cook up great. If you're in New York and you want to get your borscht fix, try Veselka in the East Village, or M & I International Foods on Brighton Beach Avenue in Brooklyn—they've always got three or four different kinds going. But I think my mom's is the best. Serve it up with thick slices of brown bread.

SERVES 6 AS AN APPETIZER

2 $^1/_2$ pounds beets (5 or 6 medium beets)
4 cups vegetable broth, chicken broth, or water
1 teaspoon salt
$^1/_2$ teaspoon fresh-ground black pepper
1 tablespoon sugar
1 tablespoon red wine vinegar
1 tablespoon sherry vinegar
$^1/_3$ cup sour cream
3 green onions, sliced thin

Preheat the oven to 400°F.

Wash the beets, then wrap each one in a piece of tin foil. Put the wrapped beets on a baking sheet, and bake them in the oven for 45 minutes to 1 hour, until a paring knife goes through the flesh easily.

Let the wrapped beets cool down on the countertop until you can handle them. Then unwrap them, put them in a bowl, and let them chill down in the fridge until they've cooled through.

Use a paring knife to cut off the stems and peel all the rough skin off the beets. (Don't try to use a vegetable peeler for this. It won't go well.)

Using a box grater or a large flat grater, grate the beets into a bowl. (This is a messy process: if you have clean rubber gloves, you might want to wear one on your grating hand so your skin doesn't turn purple.)

Warm the broth up in a medium-sized soup pot over medium heat for about 5 minutes. Add the grated beets and stir well. Then add the salt, pepper, sugar, and the red wine and sherry vinegars.

Stir everything together, and then take the pot off the heat and carefully transfer the borscht to a large bowl (watching out for catastrophic purple spills). Put it in the fridge to cool down.

When the borscht has cooled (about 15 to 30 minutes), pull it out of the fridge and ladle it into individual bowls. Put a generous scoop of sour cream in each bowl, and sprinkle the green onions over the top. Serve with thick slices of brown bread. The borscht will keep in the fridge for 5 days or so.

CHILLED YOUNG CARROT SOUP WITH GINGER

This soup has bright flavors and deep colors; it makes a really suave first course, and it's great to eat on a hot day. This is one of those dishes that really, really needs good ingredients: it's all about the carrots. If you've got lousy carrots, you're going to have lousy soup. I like to use organic carrots with tops: they're so much sweeter than the regular horse carrots, the ones that you buy loose without tops. To make sure that the flavor is pumped up as much as possible, I puree the soup so it's super-thick, and then I thin it out with carrot juice, to give back some of that fresh raw flavor. Every vegetable tastes different raw than it does cooked: without the raw juice, that sweet carrot flavor would get flattened out. If you taste the soup a minute or two after you add the broth, and then you take a swig of the fresh carrot juice, you'll see what I mean right away.

This soup is simple to make, but it's not a last-minute dish. It's a good idea to put it together the day before you plan to serve it, so that it cools thoroughly and all the flavors come together.

SERVES 4 TO 6 AS AN APPETIZER

FOR THE SOUP
2 tablespoons olive oil
1 large onion, sliced (1 $^1/_2$ cups)
$^1/_4$ teaspoon salt plus a pinch
One 2-inch piece of fresh ginger, peeled and
    rough-chopped (2 tablespoons)
1 clove garlic, peeled
$^1/_8$ teaspoon crushed red pepper flakes
1 $^1/_2$ pounds carrots, peeled and chopped
    (about 4 cups)
2 $^1/_2$ cups vegetable broth
2 cups carrot juice (one 16-ounce bottle)
Juice of 1 lime (2 tablespoons)
Fresh-ground black pepper to taste

OPTIONAL GARNISHES
Chunks of cooked lobster or crab
Cooked shrimp
Fresh cilantro leaves
Grated lime zest
. . . or whatever looks good to you

Heat the olive oil in a medium-sized soup pot over medium-low heat.

Add the onions and a pinch of salt (to stop caramelization). Cook the onions until they soften up (about 2 minutes), stirring them every few seconds so they don't darken or stick.

Add the ginger, garlic, and red pepper flakes. Stir to coat everything in the oil, and cook the mixture together, stirring regularly so nothing sticks or caramelizes, until the ginger and garlic start to soften and you can smell the flavors: about 2 minutes.

Add the carrots, and mix everything together to combine.

Add the vegetable broth and the $^1/_4$ teaspoon of salt. Turn the heat up to medium-high and cook the soup at a simmer for about 30 minutes, until the carrots are soft enough to puree. You should be able to crush the carrots against the side of the pot with a wooden spoon, but they should have some toughness left in them—if you let them cook till they're total mush, they won't have any flavor.

Puree the soup, in batches, in a blender, blending each batch on high speed for 45 seconds to a minute, until it's really smooth, with a thick yogurty consistency. (Be careful in blending hot liquids: don't fill the blender all the way to the top, and make sure you hold the top down, using a kitchen towel, so that you don't

end up with hot orange soup splattering all over your kitchen.)

Pass each batch of the pureed soup through a fine-mesh strainer into a large bowl, using the back of a ladle to push as much of the good stuff through as possible. The soup should be very thick at this point.

Put the soup in the fridge to chill, uncovered, for at least 15 minutes. (Make sure the soup has really cooled down: you don't want to end up heating the carrot juice.)

Add the carrot juice and lime juice, and whisk everything together thoroughly. Season with salt and pepper to taste.

Put the soup back in the fridge until it's really nice and chilled (you can do this the day before).

Serve up the soup in some elegant-looking bowls; if you're feeling it, toss in the garnish that looks good to you.

TOMATO-CHILE-MANGO GAZPACHO

There are a million recipes for gazpacho, but there are really only two basic kinds. There's the Spanish style, made with bread and tomatoes and garlic, which is so popular in Spain that you can find it sold in cartons in the grocery store. And then there's Mexican gazpacho, which is kind of like a salsa minus the fire-roasting. My version is a take on the Mexican style. The marinade is key here: it really deepens the flavor of the raw vegetables, so that you end up with a smooth, well-balanced, refreshing soup with a little bit of a kick. And if you pour it into a tall glass and add a generous dose of vodka, it makes a great bloody Mary. . . .

SERVES 6 TO 8

FOR THE VEGETABLE MARINADE

1 pound ripe beefsteak tomatoes, cored and chopped (about 4 cups)

2 celery stalks, tough outer layer peeled off, cut into chunks (about 1 cup)

1 ripe mango, peeled and cut away from the pit in chunks (about $1/2$ cup)

$1/2$ English cucumber, peeled and chopped (about 1 cup)

1 small or $1/2$ large Vidalia onion, peeled and chopped (about 1 cup)

1 small fennel bulb, head only, outer leaves and core removed, sliced into chunks (about 1 cup)

1 red bell pepper, cleaned and cut into chunks (about 1 cup)

1 poblano pepper, cleaned and cut into chunks (about $1/2$ cup)

1 Anaheim pepper (might be called a banana pepper, depending on what part of the country you're from), cleaned and cut into chunks ($1/2$ cup)

1 jalapeño pepper, cleaned and cut into chunks

2 cloves garlic, peeled and cut in half

$1/4$ cup fresh cilantro leaves

10 fresh basil leaves, torn into pieces

10 fresh mint leaves, torn into pieces

1 teaspoon chili powder

$1/4$ teaspoon ground cumin

TO FINISH THE GAZPACHO

2 cups tomato juice

Juice of 3 limes ($1/3$ cup)

$3/4$ teaspoon salt

$1 1/2$ teaspoons Tabasco sauce (preferably the jalapeño kind, if you can find it)

GARNISHES

1 avocado, sliced

A handful of crumbled tortilla chips

$1/4$ cup fresh cilantro leaves, torn

TO MAKE THE VEGETABLE MARINADE

Pile all of the vegetables and fruit into a large bowl or pan, and sprinkle the garlic, herbs, chili powder, and cumin over the top.

Mix everything together with your hands, so the herbs and spices coat the fruit and vegetables.

Cover the bowl with plastic wrap and put it in the fridge to marinate for 8 to 12 hours.

TO FINISH THE GAZPACHO

Put half of the vegetable mixture into a food processor fitted with the metal blade. Add 1 cup of the tomato juice, and process for about 15 seconds, until you've got a thick soup. Pour the gazpacho into a large bowl; then repeat the process with the rest of the vegetable mixture and tomato juice.

Add the lime juice, salt, and Tabasco.

Pour the gazpacho into bowls. Garnish with the avocado slices, tortilla chips, and cilantro, and serve it right away, ice-cold.

COCONUT-CURRY BUTTERNUT SQUASH SOUP WITH LEMONGRASS AND CILANTRO YOGURT

This is a perfect cold-winter-day recipe: the soup is rich and savory and a little bit spicy, and the coolness of the cilantro yogurt and the crunch of the dhana dal balance out the intense flavors of the soup. The inspiration was Indian pumpkin curry, a dish you can find in the restaurants in legendary New York Indian neighborhoods like Jackson Heights, Queens. Patel Brothers, the jumpin' Indian supermarket at the heart of the neighborhood, sells of all the ingredients—huge bags of dhana dal, fresh ginger root the size of my arm, and beautiful vibrant cilantro. But you can probably find most everything you need for this recipe at your local market.

I like to garnish this soup with dhana dal: that's the inside part of the coriander seed, roasted in ghee (clarified butter) and salted. It's got this great crunchy-salty thing going: it's perfect as a topping for all kinds of soups and vegetables. If you can't find it near you and you want that crunch, you can garnish the soup with toasted almonds, but the taste will definitely be different. A lot of supermarkets and groceries carry fresh lemongrass in the herb section these days, but if you can't get your hands any, use the dried stuff.

SERVES 6 TO 8 AS AN APPETIZER

FOR THE SOUP

2 small butternut squash (about 3 pounds, 6 cups when cut into chunks)
2 tablespoons extra-virgin olive oil
1 tablespoon unsalted butter
1 large yellow onion, rough-chopped (2 cups)
One 1-inch piece of fresh ginger, peeled and rough-chopped ($^{1}/_{4}$ cup)

$^{1}/_{4}$ stalk lemongrass, sliced ($^{1}/_{4}$ cup), or $^{1}/_{2}$ teaspoon dried lemongrass
1 clove garlic, sliced
1 tablespoon curry powder (preferably Madras)
2 small sweet apples (such as Gala or Macintosh), peeled, cored, and rough-chopped (about 2 cups)
4 cups chicken broth, vegetable broth, or water
One 14-ounce can coconut milk (1 $^{1}/_{2}$ cups)
1 teaspoon salt

FOR THE CILANTRO YOGURT

1 cup thick yogurt (preferably the thick Greek kind)
1 loosely packed cup fresh cilantro leaves, roughly chopped
Pinch of salt
1 tablespoon extra-virgin olive oil

FOR THE GARNISH

2 tablespoons dhana dal

TO MAKE THE SOUP

Cut the top and bottom off each butternut squash, using a large serrated knife. (For all root vegetables—celery root, rutabagas, large squash—a serrated knife makes things much easier.)

Cut the squash in two right where the round part meets the long part.

Peel the skin off the long part of the squash, using the serrated knife and shaving lengthwise.

Cut the round part in half. Use a spoon to scoop the seeds and guts out of the cavity of each half.

Shave the skin off the round parts of the squash, using the serrated knife: cut lengthwise, holding the squash section on top to save your fingers. Then place each piece on the cutting board, flat side down, to cut off any leftover pieces of skin.

Chop the squash into big chunks.

Heat the olive oil and butter in a large soup pot over medium-high heat.

When the butter melts, add the onions, ginger, and lemongrass, and cook, stirring frequently for about 5 minutes, until the onions begin to soften but not color and the lemongrass aroma is released.

Add the garlic and curry powder, and mix so the onions and lemongrass are coated in the curry. Toast the curry for 30 seconds, stirring frequently, until you've brought out the aromas.

Add the butternut squash, apples, broth, and coconut milk to the pot and mix well; then increase the heat to high and stir in the salt.

Bring the soup up to a low boil. Reduce the heat to low and simmer, uncovered, for about 20 to 30 minutes, until the apples and squash are soft.

Working in batches, spoon the soup into a blender, being careful to fill the blender only about halfway—otherwise, the top might blow off and hot liquid would splatter everywhere. (With my pretty standard blender, this soup took 3 batches.) I like to put a towel over the top of the blender and hold it down to make sure the hot stuff stays inside. Blend the soup until it's completely smooth, starting at the lowest speed and slowly increasing as the soup breaks down.

Strain the blended soup through a fine-mesh strainer into another pot, pushing the soup through the strainer with the back of a spoon or ladle. If it's cooled down, warm the soup again over medium heat.

TO MAKE THE CILANTRO YOGURT
Stir the yogurt, cilantro, salt, and olive oil together in a medium-sized bowl.

TO FINISH THE SOUP
Divide the soup into individual bowls. Top each one with a large dollop of the cilantro yogurt, and sprinkle the dhana dal over the top. Serve immediately.

CREAM OF MUSHROOM SOUP

If you look at old American cookbooks from the '50s and '60s, every third recipe starts with a can of cream of mushroom soup. It's like some sad American version of a mirepoix, the French base that goes in everything. So when I started cooking seriously, I didn't want to have anything to do with the stuff, or with the poor-cousin button mushrooms it was made of. When we cooked mushroom soup in my restaurant, it was all wild mushrooms all the time; I spent a fortune on chanterelles and morels hand-picked by foragers in the wilds of the Northwest. Not a single button mushroom could be found in my kitchen. Real cooks, I thought, didn't do button mushrooms. It took a French guy to prove me wrong.

For service one night, Bertrand Chemel, then a sous chef at Café Boulud (he's the chef at 2941 in Washington, D.C., now), made the exact same mushroom soup I always did—but he used white button mushrooms (though he called them *champignons de paris* on the menu, and you've got to admit that sounds like a whole different thing). The soup he made was simple and inexpensive—every single ingredient could have come from the midwestern grocery stores I grew up with—and it was the best-tasting, most unbelievable mushroom soup I've ever had. You know how sometimes you have those *duh* moments, when the most obvious thing ever stares you in the face and goes, "You idiot, don't you recognize me?" Yep.

SERVES 6 TO 8 AS AN APPETIZER

$^3/_4$ stick (6 tablespoons) unsalted butter
7 shallots, sliced (about 1 $^1/_2$ cups)
1 pound white button mushrooms, washed and sliced
$^1/_2$ cup heavy cream
2 $^1/_4$ cups chicken broth
2 fresh thyme sprigs
$^1/_2$ teaspoon salt
$^1/_4$ teaspoon fresh-ground black pepper
1 cup croutons, or 2 slices crunchy toasted bread
2 tablespoons chopped fresh chives

Melt the butter in a large soup pot over medium heat. Add the shallots and sauté them in the butter for about 3 minutes, until they're nice and soft.

Add the mushrooms, turn the heat up to medium-high, and mix everything together well, so the mushrooms are coated in the butter and shallots. Cook the mushrooms for about 5 to 6 minutes, letting them release their water and steam things up but stirring them regularly so they don't stick or color.

When the mushrooms have softened up, add the cream, the chicken broth, and 2$^1/_4$ cups of water. Stir everything together, and then add the thyme sprigs, salt, and pepper.

Bring the soup up to a simmer. Then reduce the heat to medium-low and let it cook for 20 minutes, uncovered, until the mushrooms are very soft and the flavors have come together.

Pull the thyme sprigs out of the pot. Then ladle the soup into a blender, in batches, making sure you scrape in all the good stuff on the bottom. Blend each batch for about 10 seconds on low speed to get things going, then 20 seconds on medium and 20 on high as the soup breaks down. (Be careful to hold the top down with a towel to avoid hot-liquid disasters.) When it's done, the soup should be completely smooth. As you finish each batch, pour it into a clean pot. If the soup has cooled down when you're done, reheat it over a medium flame.

Season the soup with more salt and pepper if it needs it. Serve it up in individual bowls, garnished with the croutons and chives (or with the toast on the side).

GOOD OLD GOULASH

If you don't think of goulash as American, you've definitely never been to the Midwest. There are lots of Hungarian-Americans in south Cleveland, so when I was growing up, you saw goulash on menus and at events all over the place. If you live in Cleveland (or Toledo, or Pittsburgh), you've probably seen a million variations on this dish. I know: it's as old-school as fern bars and Pac-Man—but is that necessarily a bad thing? On a cold midwestern night, what could be better than a super-soul-satisfying, slightly smoky, slightly spicy stew?

Goulash is a slow-cooking dish, the kind of thing you want to make on a snowy day when there's really no good reason to go outside. You can do this goulash with regular paprika, but it's worth hunting down the two different kinds I use here: together, they give the goulash a really interesting depth.

SERVES 6 TO 8

¹/₄ cup extra-virgin olive oil
1 ¹/₂ pounds boneless beef shoulder stew meat,
   in chunks
1 large onion, sliced (1 ¹/₂ cups)
2 cloves garlic, peeled
¹/₂ teaspoon caraway seeds, crushed with a knife
2 teaspoons sweet paprika
2 teaspoons smoked paprika
¹/₄ teaspoon salt
¹/₄ teaspoon fresh-ground black pepper
One 14.5-ounce can crushed tomatoes
   (I like Jersey Fresh)
9 cups chicken broth
1 green bell pepper, chopped (about 1 cup)
1 red bell pepper, chopped (about 1 cup)
1 pound new potatoes, peeled and cut into
   1-inch pieces (2 cups)
2 medium parsnips, peeled and cut into
   1-inch chunks (1 ¹/₂ cups)

Heat the olive oil in a large pot over medium-high heat.

Add the stew meat and cook for about 1 minute, stirring frequently so nothing sticks, until the meat begins to brown.

Mix in the onions, and then keep cooking everything together for about 5 minutes, until the onions have softened and browned up a bit (they should caramelize a little, and they'll also take on some color from the meat juice).

Mix in the garlic cloves, caraway seeds, and sweet and smoked paprika. Season with the salt and pepper, and toast everything together for a minute or so, until the juice from the onions and the meat mixes with the spices and forms a paste, and the whole kitchen smells like paprika.

Add the tomatoes and the chicken broth, and stir everything together. You should have a deep red soupy mix in your pot, with a sweet, smoky, tomato flavor. Bring the soup up to a simmer and let it cook, uncovered, for 2 hours.

Add the green and red peppers, the potatoes, and parsnips. Stir everything together and continue cooking for another 45 minutes or so, uncovered, until the meat has softened up completely and is fork-tendah.

PINO'S MEATS, SULLIVAN STREET, NEW YORK CITY

CHICKEN POZOLE

Pozole is the Spanish word for hominy: dried corn kernels with the germ and husk removed. The soup known as pozole is a staple in Mexican cooking; the different styles you find across the U.S. depend on what part of Mexico the cook's family comes from. (This version, for example, could be made, if you wanted to go that way, with veal head instead of chicken.)

My take on pozole comes from a classic family-meal staple at Café Boulud that was cooked up by some of our dishwashers, who came from Puebla. I loved it so much I actually put it on the menu.

This soup is really all about the garnishes. On its own, it has some heft from the hominy and a meaty savoriness from the chicken, but when you load it up with salsa, cilantro leaves, romaine, and tortilla chips, squeeze a good hit of lime on top, and dose it with a little hot sauce, you've really got something special. It's a great party soup: make a big pot of this, put it in the middle of the table, and let everybody throw on their own garnishes. People love that.

SERVES 4 AS A MAIN COURSE OR
6 AS AN APPETIZER

FOR THE SOUP
1/4 cup extra-virgin olive oil
1 medium onion, halved and sliced
    (about 1 1/2 cups)
1/2 teaspoon ground cumin
3/4 teaspoon chili powder
6 chicken legs, split (about 2 1/2 to 3 pounds; if you
    can't find legs that are already split, use a meat
    cleaver to divide the leg from the thigh)
4 cups chicken broth
1 tablespoon dried oregano (preferably Mexican)
1 teaspoon salt
2 1/2 cups canned hominy

One 4-ounce can diced Hatch green chiles
    (about 1/3 cup)

FOR THE SALSA
2 medium-sized ripe tomatoes, chopped
    (about 2 cups)
1/2 medium red onion, chopped (about 1/2 cup)
Pinch of salt
1 tablespoon extra-virgin olive oil
Juice of 1/2 lime (about 1 teaspoon)
Dash of your favorite hot sauce

FOR THE GARNISH
2 limes, quartered
7 radishes, diced (about 1 cup)
5 green onions, chopped fine (about 1/2 cup)
1 head romaine lettuce, sliced into thin ribbons
1 cup whole fresh cilantro leaves
1/2 bag corn tortilla chips (you can eat the rest
    of the bag in front of the TV)
Your favorite hot sauce

TO MAKE THE SOUP
Heat the olive oil in a large soup pot over a medium-high flame. Then add the onions and cook them for about 1 minute, until they start to soften up.

Add the cumin and chili powder. Cook for 10 seconds or so, until the spices release their aroma. Then add the chicken legs and mix well to coat the chicken in the spices.

Add the chicken broth and 2 cups of water, and turn the heat up to high.

When the soup comes to a boil, turn the heat down to a simmer and stir in the oregano and salt.

Cook the soup, uncovered, for about 30 to 45 minutes, until the chicken is falling off the bone.

>>>

Using a slotted spoon, pull the chicken out of the pot. Cool it down on a plate in the fridge.

In the meantime, stir the hominy and green chiles into the pot; then remove the pot from the heat.

When the chicken has cooled, pull the meat off the bones. You can throw away the skin if you want, but I like to keep it on the meat and throw it in the soup for a little more mouth-feel. Watch out for rubbery pieces of cartilage and small bones. When you've pulled out anything you wouldn't want to eat, add the chicken meat back to the pot, and bring the soup back up to a simmer.

MEANWHILE, MAKE THE SALSA

In a mixing bowl, combine the tomatoes and onions.

Mix in the salt, the olive oil, the lime juice, and the hot sauce. The result should be tangy, juicy, and rich on the tongue.

TO SERVE

I like to serve the soup in a pot in the middle of the table, with a big ladle that can pick up the chicken, hominy, and liquid all at once. Give each person a large wide-mouthed soup bowl (so they can fit in all the garnishes) and make sure everybody grabs some lime to squeeze over the top. Arrange the salsa and the garnishes in little bowls around the pot. Heap the tortilla chips in a big bowl, put a bottle of your favorite hot sauce on the side, throw some beers on ice, and let everybody go to town.

TORTILLA MACHINE AT TACQUERIA
LOS HERMANOS IN BUSHWICK

HATCH GREEN CHILES

If you drive south from Truth or Consequences, New Mexico, you'll find yourself in Hatch, home of the famous Hatch green chile. Red chiles grow here, too, but the green ones are really something special. Hatch has a chile festival every September; you'll be driving along, and suddenly you'll see a big metal tumbler—just like one of those old bingo tumblers—standing at an intersection. They put 25 pounds or so of green chiles inside the tumbler, and then they plant a propane or butane torch under the tumbler, and they start turning. The chiles roast just like that, in the open. When they're ready, the growers sell them in little bags at markets all over New Mexico. The chiles have this really deep sweet-but-spicy flavor: they say that the earth, water, and mesa air together create that special taste.

Outside New Mexico, Hatch chiles are sold all over in little tins. They're already roasted and peeled and ready to go—super-easy to work with, a great chef secret weapon.

ITALIAN WEDDING SOUP WITH CHICKEN MEATBALLS AND SAGE CROSTONE

You can't have an Italian-American wedding in Cleveland (or Pittsburgh, or Youngstown) without Italian wedding soup. When I was working in catering halls in high school, every single Italian wedding started with this soup: chicken base, pastina, escarole, Parmesan cheese, and meatballs. Everybody always said it was a tradition from the old country: it was what people had eaten at weddings for centuries, maybe millennia, you couldn't have a good marriage without it, it was good luck, yadda yadda. But when I went to Italy, I found out that Italian wedding soup has nothing to do with actual weddings at all—it's just this Italian-American invented tradition, probably started by mistake. It's true that if you make a soup like this in Naples, you call it *zuppa de matrimonio,* but that's got nothing to do with any ancient wedding feast: the marriage is between the meat and the vegetables. It's a pretty good match, though—I think it's one marriage that's going to last.

There are a lot of steps here, but don't get scared: the recipe is actually really easy.

SERVES 6 TO 8

FOR THE CROSTONE
Six 1-inch-thick slices ciabatta bread
1/4 cup extra-virgin olive oil
1/4 teaspoon salt
1/4 teaspoon fresh-ground black pepper
10 fresh sage leaves, chopped (about 2 tablespoons)
2 tablespoons grated Parmesan cheese

FOR THE MEATBALLS
1/2 pound ground chicken
1/2 pound chicken sausage, removed from the casing
1/2 teaspoon salt
1/4 teaspoon fresh-ground black pepper
2 tablespoons grated Parmesan cheese

1 egg
1/2 cup dry bread crumbs (I like panko crumbs)
1/4 cup whole milk
1/4 cup chopped fresh parsley
2 teaspoons dried oregano
1/4 teaspoon ground fennel seed
1/4 teaspoon crushed red pepper flakes

FOR THE SOUP
2 tablespoons extra-virgin olive oil
1 medium onion, roughly chopped (1 cup)
4 medium celery stalks, roughly chopped (1 cup)
4 small carrots, peeled and roughly chopped (1 cup)
6 cups chicken broth
1/2 teaspoon salt
1/4 teaspoon fresh-ground black pepper
1/2 cup pastina (a very small star-shaped pasta)
1 head escarole, outer leaves discarded, washed well, torn into medium-sized pieces

TO FINISH THE DISH
1/2 cup grated Parmesan cheese

TO MAKE THE CROSTONE
Preheat the oven to 350°F.

Lay the ciabatta slices out on a baking sheet. Drizzle the olive oil over the bread, and then sprinkle on the salt, pepper, and sage. Sprinkle the grated Parmesan over the top. Then put the sheet on the middle rack in the oven, and bake until the top is nice and crispy; about 20 minutes, depending on your oven.

TO MAKE THE MEATBALLS
Combine the ground chicken and chicken sausage meat in a large mixing bowl. Add the salt, pepper, and grated Parmesan.

Beat the egg and add it to the bowl.

Put the bread crumbs in a small bowl. Pour the milk over them, mix everything together lightly with your fingers, and let the milk and bread crumbs sit together for 3 minutes or so, until the milk is absorbed and you have a wet, bready paste.

Add the parsley, oregano, fennel seed, red pepper flakes, and milky bread crumbs to the meat mixture and mix everything together well, using both hands, until combined.

Lay a piece of plastic wrap or wax paper on a baking sheet. Form the meatballs by taking a little bit of meat and rolling it between your hands, just like you're making a snowball. The meatballs should measure about

1 to 1$\frac{1}{2}$ inches in diameter; you should have 25 to 30 of them. As you form them, place them on the baking sheet.

TO MAKE THE SOUP

Put a large pot of salted water on to boil for the pastina.

Heat the olive oil in a large pot over medium heat. Add the onions, celery, and carrots, mix well to coat the vegetables in the oil, and cook, stirring frequently, for about 3 to 4 minutes, until the vegetables start to soften.

Add the chicken broth, salt, and pepper, turn the heat to medium-high, and bring the soup up to a simmer. Cook at a low bubble for about 3 minutes, until the flavors come together. Then add the meatballs to the pot and poach them in the soup for about 5 minutes, until there's no pink on the inside when you cut one open.

Meanwhile, when the pot of water comes to a boil, add the pastina, cook it according to the directions on the box, and then drain the pasta. Don't rinse it! You want the sticky glutens to stick around.

Add the pastina and escarole to the soup, pull the pot off the heat, and mix everything together.

TO FINISH THE DISH

Ladle a generous portion of the soup, with lots of meatballs and escarole, into each bowl.

Sprinkle the grated Parmesan on top. Put a crostone on the side of each bowl. Serve right away.

ITALIAN WEDDING SOUP WITH CHICKEN MEATBALLS AND SAGE CROSTONE, PAGE 52

MIDWEST WHITEFISH CHOWDER, page 56

MIDWEST WHITEFISH CHOWDER

Lots of people think that chowder is a New England thing—but those people don't live in the Midwest. When I was a kid, we used to go camping in Michigan's Upper Peninsula (where Lake Superior and Lake Michigan meet). We'd go canoeing and hang out in Frankenmuth (a little bit of old Bavaria in the Midwest, complete with period architecture, girls in lederhosen, and places called "Cheese Haus"), and we'd always make the required stop at the Shipwreck Museum on Whitefish Point, near where the *Edmund Fitzgerald* went down. And, being on Whitefish Point, we'd get ourselves some whitefish chowder at one of the fish joints near the lake up there. So whitefish chowder is all about summer for me—and I love to throw a couple of handfuls of fresh summer corn in, to sweeten things up.

This recipe isn't complicated, but the timing is important: you need to follow all the steps in order. The fish, on the other hand, is pretty much up to you: I like to use smoked whitefish, but you could also use smoked haddock, smoked sable, smoked trout—even smoked salmon, though that will, of course, change the color a little bit.

This is great with crackers or crunchy bread—or you can go really Midwest and throw in some Goldfish crackers.

Chowders are traditionally thickened up with a flour roux, but here I use pureed potato instead. That's because the starch in the potato thickens the soup but doesn't add any weight, so the chowder's a little lighter.

SERVES 6 TO 8

FOR THE POTATO MIXTURE
1 pound Yukon Gold potatoes, peeled and cut into
    ¹/₂-inch chunks (2 cups)
1 cup heavy cream
1 cup whole milk

¹/₄ teaspoon salt, or more to taste
¹/₄ teaspoon fresh-ground black pepper

FOR THE CHOWDER
3 slices bacon, diced (about ¹/₂ cup)
1 tablespoon butter
1 medium onion, diced (about 1 cup)
3 celery stalks, diced (about 1 cup)
1 leek, cut in half, cleaned, and diced (about 1 cup)
1 cup dry white wine
1 teaspoon fresh thyme leaves
3 cups chicken broth, clam juice, or water
¹/₂ teaspoon salt
¹/₄ teaspoon fresh-ground black pepper
Kernels from 4 ears fresh corn (about 2 cups)
1 pound smoked whitefish (or other smoked fish),
    deboned and shredded into large chunks (about
    2 cups)
5 drops Tabasco sauce
2 tablespoons chopped fresh dill
2 tablespoons chopped fresh parsley

TO COOK THE POTATOES
Put the potatoes in a medium-sized pot, pour in the cream and milk, add the salt and pepper, and cook the mixture over medium-high heat for about 10 minutes, until it comes up to a simmer.

Lower the heat to medium-low and keep cooking for about 20 minutes, until the potatoes are cooked through and soft. Keep an eye on the pot to make sure the mixture doesn't burn or bubble over. Taste the liquid as it cooks, and if you're feeling it, add another ¹/₄ teaspoon salt (depending on the saltiness of your fish).

TO MAKE THE CHOWDER
While the potatoes are cooking, fry up the bacon in a large pot over medium-high heat for about 5 minutes,

so the fat renders, stirring it around occasionally to make sure it doesn't stick.

When the bacon has started to crisp, add the butter and let it foam up (about 30 seconds).

Add the onions, celery, and leeks. Mix everything together so the vegetables are coated in the fat; then turn the heat down to medium. Sweat the vegetables for about 2 minutes, until they soften up, stirring them every so often so they don't color too much.

Add the white wine and thyme. Keep cooking for about 5 minutes, until the liquid reduces by about three quarters. Then add the broth, the salt, and pepper, and let the chowder cook at a simmer until the onions, celery, and leeks are tender (about 5 to 7 minutes).

TO PUT THE CHOWDER TOGETHER AND FINISH THE DISH
When the vegetables are soft, pull the pot of potatoes off the stove. Using a slotted spoon, scoop out half of the potatoes and add them to the chowder. (Try not to transfer too much liquid: you don't want to add much of the unblended cream to the soup.)

Put the rest of the potatoes and the cream in a blender. Cover the top with a towel and hold it down;

blend the potatoes and cream on medium speed for about 15 seconds, until you have a smooth, milkshake-like sauce.

Pour the potato-cream mixture into the soup pot, add the corn, and mix everything together well. Keep cooking for about 3 minutes, until the corn is cooked and the flavors come together.

Turn the heat off, add the whitefish and Tabasco, stir everything together, and let the chowder sit, off the heat, for 5 minutes, so the smoky fish flavor infuses the soup.

Ladle the chowder into bowls, garnish each one with some of the dill and parsley, and serve it right away.

Don't let the chowder sit around for too long: after a day or two in the fridge, the corn will start breaking down and the chowder will sweeten up.

BONES

If you're using smoked whitefish or trout, you've got to be really careful about bones. Here's my method for bone removal: I put a bowl of water on the counter next to my cutting board. I pull off a chunk of fish, pull it apart with my hands, and flake apart the fish, pulling the bigger bones out. The tiny bones—the real menaces to society—are harder to get rid of because they stick to the fish; when you pull them out, they stick to your fingers, and they can end up right back in with the fish. That's where the water comes in: let the little bones stick to your fingers, then dip your hands in the water so they float way.

LENTIL SOUP WITH BACON, APPLE, AND MUSTARD

People usually think of lentil soup as some sort of sad East Village thing: an old-school hippie dish with no backbone. Well, this is lentil soup with cojones. The mustard gives it depth and sharpness to balance the thick comfort-foody-ness of the lentils; the apples make it interesting, giving the soup texture and freshness. Bacon is traditional in lentil soup, and it gives everything a nice smokiness, but you can leave it out to make a veg version: just add another ³/₄ cup of chopped vegetables to bulk it up.

The soup can be made ahead of time and stored in the fridge for up to 4 days, or in the freezer for up to a month—so you can always have some ready for a cold winter night. Follow it up with a shot of Irish whiskey and you'll get through the dark just fine.

SERVES 6 TO 8 AS AN APPETIZER

FOR THE SOUP

2 tablespoons extra-virgin olive oil
5 slices bacon, diced fine (³/₄ cup)
¹/₂ medium onion, chopped small (¹/₂ cup)
1 medium carrot, peeled and chopped small (¹/₂ cup)
2 celery stalks, chopped small (1 cup)
³/₄ teaspoon dry English mustard
1 pound dried green lentils (about 2 ¹/₂ cups)
3 fresh thyme sprigs
1 bay leaf
9 cups low-sodium chicken broth, vegetable broth, or water
1 teaspoon salt
³/₄ teaspoon fresh-ground black pepper
1 tablespoon red wine vinegar

FOR THE GARNISH

1 tablespoon grainy mustard
1 tablespoon extra-virgin olive oil

1 ¹/₂ teaspoons balsamic vinegar
1 medium Gala or Fuji apple, peeled, cored, sliced, and then cut in long thin strips
6 to 8 tablespoons sour cream (1 per serving)
2 tablespoons chopped fresh chives

TO MAKE THE SOUP

Heat the olive oil in a medium-sized pot over medium-high heat.

Add the bacon and allow it to render for about 2 minutes, until it starts to crisp up.

Turn the heat down to medium and add the onions, carrots, and celery. Cook, stirring to make sure nothing sticks, until they start to soften up: 2 minutes or so.

Add the mustard, lentils, thyme, bay leaf, and broth.

Stir to combine, raise the heat to medium-high, and cook the soup, uncovered, for about 20 minutes, stirring every so often to keep it from sticking.

Mix in the salt and pepper, and keep cooking for another 20 minutes or so, until the soup is thick and the lentils are softened but not mushy (they should still be chewable). You don't want to let the lentils boil for too long, so they get that muddy middle-school-cafeteria look: you want them to stay bright, so keep an eye on them as they cook.

Pull the pot off the heat and take out the bay leaf and the thyme sprigs.

Ladle about a quarter of the soup into a blender. Hold the top of the blender down with a towel to prevent hot-soup disasters, and blend on medium speed for about 15 seconds, until you've got a thick liquid.

Pour the blended soup back into the pot with the unblended soup, and mix everything together. (The idea is to create an instant puree, so you get smoothness alongside the texture of the lentils.)

Warm the soup through on the stove over medium-high heat.

Mix in the red wine vinegar.

TO MAKE THE GARNISH AND FINISH THE DISH
Just before you're ready to serve the soup, combine the mustard, olive oil, vinegar, and 1¹/₂ teaspoons of water in a small mixing bowl.

Add the apples and mix around to cover all the pieces in the mixture.

Serve the soup in individual bowls, with a scoop of sour cream and a sprinkle of apples and chives on each one.

TOFU STEW WITH MISO AND SHIITAKE

Back in the day, Japanese food was exotic to most Americans, the kind of thing you could only find in New York or California or Hawaii. I remember sitting in front of the TV one night with my dad when I was a kid. The news was on, and some airbrushed newscaster was talking about this crazy-popular new restaurant in California—a place that served raw fish. My dad stared at the screen, stared at me, and said, "Who would eat bait?"

Well, these days, everybody eats "bait." Teriyaki places and Japanese steakhouses dot strip malls across America; ramen noodles simmer in dorm-room microwaves everywhere; and you can buy sushi rolls in just about any suburban supermarket. Japanese cooking, in other words, is now officially a part of the American culinary landscape.

The flavors of this dish are what the Japanese call umami—dense, salty, rich, and complex, a little bit fishy in a good way—with a sharp kick from the pickled ginger. And it's super-easy: from start to finish, it'll take you about 20 minutes, all in. The key to this dish is dashi, a broth made with kombu and bonito flakes. It's one of the fundamentals of Japanese cooking. If you can't find furikake, just leave it out—or use toasted sesame seeds to get that furikake texture. You can eat this on its own as a brothy stew full of tofu and mushrooms, but it's also great with a bowl of steamed rice.

SERVES 4 TO 6

2 sheets (about 1 ounce) kombu (Japanese dried
   seaweed)
1 pound fresh shiitake mushrooms
4 cups loosely packed bonito flakes
1/2 cup miso paste
1 pound medium or firm tofu, drained and cut into
   1-inch chunks

3 green onions, sliced thin (about 1/2 cup)
4 to 6 tablespoons furikake (1 tablespoon per
   person; see Notes)
2 tablespoons pickled ginger, sliced

Lay the kombu out on a cutting board. Use a damp cloth to wipe off any grit (sand, tiny pebbles, and so forth) on both sides of each sheet.

Combine the kombu with 6 cups of water in a large saucepan, and place it over medium-high heat.

While the water is heating, clean the shiitakes, remove the stems, and quarter them.

Just before the water comes to a boil, use a pair of tongs to pull the kombu out of the pot and throw them away. (This is the most important direction in every single dashi recipe I've ever read. I've asked many Japanese cooks why it's so important to pull the kombu out before the water boils, and nobody's ever been able to tell me, but they all agree it's crucial, and I believe them.)

Add the bonito flakes to the hot water and cook for about 1 minute, until the water is almost simmering again. Pull the pot off the heat and let the bonito flakes fall to the bottom. Steep the bonito flakes for 5 minutes, until the flavors have infused the dashi.

Strain the liquid into a large bowl and toss the bonito flakes.

Return the dashi to the cooking pot and turn the heat to medium.

When the dashi comes up to a simmer, whisk in the miso, so that the liquid takes on that slightly broken-up look you see in miso soup in Japanese restaurants. The liquid should now be salty-tasting as well as bonito-flake-tasting.

>>>

Stir in the shiitakes, and let the soup cook for about 3 minutes, until the mushrooms just start to soften and are a little bit silky on the tongue.

Add the tofu and keep cooking for about 2 minutes, until the tofu is warmed through.

Stir the soup in the pot so that the miso doesn't settle on the bottom; then ladle the soup into individual bowls.

Top each bowl of soup with a scattering of green onions, 1 tablespoon of the furikake, and a pinch of pickled ginger. Serve right away.

NOTES

Some ingredients for this dish may not be available at your local supermarket, but they're pretty standard issue at Asian food stores (the furikake, bonito flakes, and kombu are all with the dry goods; pickled ginger, the same stuff you get on your plate at a sushi joint, comes in a sealed plastic pouch).

Furikake is a flaky dry seasoning mixture containing toasted sesame seeds, nori seaweed, and dried egg. I like Urashima brand.

SOUP DORIA

When I worked in Gray Kunz's kitchens at Lespinasse, there was an honest-to-God Swiss princess living at the St. Regis Hotel. Her name was Princess Doria, and every night, she would phone down to the kitchen and tell us what she wanted to eat for dinner. In the beginning, Gray would cook for her himself: he was Swiss, she was Swiss, it was a whole Swiss thing going on. But after a while, he got tired of taking her calls, and the job devolved to me and the sous chefs. Every night, that phone would ring, and I would say, "Good evening, Princess," and she would tell me what she wanted to eat that night. Princess Doria wasn't into super-fancy creative cooking: her thing was refined-but-homey. Sometimes, for example, it would be a roast *pintade* for two: I would plate the breast for her, and the thighs for her cat. So I developed some dishes that were just for her. I named them after her: Salad Doria, Chicken Doria. And sometimes on cold winter nights, she would call down and say, "Andrew, I would like some Soup Doria tonight, please."

Time passed. I left Lespinasse to travel and cook in France. When I got back to New York, I helped open Le Cirque 2000 in the Palace Hotel. We'd been up and running about two weeks when the kitchen phone rang by my station one night, right in the middle of the busiest part of service. I heard a familiar voice say, in French-accented tones, "Andrew?" Princess Doria on the line. She'd moved on to the Palace right behind me, and she would be pleased, she said, if I would send up some Soup Doria for her.

This soup is just Princess Doria's style. It's really a *potage*—a French minestrone, a chunky winter vegetable soup. I like to sprinkle Parmesan cheese on top and serve it with some crusty, crunchy French bread.

SERVES 6 TO 8

2 tablespoons extra-virgin olive oil
10 slices bacon, diced large (2 cups)
1 large sweet onion, quartered and sliced (about 2 cups)
2 large leeks, cut in half, cleaned, and roughly chopped (about 2 cups)
1/4 teaspoon crushed red pepper flakes
6 medium carrots, peeled and sliced (about 2 cups)
1 large celery root, peeled, cut lengthwise into 6 pieces, and sliced thin (about 2 cups)
2 2/3 pounds mixed potatoes (red, yellow, wax), washed but not peeled and sliced thin (about 2 cups)
10 Jerusalem artichokes, peeled or scrubbed and sliced into thin rounds (about 2 cups)
1 teaspoon salt
1/2 teaspoon fresh-ground black pepper
8 cups low-sodium chicken broth
Herb packet: 3 dried bay leaves and 10 fresh thyme sprigs, tied together with string
1 bunch kale, washed, stemmed, and torn (about 6 cups)

OPTIONAL
Hazelnut or pumpkin-seed oil for drizzling
2 tablespoons freshly grated Parmesan cheese

Heat the olive oil in a large pot over medium heat.

Add the bacon and let it render slowly in the olive oil, stirring every so often to keep it from sticking, for about 5 minutes, until it starts crisping up.

Add the onions, leeks, and red pepper flakes. Turn the heat up to medium-high, mix the vegetables and the bacon together well, and let them cook for about 3 minutes, stirring every so often, until the onions and leeks have started to soften but the onions have not colored.

Add the carrots, celery root, potatoes, Jerusalem artichokes, salt, pepper, chicken broth, and the herb packet. Mix everything together. Then turn the heat to high and let the soup cook at a low bubble for about half an hour, until the vegetables soften up (but before they get super-mushy).

Add the kale, stir it into the soup, and cook it down for about 10 minutes, until it's soft and cooked all the way through. Pull out the herb packet.

Serve the soup with some good bread on the side. I like to top each bowl with a drizzle of hazelnut or pumpkin-seed oil and a sprinkling of cheese.

GARDEN SALAD WITH GRANDMA'S DRESSING

This salad is all about what's fresh from the garden (or the farmers' market, if you're garden-deprived like me). The dressing is more or less the same one my grandma in Miami taught me to make.

The garlic prep method here is also a lesson from my grandma. The salt gives you some grit when you grind the garlic and pulls the liquid out, so it turns into a paste more easily.

SERVES 4 TO 6

FOR THE SALAD
About 8 cups of whatever's good from the garden (except potatoes), for instance:
8 radishes, sliced thin
$^1/_2$ cup cherry tomatoes, sliced thin
1-2 red bell peppers, sliced thin
1 yellow bell pepper, sliced thin
1 fennel bulb, trimmed, cored, and sliced thin
$^1/_2$ cucumber, sliced thin
1 head arugula, washed and torn
1 head of any other kind of lettuce you like, washed and torn

FOR THE GARLIC
2 cloves garlic, peeled
Pinch of salt

FOR THE DRESSING
1 tablespoon Dijon mustard
$^1/_4$ cup red wine vinegar
$^1/_4$ cup balsamic vinegar
1 tablespoon mixed dried herbs (I like to use herbes de Provence, but Italian seasoning is fine)
$^3/_4$ cup extra-virgin olive oil
$^3/_4$ cup corn oil
$1^1/_2$ teaspoons sugar
$^1/_4$ teaspoon salt
$^1/_4$ teaspoon fresh-ground black pepper

TO FINISH THE SALAD
$^1/_2$ to $^3/_4$ cup grated Parmesan cheese

TO MAKE THE SALAD
Assemble all the ingredients in a large bowl and toss them together, using your hands.

TO PREPARE THE GARLIC
Mince the garlic superfine. Then sprinkle a pinch of salt over it and give it a few more chops.

Using the flat side of a large knife, crush the garlic over and over, rocking and pressing the side of the knife down and mashing the garlic into the cutting board, until you have a fine paste.

TO MAKE THE DRESSING
Put the garlic in a mixing bowl and add $^1/_4$ cup water, the mustard, red wine vinegar, and balsamic vinegar. Whisk everything together, and then whisk in the dried herbs. (You can also do this in the blender, working on a very low speed.)

Pour the olive oil and corn oil into a liquid measuring cup so they mix together, and then pour them slowly into the garlic mixture, whisking or blending constantly.

Add the sugar, salt, and pepper, and whisk or blend well. You want the oils and the vinegars to be completely blended.

TO FINISH AND SERVE THE SALAD
Pour the dressing over the salad, toss it well, and serve it up in individual bowls, with about 2 tablespoons of the Parmesan sprinkled over each salad.

If you've got more dressing than you need (depending on how heavily you like your salad dressed), store any extra in a covered container in the fridge; it will keep for up to a week.

MOM'S FLORIDA AVOCADO AND ORANGE SALAD

My grandma's house was in the Miami neighborhood that used to be called Little River (it's known as Little Haiti now). She had a big yard that was full of fruit trees: you could walk out into her backyard and pick grapefruit, sour oranges, sapodillas, mangos—even Cuban bananas. We would drive down to Florida a couple of times every winter when I was a kid, and as soon as we got out of the car, I would head right through the house to the yard, where I would run around in that little jungle. My mom loves citrus and avocados, so she made up this salad while we were down South visiting. She would only make it when we were in Miami, with citrus from my grandma's yard and big smooth-skinned green Florida avocados, which are meatier than the little Hass guys you find in most grocery stores. This salad takes me right back there. It's Florida in a bowl: the sharp fresh flavor of citrus meets the richness of avocado and a little bit of a kick from the onion and hot sauce. I like to use navel oranges and Florida avocados, but Hass avocados work fine, and you can use any kind of orange, or even grapefruit.

SERVES 4

2 Valencia or navel oranges
1 Florida avocado or 2 Hass avocados, sliced in half and pitted
1 cup cherry tomatoes, halved
1/2 small red onion, sliced thin (about 1/4 cup)
Juice of 1 lime (2 tablespoons)
1/4 cup extra-virgin olive oil, plus some for drizzling
1/4 teaspoon salt
1 teaspoon of your favorite hot sauce
1 tablespoon dried oregano (preferably Mexican)
A handful of fresh cilantro leaves for garnish (optional)

Slice the ends off the oranges (with the peel on).

Stand an orange on one end and, with a small sharp knife, slice off the orange peel, taking the white pith with it.

Holding the peeled orange in your hand, cut the membrane away just to the inside of each white segmenting line. As they come loose, let the "supremes" drop into a large bowl, leaving all the white attached to the "skeleton" with a thin membrane of flesh.

Squeeze all the juice out of the "skeleton" into the bowl with the supremes. Then throw away the skeleton.

With a dinner knife (*not* the sharpest knife in your kitchen—you don't want to cut right through the skin and into your hand), cut each avocado half into segments lengthwise, cutting through the meat to (not into) the skin. Then cut around the outside of the avocado meat, and, using the knife, push the pieces out of the skin and into the bowl containing the oranges.

Add the tomatoes and the onions to the bowl.

Squeeze the lime over the top, twisting a fork in the flesh to get all the juice out.

Add the olive oil, salt, hot sauce, and oregano, and mix everything together.

Pile the salad into a serving bowl. Garnish it with fresh cilantro leaves, drizzle more olive oil over the top, and serve it right away.

SPICY SUMMER MELON SALAD

Nothing's better than a super-ripe local melon—unless it's a melon with a kick. This recipe has its roots in Southeast Asian cooking: the cool sweetness of the fruit, basil, and mint together with the heat of the Sriracha are guaranteed to cool you down on a hot summer day. (You know that old argument about whether eating spicy things on a hot day cools you down more than eating cool things? Here you get both, so everybody wins.) Don't get freaked out by the fish sauce in this recipe: you won't actually taste it, but it gives everything a lot more balance.

Don't let the fruit marinate too long, and make sure you serve this supercold, with the melon right out of the fridge.

SERVES 6 AS AN APPETIZER

6 cups mixed melon (cantaloupe, honeydew, watermelon . . . whatever's in season and delicious, cut into chunks)
Juice of 4 limes ($1/4$ cup)
$1 1/2$ teaspoons Sriracha (Thai hot sauce; see page 85)
$1/4$ cup peanut oil
1 teaspoon fish sauce (see page 72)
$1/2$ teaspoon salt
20 fresh basil leaves, roughly torn (about $1/2$ cup)
20 fresh mint leaves, roughly torn (about $1/4$ cup)
$1/2$ cup unsalted peanuts, chopped

Chill down the melon chunks in the fridge until they're really cold.

Squeeze the lime juice into a small mixing bowl, and then whisk in the Sriracha.

Pour the peanut oil slowly into the bowl, whisking constantly until it's completely blended.

Add the fish sauce and salt, and whisk everything together.

Toss in the basil and mint leaves, and mix everything together.

Just before you're ready to serve it, take the melon out of the fridge and pile it in a big serving bowl.

Pour the dressing over the melon and mix it in with your hands.

Scatter the chopped peanuts over the salad, and serve it right away.

FISH SAUCE

If you don't have fish sauce in your refrigerator, you're really missing out. Fish sauce is a Southeast Asian thing: it's made from anchovies, salt, and water, fermented outside in the sun. And believe it or not, it makes everything better.

Fish sauce isn't just an Asian thing. There's an old European tradition along these lines, too. The Romans called it *garum,* and they made it with exactly the same mix of ingredients. And you'll find a version of fish sauce in every steakhouse: good old Worcestershire relies pretty heavily on fermented anchovies, too.

Fish sauce is kind of like natural MSG: it has a very high glutamate content, and that makes things taste good. It doesn't give dishes a fishy flavor; it just kick-starts your palate, rounds out the tastes, and brings *umami*—that famous Japanese "fifth flavor"— into the mix. I use fish sauce in the melon salad on page 71, the mussels on page 94, the pork on page 153, and the steamed snapper on page 84, but you can use it in all kinds of dishes. You can find fish sauce in the Asian section of your grocery store; my favorite is Squid brand.

TOMATO SALAD WITH BUTTERMILK DRESSING

I'm a big fan of buttermilk dressing: if you're going to dress really great tomatoes with more than just salt, pepper, olive oil, and vinegar, this is the way to go. This salad combines the smooth flavor of the dressing and the freshness of the tomatoes with a kick from the garlic and red onion. When the tomatoes are really ripe and beautiful, it's a perfect summertime dish.

SERVES 6 TO 8 AS A SALAD COURSE

FOR THE BUTTERMILK DRESSING

1/2 cup whole-milk or low-fat yogurt

1/2 cup mayonnaise

1/2 cup buttermilk

3 cloves garlic, minced (2 tablespoons)

1/2 teaspoon Sriracha (Thai hot sauce; see page 85) or other hot sauce

Juice of 1 lemon (2 tablespoons)

1/4 teaspoon salt

1/4 teaspoon fresh-ground black pepper

2 green onions, chopped (about 1/3 cup)

10 fresh basil leaves, chopped

FOR THE SALAD

6 super-ripe beefsteak tomatoes (1 1/2 to 2 pounds) or any really great ripe local tomatoes

1/2 teaspoon salt (preferably coarse sea salt)

1/2 teaspoon fresh-ground black pepper

1/4 cup extra-virgin olive oil

1 small red onion, sliced thin (about 1/3 cup)

10 fresh basil leaves, chopped

2 tablespoons chopped fresh chives

2 tablespoons fresh parsley leaves

TO MAKE THE BUTTERMILK DRESSING

Combine the yogurt, mayonnaise, buttermilk, garlic, Sriracha, lemon juice, salt, and pepper in a medium-sized bowl.

Whisk everything together until you have a smooth, thick mixture. The dressing should taste tangy and a little spicy.

Gently stir in the green onions and basil.

Let the dressing chill in the fridge for about an hour, so that the flavors come together.

TO MAKE THE SALAD

Cut the tomatoes into thick slices and lay them out on a tray.

Season the tomatoes with the salt and pepper, and drizzle the olive oil on top.

Take the dressing out of the fridge and spoon it over the bottom of a serving dish (or onto individual plates)—it looks nicer to have the color up top and the white dressing on the bottom.

Lay out the tomatoes on top of the dressing.

Spread the onion slices across the tomatoes.

Sprinkle the basil, chives, and parsley on top. Serve the salad right away.

BUTTERMILK

Buttermilk is all over the American culinary oeuvre: we love buttermilk chicken, buttermilk biscuits, buttermilk mashed potatoes . . . and buttermilk dressing. (That's basically what you're getting when you buy ranch dressing, which is the number one salad dressing in the country.) Like so many American foods, buttermilk is an immigrant: lots of culinary traditions use it, but it's a real star player in Irish and English cooking. That's how it got to the South and Appalachia, where American buttermilk cooking is strongest.

ENDIVE, APPLE, AND FARMHOUSE CHEDDAR SALAD WITH COUNTRY HAM AND WHEAT BEER DRESSING

Like every New Yorker, I sometimes need to get outta town. This salad is like a trip to a Vermont country inn on a chilly fall afternoon. Vermont-made Cabot cloth-bound cheddar cheese creates a good contrast for crisp, juicy fall apples—the kind New Yorkers pay a fortune to pick off trees out in the country. I know the beer dressing seems a little weird, but if you use a good local wheat beer for this (I like Ommegang Witte, from Cooperstown, New York), the brightness of the beer actually keeps the ham and cheese from getting too heavy.

SERVES 6

FOR THE DRESSING

$^1/_3$ cup wheat beer
1 tablespoon honey
1 tablespoon Dijon mustard
Juice of 1 lemon (2 tablespoons)
$^1/_3$ cup grapeseed or corn oil
$^1/_3$ cup extra-virgin olive oil
$^1/_4$ teaspoon salt
$^1/_4$ teaspoon fresh-ground black pepper

FOR THE SALAD

1 head Belgian endive, leaves cut into large pieces
1 head radicchio, cut into chunks
$^1/_4$ pound thin-sliced country ham or prosciutto
2 Gala apples (or whatever's local, crunchy, and in season), sliced thin
$^1/_4$ pound sharp farmhouse cheddar, sliced thin
$^1/_4$ cup fresh parsley leaves
Salt to taste
Fresh-ground black pepper to taste

TO MAKE THE DRESSING

In a medium-sized bowl, whisk together the beer, honey, Dijon mustard, and lemon juice.

Whisk in the grapeseed and olive oils, pouring slowly and whisking constantly so that everything emulsifies.

Add the salt and pepper, and whisk again.

TO MAKE THE SALAD AND FINISH THE DISH

Pile the endive, radicchio, ham, apples, cheddar, and parsley into a large bowl, leaving aside a slice or two of the ham for each person.

Taste the salad and season it with salt and pepper to your taste.

Scoop the salad onto individual plates. Drizzle the dressing over the salad, and then drape a little ham on top of each serving. Adjust the seasoning if you like, then serve it up right away.

GAZPACHO SALAD

This salad is a cross between gazpacho and an updated version of that '70s classic, the taco salad. Old-school taco salad was usually a combo of ground beef, taco seasoning mix, iceberg lettuce, chopped beefsteak tomatoes, cheddar cheese, and chopped-up taco shells—literally a taco in a salad. My salad begins with the same basic idea, but what's deconstructed here is gazpacho.

You want to make this salad in the summertime, when the farmers' markets are full of super-ripe tomatoes. When the tomatoes are fresh and seasonal, it's so delicious—clean-tasting but with lots of cilantro, a rich mouthfeel from the avocado and mango, and some tang and crunch from the crumbled cheese and tortillas—that you don't miss the beef that was the heart of that '70s salad. But like the old taco salad, this one is great with a nice cold Corona.

SERVES 4 TO 6

FOR THE SALAD

1 medium yellow bell pepper, cut into matchsticks
1 medium orange bell pepper, cut into matchsticks
1 English cucumber, cut into thin flat strips
$^{3}/_{4}$ pound cherry tomatoes, halved or quartered, depending on the size of your tomatoes (about 2 cups)
3 medium celery stalks, sliced (about 1 $^{1}/_{4}$ cups)
$^{1}/_{2}$ medium red onion, sliced (about $^{1}/_{2}$ cup)
1 medium mango, peeled, cut away from the pit, and sliced thin
12 large fresh basil leaves, washed and torn
$^{1}/_{4}$ cup fresh cilantro leaves
2 ripe avocados

FOR THE DRESSING

Grated zest of 3 limes
Juice of 3 limes ($^{1}/_{3}$ cup)
Grated zest of 2 lemons
Juice of 2 lemons (5 tablespoons)
$^{1}/_{3}$ cup extra-virgin olive oil
$^{1}/_{4}$ teaspoon jalapeño-flavored Tabasco sauce, or more if needed
$^{1}/_{4}$ teaspoon salt, or more if needed
1 tablespoon dried oregano

TO CRUMBLE ON TOP

1 cup Cotija cheese
2 cups tortilla chips

Pile all of the salad ingredients, except the avocados, into a large bowl.

Whisk all of the dressing ingredients together in a small bowl.

Cut each avocado in half and remove the pit. Then use a knife to make lengthwise and widthwise cuts in the avocado meat of each half while it's still in its skin. Scoop out the meat with a large spoon and let it fall, already cut into pieces, into the salad bowl. (Do this right before you're ready to serve the salad—otherwise, the avocado will turn brown.)

Pour the dressing over the salad and mix it well with your hands, so that all the vegetables are coated in the dressing. Taste a piece to see if you want to throw in a little bit more Tabasco or salt.

Crumble the cheese and tortilla chips over the top, and serve the salad right away.

BULGUR SALAD

When I was growing up, there was an old lady named Sadie Shakour who lived down the street. Sadie liked to check up on us: she stopped by all the time, usually letting herself right into the house. She'd get all the way to the kitchen before she started yelling our names to see if we were home. Sometimes she brought us food, though, and it was pretty good. In fact, it was Sadie who introduced me to tabouli, the Lebanese parsley and bulgur wheat salad. This is my juiced-up version of her salad, with a nod to the great Middle Eastern neighborhoods of New York and L.A.

This is a simple salad, but it's really surprising—it's nutty, sweet, salty, fresh, and vegetably all at once. I've added the sunflower seeds and feta to give the salad a little more texture and salt. The dash of spice gives the dish a really nice undertone, and the fresh lemon juice tarts everything up.

SERVES 4 TO 6

1 cinnamon stick
2 cardamom pods
Pinch of cayenne pepper
1 cup bulgur wheat
$^3/_4$ teaspoon salt
$^1/_4$ English cucumber, quartered and sliced thin
   (1 cup)
15 cherry tomatoes, halved (1 cup)
2 green onions, chopped (2 tablespoons)
10 fresh mint leaves, chopped (2 tablespoons)
10 fresh basil leaves, chopped ($^1/_4$ cup)
$^1/_3$ cup roasted salted sunflower seeds
Juice of 2 lemons (5 tablespoons)
$^1/_4$ cup extra-virgin olive oil
A few drops of your favorite hot sauce
$^3/_4$ cup feta cheese

In a small pot, combine 2 cups of water with the cinnamon stick, cardamom seeds, and cayenne. Bring the mixture up to a boil over high heat.

Meanwhile, mix the bulgur wheat with $^1/_4$ teaspoon of the salt in a medium-sized heatproof bowl.

When the water boils, pour it directly over the bulgur wheat. Stir the mixture around with a spoon or a fork so the water goes everywhere, and then cover the bowl tightly with plastic wrap. Let the bulgur steam like this for about 12 minutes, until all the water has been absorbed and the grain is tender.

Fluff the bulgur with a fork to loosen it up and stop it from sticking. Pull the cinnamon stick and the cardamom pods out of the bowl, and then put the bulgur in the fridge, uncovered, to chill it (about 15 minutes).

Add the cucumber, cherry tomatoes, green onions, mint, basil, and $^1/_4$ cup of the sunflower seeds. Mix everything together well.

Squeeze in the lemon juice and add the olive oil, the hot sauce, and the remaining $^1/_2$ teaspoon of salt.

Sprinkle the remaining 2 tablespoons of sunflower seeds over the salad, crumble in the feta cheese on top, and serve it right away.

TUNA POKE

Poke is like Hawaiian sushi: the term means "to slice or cut into pieces," and the dish is all about fresh raw fish, usually served with rice. Poke comes in every form you can think of (and a few that probably never occurred to you if you're not Hawaiian): out there on the Islands, they eat everything from ahi (tuna) poke to sea snail kimchee poke. When you walk into a store that sells poke, you'll see a line of buckets, each filled with a different version. In this one, I use tuna, since that's pretty traditional, but you can also use any super-fresh sushi-grade fish: fluke, snapper . . . whatever's freshest at your fishmonger's. Serve it up in a big bowl with rice on the side.

Poke is pronounced *poh-kay*, not *poke* or *pokee*. Be authentic, yo.

I use Hawaiian red salt here because the big granules don't melt too fast, so the salt has a good crunch to it. If you can't find it, you can use regular kosher salt or rock salt, or any other salt with big granules.

SERVES 4 AS AN APPETIZER

1/2 cup dried ogo (Hawaiian seaweed; I like Noh Foods)
1 pound sashimi-grade tuna (about 3 cups cubed)
1/4 cup soy sauce (regular or low-sodium)
2 teaspoons sesame oil
1/4 medium Maui or Vidalia onion, sliced thin (1/4 cup)
2 green onions, sliced thin (1/4 cup)
1 small (1-inch) fresh Thai red chile, seeded and minced (or 1/4 teaspoon crushed red pepper flakes)
2 teaspoons toasted sesame seeds
1 teaspoon grated fresh ginger (1/2 inch knob, peeled)
1 teaspoon Alaea Red Hawaiian salt, kosher salt, rock salt, or other coarse salt

Rehydrate the ogo in enough water to cover for about 5 minutes, until it softens up.

Cut the tuna into 1-inch cubes and transfer them to a medium-sized mixing bowl.

Pour the soy sauce and sesame oil over the tuna, and add the sweet onions, green onions, chile, sesame seeds, grated ginger, and salt.

Drain and roughly chop up the ogo, and sprinkle it over the top.

Mix the poke well with a wooden spoon so that all the ingredients are combined. Cover the bowl tightly with plastic wrap and let it marinate in the fridge for an hour or two, so the flavors come together. The longer you let it sit, the stronger the flavors will be. It can keep in the fridge for up to 24 hours.

OGO

Ogo, Hawaiian seaweed, is used fresh on the Islands: people cut it up and throw it into the poke. But you can't find fresh ogo more than a few miles from the ocean, so we use the dried stuff here. Ogo comes in a range of colors, from green to purple; any one will give you that elastic bounce between the teeth. If you can't find it, you can substitute dried seaweed salad mix (available in Japanese grocery stores). If you can't find that, just leave it out. Don't use the poke mixes that have all the chiles and seasonings mixed in—they won't work with this recipe.

SEAFOOD

STEAMED SNAPPER WITH SPICY PEANUT SAUCE AND LIME

I love eating in New Orleans. I can't get enough of the heavy, French-influenced food, the dark spice of Cajun cooking, the sweet Southern stuff, the crazy only-in-New-Orleans foodways. One of my favorite things to eat down in Louisiana is pecan-crusted Gulf fish: it's sweet and savory and crunchy and succulent and delicious. In New Orleans, they do this with catfish, sheepshead, snapper—just about any kind of white flaky fish. (See page 90 for my take on pecan-crusted cod.)

But I also love the off-the-beaten-path food of New Orleans, the stuff you don't think about when you think about the American South. There's a big Vietnamese community down on the Gulf, for example, and in Vietnamese restaurants, you find lots of steamed fish cooked up with lime, ginger, and lemongrass.

I figured, why not try to get the best of both worlds? So I've put the two traditions together here: I steam the fish Vietnamese-style and add lots of traditional Southeast Asian flavors—and instead of a pecan crust, I use a spicy peanut sauce. The New South for real, right?

SERVES 6

FOR THE PEANUT SAUCE
1/4 stalk lemongrass
3/4 cup peanut oil
One 2-inch piece fresh ginger, peeled and finely
    chopped (about 2 tablespoons)
1/3 cup rice vinegar
1 tablespoon fish sauce (see page 72)
1 tablespoon sugar
1 clove garlic, sliced
1 cup creamy peanut butter
2 teaspoons Sriracha (see page 85)
Juice of 2 limes (1/4 cup)

FOR THE FISH
1 tablespoon fish sauce
Juice of 2 limes (1/4 cup)
2 tablespoons peanut oil
2 green onions, chopped
6 snapper fillets (7 ounces each)

TO FINISH THE DISH
1/3 cup fresh cilantro leaves

TO MAKE THE PEANUT SAUCE
Crush the lemongrass stalk with the back of a knife, so it flattens; then fold and crush the stalk in your fist, and use string to tie it up in a bundle.

Heat the peanut oil in a medium-sized pot over low heat. Add the lemongrass and ginger, and cook for 5 minutes, until the flavors come together.

Add the rice vinegar, fish sauce, sugar, garlic, peanut butter, and 1 cup of water. Bring the mixture up to a simmer and let it cook for 10 minutes, uncovered, until the flavors come together and the aroma is released.

Pull the lemongrass out of the pot, and then pour the peanut sauce into a blender.

Add the Sriracha and lime juice, and blend the sauce on high speed for about 30 seconds, until it smooths out. Make sure you hold down the top of the blender with a towel to avoid hot-liquid disasters.

TO STEAM THE FISH
Bring water to a boil in the bottom of a steamer.

Mix the fish sauce, lime juice, peanut oil, and green onions together in a small bowl.

Lay the snapper fillets on a plate, and pour the fish sauce mixture over them.

Put the plate into the steamer, and let it steam for about 4 minutes, until the inside of the fish is opaque when you cut into it with a knife.

TO FINISH THE DISH
Pull the plate out of the steamer.

Lay out 6 dinner plates, and spread about ¼ cup of the peanut sauce on each plate, using a spoon to make a shallow circle in the center of the plate.

Lay a snapper fillet on each circle of sauce. Scatter a little cilantro on top of each fillet, and serve the fish right away.

SRIRACHA

Sriracha is the go-to hot sauce for a lot of chefs these days: you find it in fancy kitchens and little dives, and people squirt it on everything from fried eggs to tacos to noodles. That's because Sriracha isn't just a hot-hot-hot hot sauce: it's got an unbelievable balance between vinegar and heat. You can give just about anything a great little kick with it. It's a great way to pump up the flavor in just about any sauce; it works very well in salad dressings and soups; I really like it on grilled chicken.

Sriracha is pretty commonly available: it's the bright red hot sauce in the squeeze bottle with a green cap and a rooster on the front. And it's not a foreign import, either: people think it comes from Thailand or Vietnam or China, but it's actually made in California.

PAN-FRIED SKATE WITH PICKLED RAMPS

You've probably seen skate on a thousand restaurant menus, but I bet you've never cooked it at home. I guess people think that skate—a type of stingray—is hard to deal with, but actually it's super-easy. It's also cheap to buy, good for the environment (skate is definitely a sustainable fish), and—if you make it right—very very delicious. It's a meaty white fish, without a strong flavor, and it goes really well with a great sauce and some veg on the side. You buy skate in fillets: each fillet is one "wing" of the fish (so it's not like you're dealing with stingers). You can bake it or poach it, but I think the best way to eat skate is pan-fried.

The sauce I use here is a true French-American fusion. It's based on the classic French *grenobloise,* made with brown butter and lemon juice. I've added pickled ramps and their juice, which bring a great sweet-and-sour flavor to that old-school buttery French taste. The tomatoes and ramps make this dish fresh . . . tart . . . American. Add some rice or potatoes on the side and you're golden.

Skate cooks up really really fast, so make sure you have everything prepped ahead of time: you don't want to be letting your fish overcook while you chop your parsley.

SERVES 4

FOR THE FILLETS
1/4 teaspoon salt
1/4 teaspoon fresh-ground black pepper
4 skate fillets (about 2 pounds)
1 cup all-purpose flour
2 tablespoons extra-virgin olive oil

FOR THE SAUCE AND FINISHING THE DISH
2 tablespoons unsalted butter
2 tablespoons pickled ramp juice (see page 306)
1 cup cherry tomatoes, sliced in half
1/4 cup pickled ramps (see page 306), chopped
Juice of 1 lemon (2 tablespoons)
2 tablespoons chopped fresh parsley
1 tablespoon capers

TO COOK THE FISH
Preheat the oven to 175°F.

Sprinkle the salt and pepper over both sides of each skate fillet.

Pour the flour onto a big flat plate, and lay a fillet on top of the flour, so it's floured on one side. Repeat with a second fillet. (You'll probably have to cook the skate in batches, unless you have a really enormous pan in your kitchen: the average pan can't handle more than 2 wings at a time.)

Heat a nonstick skillet over high heat, and then add 1 tablespoon of the olive oil.

Shake the excess flour off the fillets, and then add them to the skillet, flour side down.

Let the fish cook for about 1½ minutes, until it's golden brown on the bottom. Flip the fillets over and keep cooking for another minute or so, until the second side has browned up.

Pull the fish out of the skillet, lay it on a plate, and put it in the oven to keep it warm while you cook the rest of the fillets.

Add the remaining tablespoon of olive oil to the pan, and repeat this process until all the fish is cooked;

then hold all the fillets in the oven while you make the sauce.

TO MAKE THE SAUCE AND FINISH THE DISH

Put your skillet back on the stove, lower the heat to medium, and add 1 tablespoon of the butter.

Let the butter cook down for 10 seconds or so, shaking the skillet pretty vigorously or stirring well, until it turns a hazelnut color and bubbles up.

Deglaze the skillet by adding the ramp juice.

Add the tomatoes, ramps, lemon juice, parsley, and capers to the skillet.

Turn the heat to low, add the remaining tablespoon of butter, and stir until the butter melts. The sauce should be buttery, but with a bite from the vinegar and lemon.

Remove the fish from the oven, serve it out onto individual plates, and pour the sauce over the top. Serve this right away.

CLEANING SKATE

Skate is usually sold pretty clean, but I like to make sure the fillets are really ready for action. I use the tip of a knife to cut away the silverskin at the top of the fish, where the skate wing was close to the body before it was butchered. If you let the silverskin cook on the fish, it will end up a little tough.

I like to keep each skate wing whole, but if you think your wings might be too big for your pan, or just too much to handle, cut each one in half widthwise.

NOT *DIRTY DANCING*

There are a lot of decisions that go into choosing your first internship at culinary school: geographic location, quality of cooking, type of cuisine. Then there are what we might call the lifestyle issues. For example: I was very interested in finding some way of working girls into my professional life. Back when I was at the Culinary Institute of America, in Hyde Park, New York, the place had about as many women as a Rush concert. And for some reason, the women from Vassar, down the street, weren't very interested in hanging out with a bunch of sweaty, dirty kitchen boys. So when I thought about how I was going to spend my summer, did I picture a kitchen full of boys? No way. I was keeping my leisure time in mind. That's why I picked a resort in Virginia. I'd seen *Dirty Dancing*. I knew all about it. While my friends busted their butts in air-conditioning-deprived restaurant kitchens in the Northeast, I would be hanging around the employee swimming pool, chatting up lithe, toothsome hotties in retro bikinis. Visions of all-night staff parties and stolen evenings with the highly corruptible young daughters of guests danced in my head. What better way to get a little bit of culinary training?

Well, turns out there was no staff swimming pool.

The hotel was a sprawling, stately place way up in the Virginia mountains, a railroad resort from the turn of the century. No staff pool, but there was a golf course, a skeet-shooting range, and . . . lawn bowling!

Some of the lawn bowlers might have been corruptible. I wouldn't know.

The staff weren't really the all-night-party types, either. It was one of those places that hire the same locals back season after season; the chambermaids were all over fifty, and the guy who parked cars had a kid in college. The staffers who weren't local lived in one of three big white houses in a row at the edge of the property, far, far away from the guests (at least *Dirty Dancing* got that part right: Jerry Orbach would have had to travel some serious distance to help out Baby and her friends).

The house next door to mine was full of musicians. Frank, the piano player in the main lounge, told everybody who would listen that he'd performed with Frank Sinatra at the Fontainebleau in Miami in 1950. He'd been a Broadway player, too; he had a million stories, and nearly every one of 'em featured some poor girl from the Midwest who got off the bus in New York ready to be a star and ended up on the casting couch with a crooked director or choreographer or dance captain. There was a guitar player from Rhode Island and an upright bass player from Georgia—good guys and good musicians. And then there was Billy. He lived with the musicians even though his official job was groundskeeper on the golf course. When he wasn't working, he was playing the Dobro. Every night, he would sit out on the front porch of his house and pick out bluegrass and country-and-western tunes on that Dobro. He used to make up songs on the spot, all true-life tales. You know how the basic country song has to have a done-me-wrong theme, or a lost-my-money theme, or an I'm-sorry-I-drank-too-much theme, or else has to refer to a coal mine? Well, Billy was a walking country-and-western song. His wife had left him; he'd got kicked out of his house; he'd lost all his money. There was something about a coal mine, too. I can't remember exactly how that part went, but I'm sure it was tragic.

Sometimes I would go over there with my guitar and we would jam, Billy and I. That was a big night for me in Virginia.

Once I got friendlier with the local guys, there were some outings, too. One hot day when I wasn't working, for example, somebody said, "Let's go inner-tubing!" They told me it was a local tradition—shooting the mountain rapids on inner tubes. They said it was awesome, a huge rush. They didn't say the water was about forty degrees. Or that they liked to inner-tube naked. "Skinnytubing," they called it. That was part of the tradition, too.

But there were some better local traditions. Virginia is where I started learning about picking mushrooms. A couple of the locals used to go on picking expeditions; they'd sell what they found to the hotel, and for a pretty good buck, too. Those guys taught me how to pick chanterelles: they grow on the sides of some pretty steep hills, so you climb and climb until you see a little bit of gold sticking up above the ground cover. Where there's one chanterelle, there's always more: you'd see a mushroom poking its head up, and then you'd brush aside the leaves and find a whole vein of gold running up the mountain. We picked lobster mushrooms, and we picked morels, too, which were trickier: to get this right, you needed to know the difference between actual, good, delicious local morels and the stuff they called false morels, which would kill you. If you sold false morels to the hotel, things would not go well for you.

We picked ramps on those trips, too, and back in the kitchen, I learned how to pickle them—something I still love to do every spring. And towards the end of my time in Virginia, one of the guys I got to know really well showed me how to pick ginseng. This was a big deal: ginseng is rare and expensive, and people guard their spots pretty carefully. But I was more interested in eating it raw then selling it, because I wanted to see if it did what it was rumored to do, which was to act like a supersonic aphrodisiac. This being the Virginia mountains, unfortunately, I never did get a chance to try it out.

PECAN-CRUSTED COD WITH ROSEMARY

Southerners love their pecans, and pecan-crusted fish is kind of a Southern classic: they serve it all over below the Mason-Dixon line. The nuts are a little bit sweet, and they give the fish a great texture. I've had pecan-crusted halibut and pecan-crusted sheepshead, but in my version, I use cod. It's great with Mustard Sauce, too (page 302).

(For another spin on nuts with fish, see the Vietnamese Steamed Snapper with Spicy Peanut Sauce and Lime on page 84).

This recipe makes more pecan crust than you'll need—probably enough for 10 fillets—so if you've got a crowd you can increase the number of fillets. Otherwise you can always freeze it. The crust mixture will keep in the freezer for up to a month.

SERVES 4 TO 6

FOR THE SAUCE

2 tablespoons extra-virgin olive oil
1/2 medium Vidalia onion, diced (about 1/2 cup)
Pinch of salt
Pinch of fresh-ground black pepper
2 teaspoons Dijon mustard

FOR THE PECAN CRUST

2 cups pecans
1 cup panko bread crumbs
7 tablespoons butter, at room temperature (3/4 stick)
1 tablespoon fresh rosemary, chopped fine
2 teaspoons Old Bay seasoning
1/4 cup fresh parsley leaves
1/2 teaspoon salt
1/4 teaspoon pepper

FOR THE COD

4 to 6 cod fillets (6 to 8 ounces each)
3/4 teaspoon salt
1/2 teaspoon fresh-ground black pepper

TO MAKE THE SAUCE

Preheat the oven to 350°F.

Heat the olive oil in a small pan over medium heat.

Add the onions, salt, and pepper. Cook the onions over medium-low to medium heat for about 3 to 4 minutes until they soften up, stirring them regularly so they don't color or stick.

Add the Dijon mustard and stir it around so the onions are coated in it. Then take the pan off the fire.

TO MAKE THE PECAN CRUST

Pour the pecans and bread crumbs into a food processor fitted with the metal blade, and pulse for 15 seconds, so the pecans form a fine meal.

Add the butter, the onion-mustard mixture, and the rosemary, Old Bay, parsley, salt, and pepper. Pulse for 15 to 20 seconds, until the mixture has a soft, pebbly texture, like tabouli.

TO COOK THE FISH

Blot the fish fillets with a paper towel to get rid of any extra moisture. Season the fillets with the salt and pepper on both sides.

Use your hands to top the fish with a thick layer of the pecan mixture—about 2 tablespoons for each fillet. (You want to pat it on like you're making a sand castle.)

Lay the fillets on a rack in a baking dish.

Bake the fish on the middle oven rack for about 12 minutes, until there's some bounce-back to the touch and a fork or knife will go in easily and will be warm to the touch when inserted in the center. (If you've got a food thermometer, the internal temperature should be about 115°F.)

Serve the fish right away, with Mustard Sauce.

CORTEZ FISH CHOWDER

Florida is home to a million waterside seafood joints. You know the kind of place I'm talking about. Everything is fried way past identification, the decor is nautical with fake-wood paneling, the wait on Saturday nights is epic, the waitresses call you "hon," and they serve two kinds of beer: pale and paler. But Starfish Seafood Company is not your average waterside seafood joint.

Starfish is in the tiny village of Cortez on the west coast of Florida, one of the last commercial mullet-fishing ports in the U.S. To get there, you turn off a busy highway and drive through a maze of quiet, shady streets lined with old-school Florida houses, with boats and fishing gear in the front yards. You park in a lot full of big trucks with boat hitches. Then you walk right onto the dock at the fishing port, order your food at the window, and sit yourself down at a picnic table or at the bar. Pelicans waddle around by the fishing boats, seabirds circle overhead, and fishermen work on their rigs or haul in their catch.

When Gwen's family found this place ten years back, you could sit at the bar at Starfish, nursing a beer and eating yourself sick on mullet or grouper sandwiches and hush puppies, with no one around to bother you but a couple of old-timers and some smart snowbirds. These days, it's always packed with guidebook-wielding tourists in walking shorts and practical shoes, ready to fight for their picnic tables. But it's still worth the wait.

One of my favorite dishes at Starfish is a fish chowder that's kind of a cross between a Manhattan-style chowder and a gumbo, with chunks of potato and corn and flakes of mullet inside. Mullet is probably hard to find in your local grocery, but this version will work with other kinds of whitefish. This isn't a long-simmer soup: the fish cooks really quickly, and you want the fresh taste of the vegetables (and a little bit of crunch).

SERVES 6 TO 8 AS AN APPETIZER

1/4 cup extra-virgin olive oil
1 medium onion, chopped (about 1 cup)
2 celery stalks, chopped (about 1 cup)
1 small green bell pepper, chopped (about 1 cup)
2 cloves garlic, sliced superfine
1/2 teaspoon paprika
3/4 teaspoon chili powder
1/2 teaspoon fresh-ground black pepper
2 bay leaves
One 28-ounce can chopped tomatoes with their juice
1 pound new potatoes, skin on, cut into 1/2-inch chunks (about 2 cups)
4 cups chicken broth
1 pound whitefish (cod, halibut, snapper, mullet), skin and bones removed
Kernels from 4 ears fresh corn (about 2 cups)
1 cup French green beans (haricots verts), trimmed and cut into 1-inch pieces
1/2 teaspoon of your favorite hot sauce

Heat the olive oil in a large saucepot over medium heat. Add the onions, celery, and green pepper, and stir to coat the vegetables in the oil. Cook until the vegetables start to soften, about 5 minutes, stirring occasionally to make sure nothing sticks.

Stir in the garlic. Then mix in the paprika, chili powder, black pepper, bay leaves, chopped tomatoes, potatoes, and chicken broth. Turn the heat up to medium-high and let the mixture come up to a simmer.

Cook the soup for about 15 minutes at a low bubble, until the vegetables have softened up, the flavors have come together, and the stock has reduced a little bit.

While the soup is cooking, lay the fish out on a cutting board. Using a long sharp knife, cut it into thirds. Cut each piece along the spine, and then cut the fish into small chunks, about 1-inch square.

When the soup is ready, add the corn and green beans to the pot. Give everything a stir, and let the soup cook for about 5 minutes, until the corn and green beans have softened up.

Add the fish and hot sauce to the pot. Stir everything together, and cook the soup for another 5 minutes, until the fish starts to flake apart.

Pull out the bay leaf and serve right away in true Florida style (wearing an ugly Hawaiian shirt), with a package of saltines or a crunchy piece of toasted bread on the side.

MAINE MUSSELS WITH LEMONGRASS AND CHILES

Mussels are a big traditional food in this country, from way back when the first European settlers ate them for dinner. A lot of people are purists about their mussels: they just steam 'em and eat 'em, maybe with some lemon juice, and that's OK. The Europeans like to steam mussels with white wine, cream, and maybe a splash of tomatoes: that's OK, too. But I thought we'd bring some good old American innovation to this old-time American dish. So I've incorporated Southeast Asian flavors to give it some freshness and spark. It's not authentic Asian, or authentic traditional-American, or authentic anywhere else, really, but it's simple and delicious and really damn good—especially with steamed rice and cold beer.

The most important direction in this recipe: don't cook the mussels to death. People get nervous about shellfish, but fresh mussels that are unopened before you cook them will not make you sick. I promise. If you overcook your mussels, the proteins in the meat will tighten up and the mussels will be tough and chewy, instead of soft and luscious, the way they should be.

SERVES 4

2 1/2 pounds mussels
1 cup canned coconut milk (half a 14-ounce can)
2 tablespoons fish sauce (see page 72)
2 tablespoons corn oil or canola oil
2 shallots, sliced (about 1/4 cup)
1 stalk lemongrass, chopped superfine (about
    2 tablespoons)
1 Fresno or Thai chile, chopped superfine
2 cloves garlic, minced
2-inch piece fresh ginger, chopped superfine
    (2 tablespoons)
Grated zest and juice of 3 limes (1/4 cup)
1/2 cup chopped fresh cilantro leaves

Mussels are usually sold pretty clean, but there's nothing worse than a sandy mussel, so double-clean them by setting them in a big bowl in the sink and leaving them under a stream of running water for about 3 minutes, until the water in the bowl is clear. Throw away any mussels that are cracked or already opened. If any of your mussels have a hairy bit (the "beard") sticking out of the closed shell, pinch it between two fingers and pull it out.

Pour the coconut milk into a small bowl and stir in the fish sauce.

Heat the oil in a large pot over low heat. Add the shallots, lemongrass, chile, garlic, and ginger. Sauté for about 2 minutes, stirring constantly, until the shallots soften but don't color and you can smell the chile.

Add the mussels to the pot, turn the heat up to medium-high, and stir everything around.

Add the coconut milk mixture and 1/2 cup of water, and stir again. Then cover the pot and let the mussels cook for about 3 minutes. But keep an eye on the pot: they're done as soon as they're all open.

Pull the pot off the heat, grate in the lime zest, squeeze in the lime juice, add the cilantro, and stir everything around so the lime-and-cilantro flavor hits everywhere.

Pour the mussels into a big serving bowl and eat 'em while they're hot.

SCALLOPS WITH GRAPEFRUIT BUTTER

This dish is an ode to Miami, circa 1982. When I was a kid, my family used to drive down to Florida a couple of times every winter, to see my grandma and to get out of the Cleveland weather. We always stopped at a citrus grove in Fort Pierce called Boudrias Groves. They sold amazing Indian River citrus: we'd buy navels, Honeybells, temples, and this unbelievable red orange juice, crazy-good stuff. When we got to Miami, we'd get to go out to a fancy restaurant as a treat—one of those places that served amazing fresh seafood, stuff you just couldn't get in Cleveland back then. So this dish brings together two of my favorite Florida things. And it's got a little bit of retro going on: the butter sauce is definitely old-school.

You can serve this citrus sauce with just about any fish or seafood—lobster, mahi mahi, anything that makes you think of the beach. (You can prep the fish any way you like, too: grilled, broiled, sautéed, whatever.)

SERVES 4

FOR THE GRAPEFRUIT BUTTER
1 cup white wine
1 large shallot, diced (2 tablespoons)
Juice of 3 ruby red grapefruits (about 1 cup)
1/4 cup bitter orange juice (Goya has one called Naranja Agria Bitter Orange Marinade, see Note); or juice of 1 orange and juice of 1 lime, mixed together
3/4 stick (6 tablespoons) salted butter

FOR THE SCALLOPS
16 sea scallops
1/2 teaspoon salt
1/2 teaspoon fresh-ground black pepper
2 tablespoons extra-virgin olive oil (or 1 tablespoon for each batch of scallops)

2 tablespoons unsalted butter
2 fresh thyme sprigs
Juice of 1 lime (2 tablespoons)

TO FINISH THE DISH
2 ruby red grapefruits, segmented (about 1 cup segments; see page 68)
2 tablespoons chopped fresh parsley

TO MAKE THE GRAPEFRUIT BUTTER
Heat the white wine in a large saucepan over medium-high heat. Add the shallots, stir to coat them in the wine, and let them cook for about 5 minutes, until the wine has evaporated completely—there should be no more liquid left in the pan at all.

Add the grapefruit juice and bitter orange juice, and cook for about 5 to 6 minutes, until the mixture thickens up and reduces to about 1/4 cup.

Pull the pan off the heat and whisk in the butter a tablespoon at a time, whisking continuously until each pat is melted, then adding the next one.

TO COOK THE SCALLOPS
Preheat the oven to 175°F.

Season the scallops with the salt and pepper on both sides.

Heat 1 tablespoon of the olive oil in a saucepan over medium-high heat until it starts to smoke; then add half of the scallops. (If you put a scallop in and it sticks, the oil isn't hot enough.)

Let the scallops cook for about a minute and a half, until they brown up on the bottom, then flip them over and keep cooking for another minute and a half, until the tops and bottoms are brown but the sides are still white.

butter, another thyme sprig, plus another tablespoon of lime juice.

TO FINISH THE DISH
If the sauce has cooled down, heat it up again.

Add the grapefruit segments to the sauce and mix everything together well, so the grapefruit is coated.

Add the parsley, mix again, and then pour the grapefruit butter over the scallops. Serve right away.

Add half the butter and half the thyme. Shake the pan around as the butter melts, so it gets everywhere, then squeeze half the lime juice. Tilt the pan so the juice slides to one side, and use a deep spoon to catch the sauce and spoon it over the scallops so they're shining and glazed.

Pull the pan off the heat and slide the scallops onto a plate. Hold them in the oven while you do the same with the second batch, adding another tablespoon of

NOTE

You can find frozen sour orange concentrate online, but it's almost impossible to find fresh sour orange juice north of the Mason-Dixon Line. I found sour orange juice at Kalustyan's, an amazing specialty store in Manhattan. If you can't get your hands on any of the real stuff, you can substitute the orange/lime juice mix. It will be just as good.

CRAB ON TOAST, PAGE 100

CRAB ON TOAST

The crab crostini at Locanda Verde is our most popular dish—not to mention the one that food writers talk about the most. Which is kind of funny because, except for the name, there's nothing Italian at all about crab crostini. It's pure America: all the flavors from a really good crab boil, on toast. Funny, too, because after we spent months and months planning the menu, this was a dish that we really came up with on the fly. It just goes to show you: sometimes the best dishes are the ones you don't think too much about.

The crostini make a great start to a big fun summertime party or meal. And they go really well with ice-cold beer.

SERVES 6

FOR THE GARLIC CREAM

1 tablespoon extra-virgin olive oil

2 cloves garlic, sliced thin

1 cup heavy cream

$1/4$ teaspoon salt, plus a bit more to your taste

$1/8$ teaspoon fresh-ground black pepper, plus a bit more to your taste

$1/8$ teaspoon cayenne pepper, plus a bit more to your taste

6 ounces lump crabmeat

FOR THE CRAB TOASTS

12 slices ciabatta bread

4 tablespoons extra-virgin olive oil

$1/2$ medium zucchini, halved lengthwise and sliced thin (about 1 cup)

Pinch of salt

Pinch of fresh-ground black pepper

$1/2$ cup canned crushed tomatoes (I love Jersey Fresh)

$1/2$ jalapeño pepper, halved, seeded, and sliced thin

TO MAKE THE GARLIC CREAM

Heat the olive oil in a medium-sized saucepan over medium heat.

Add the sliced garlic and sauté for about 2 minutes, stirring constantly, until the garlic slices have turned golden in the center and brown on the edges. They'll crisp up a little, but you don't want to let them burn.

Add the heavy cream, turn the heat up to high, and let it boil for about 7 minutes, until the cream has thickened and reduced to about $1/4$ cup.

Stir in the salt, black pepper, and cayenne pepper.

Spoon the crabmeat into a small bowl, pour the garlic cream over it, and stir the cream completely into the crab. Check the seasoning, and add more salt, pepper, or cayenne as you're feeling it. Then cover the bowl with plastic wrap and set it aside on the counter while you make the toast (not in the fridge: if you cool it down, the cream will break).

TO MAKE THE TOAST AND FINISH THE DISH

Preheat the oven to 350°F or heat up the grill.

Brush the bread slices on one side with 3 tablespoons of the olive oil (brush both sides of each slice if you're using the grill).

Lay the slices on a baking sheet or straight on the grill, and toast them up till they're crisp and golden (about 5 to 7 minutes in the oven; a couple of minutes on the grill, turning the bread so you get nice grill marks on both sides).

Heat the remaining tablespoon of olive oil in a medium-sized saucepan or skillet over medium-high heat. Add the zucchini and sauté for about a minute, until the slices just begin to soften. Then toss in the salt and pepper.

Keep cooking the zucchini, tossing or stirring constantly, until it's just soft and the green color has intensified—about another 30 seconds.

Slide the zucchini from the pan onto a plate, spreading the slices out in a single layer, and put the plate in the fridge for a couple of minutes to stop the cooking process.

Lay the toast out on a board. Spread each slice with about 1 tablespoon of the crushed tomatoes. Scoop 2 evenly spaced spoonfuls of the crab mixture overtop. Cut the toast in half (so each half has 1 spoonful of crab), and then place 2 or 3 pieces of the zucchini on top of each crab mound. Add a slice or two of jalapeño, and serve right away.

HOW TO COOK SHRIMP LIKE A PRO, NOT A JERK

In Miami, believe it or not, there are still a couple of shrimpers who work the waters of Biscayne Bay, just south of the heart of the city. That's where I've had the best, sweetest shrimp I've ever tasted in my life. And when shrimp are that fresh and that good, you definitely, definitely don't want to overcook them: nothing's worse than tough, rubbery shrimp. But the fact is that most people cook shrimp too hard and too long, because they've got the seafood fear. Trust me: if your shrimp are super-fresh and they don't smell like ammonia, they're not going to kill you. So please don't, as some members of my family put it, "boil the germs out of 'em."

My method here is a foolproof anti-overcooking approach. Instead of boiling (which tightens up the proteins in the meat and makes it rubbery), I poach the shrimp in the shells, with the water just steaming. It's important to keep the heads on, too, so the meat is extra-protected. The bouillon gives the shrimp just a little bit of light savory flavor. Serve them with a little New Orleans Rémoulade for dipping.

SERVES 6

1 large onion, roughly sliced
1 orange, cut into large chunks
1 lemon, cut into large chunks
1 head garlic, sliced in half horizontally right
    through the bulbs
10 fresh thyme sprigs
10 fresh parsley sprigs
3 bay leaves, crumbled
1 cup white wine
1 cup white wine vinegar
3 tablespoons Old Bay seasoning
1 teaspoon crushed red pepper flakes
1 tablespoon salt
3 pounds shrimp, in their shells with heads on

2 cups New Orleans Rémoulade (page 303), for serving

Pour 12 cups of water into a large pot and set it on the stove over high heat. Add all the ingredients except the shrimp and the rémoulade, stir to combine, and let the broth come up to a boil (the fancy French name for this broth is *court bouillon*).

Turn the heat down to low and let the mixture cook for 5 minutes, so the flavors come together. (You definitely don't want a hard boil here: you want to get the temperature down till bouillon is just steaming—about 140° to 160°F on a food thermometer—so that the shrimp poaches right. If you drop them in when the water's still boiling, the proteins in the meat will seize up and your shrimp will be rubbery.)

Pull the pot off the heat and drop in the shrimp, shells and heads still on. Let them cook in the hot liquid, uncovered and off the heat, for about 8 minutes. They're ready when you can pull a shrimp apart and it's slightly opaque in the center.

Use a strainer to pull the shrimp from the pot, and put them right on a plate or tray. (Don't worry if the citrus, herbs, and so forth come out with the shrimp—that's just extra flavor.) You can serve the shrimp hot, as they are, or cool them down in the fridge before you eat them—it's all about what you like. Either way, don't let them sit around: they're only good for a day or so in the fridge. Put 'em in the middle of the table with a big bowl of New Orleans Rémoulade on the side, peel, dip, and eat.

BROILED LOBSTER WITH RED CURRY AND LIME

This dish is a nod to the red lobster curry at SriPraPhai, a serious Thai restaurant in Woodside, Queens, that I've been going to for years. (Arun's in Chicago does a great version, too.) It's buttery, hot, and savory, with a kick of citrusy freshness from the lime and herbs.

If you're cooking lobster, you should kill it like a pro—none of this boiling your crustaceans alive, making them scream, etc. I like to plunge a knife between the eyes.

SERVES 4

1 1/2 sticks (12 tablespoons) butter, at room
    temperature
2 tablespoons red Thai curry paste
1 cup fresh cilantro leaves, chopped fine
    (about 1/2 bunch)
1/2 cup fresh mint leaves, chopped fine
    (15 to 20 leaves)
Grated zest of 1 lime
Juice of 1 lime (1 tablespoon)
4 lobsters (1 1/4 to 1 1/2 pounds each)
1/2 cup panko bread crumbs

Put a large pot of well-salted water on to boil, and preheat the oven to 425°F.

Mix the butter, curry paste, cilantro, and mint together in a small bowl. Shave the lime zest into the bowl, squeeze in the lime juice, and mix everything together so you have a thick, herby orange paste.

Place a lobster on a cutting board. Hold the point of a large heavy knife (not your best knife) about an inch from the tip of the head, behind and between the eyes. Using your other hand to stabilize the lobster's back, plunge straight down and then press the knife forward through the front of the lobster's head. When you press down, liquid will come spurting out. (Once you do this, the lobster is definitely dead.)

Starting from the point where you first put the knife in, cut straight back, splitting the lobster in half. The inside will be flesh-colored, yellow, and green.

Place your knife right at the joint where the claw meets the "arm" of the lobster, press the knife down hard with your other hand, and cut the claw off. Repeat for the other claw.

Remove the green and yellowish stuff from inside the lobster, using the tip of a spoon to scrape it out. (That's the "tomalley," or liver, and the "coral," or roe. You don't need to get every single bit out—it won't hurt you, and some recipes actually use the roe to make a sauce—but it can be bitter if it cooks.)

Lay the lobster out on a sheet tray, open side up. Repeat with the remaining lobster.

When the water comes to a boil, toss the claws in. Small claws (on a 1 1/2-pound lobster) will be done in 4 minutes; larger claws will be done in about 6 minutes. Meanwhile, fill a bowl with ice water.

Pull the claws out of the pot and plunge them into the bowl of ice water. Let them cool for about 5 minutes, so they stop cooking completely. Then remove the rubber band holding each claw closed, and crack the claw by pulling on the smaller piece until it comes right out. You can throw that piece away.

Crack the big piece of each claw by standing the claw on its longest end and bringing the butt of the knife (the part closest to the handle) down hard right where the long part of the claw meets the wider part. Then twist the shell apart at the crack and pull it off. Throw away the shells.

>>>

Use a small sharp knife to chop up the claw meat.

Use your fingers to stuff the meat into the cavities of the lobster bodies, anywhere there's open space.

Using your hands, a small spatula, or a brush, cover the lobster meat thickly with the curry butter—about 2 to 3 tablespoons for each lobster. You want to really coat all the meat, fill in all the gaps, and pat the thick butter down—it's like spackling your lobster.

Sprinkle the bread crumbs thickly on top of each lobster, like a heavy snow, so that the butter is completely coated.

Bake the lobsters on the middle rack of the oven for 5 minutes. Then turn on the broiler and broil them for about 2 minutes, till the top turns golden brown.

Pull the lobsters out of the broiler and let them rest for 3 minutes, so that the heat trapped in the shells finishes cooking the meat. Serve the lobsters in their shells, picnic-style.

THE LOBSTER TANK AT PIERLESS FISH IN BROOKLYN

POULTRY AND MEAT

MY CHICKEN POT PIE

Back when I was cooking at Café Boulud, I had a vegetable-truffle pot pie on the menu. It was this rich, yummy veggie dish—but eight times out of ten, people would ask me to add chicken. People just really, really love chicken pot pie. (Sorry, vegetarians: you lose this one.)

Old-school chicken pot pie is made with biscuit dough on top, but I'm not a fan of that: biscuit dough is really heavy, and it gets mushy when it falls into the pie. Nobody, really, likes mushy chicken pot pie. In this recipe, I've changed it up. The dough here is more like a cracker—so when you break into the pot pie, you get something a lot like crackers and soup. And who doesn't like crackers and soup?

My dough is ridiculously easy, but you need to make it the night before: this is definitely a two-step process. And be careful to cut all the vegetables to the same size, so they cook evenly. You don't want to be biting into undercooked or overmushy veggies.

I like to do the pot pies in individual casseroles, so everybody gets lots of dough, but you can also make it in one big casserole.

MAKES 4 POT PIES,
OR I LARGE POT PIE THAT SERVES 4

FOR THE DOUGH

1 1/2 sticks (12 tablespoons) salted butter
3 1/2 cups all-purpose flour, plus some for flouring
    your work surface
1/2 teaspoon salt

FOR THE FILLING

6 chicken legs (about 3 pounds)
7 cups chicken broth
1/2 teaspoon salt
1/4 teaspoon fresh-ground black pepper

5 tablespoons salted butter
1/3 cup all-purpose flour
5 small carrots, or 2 to 3 large carrots, peeled and
    chopped (1 cup)
1/2 medium sweet onion, chopped (1 cup)
2 medium celery stalks, chopped (1 cup)
1/2 pound cremini mushrooms (about 12 mushrooms),
    stems removed, caps quartered (2 cups)
1/2 pound new potatoes, cut into small chunks (1 cup)
2 tablespoons fresh thyme leaves
1 cup fresh peas
1 tablepoon chipotle-flavored Tabasco sauce

TO FINISH THE DISH

1 egg
Pinch of salt
Pinch of fresh-ground black pepper
1/3 cup grated Parmesan cheese

TO MAKE THE DOUGH

Melt the butter in the microwave or in a small pot on the stove so it's just liquified.

Using a tabletop mixer fitted with the paddle attachment, combine the flour, salt, butter, and 1/2 cup water. Mix everything together on medium-low speed (#2 on a KitchenAid) for about 2 minutes, until the mixture forms a rough dough. If it's too crumbly, add a bit more water; if it's too wet, add a little more flour.

Turn the dough out onto a floured surface and use your hands to bring it together into a ball; then flatten it out. Knead the dough, pushing it flat with the heels of your hands, forming it back into a circle, turning and flattening it again, until you have a pretty smooth ball.

>>>

Wrap the dough well in plastic wrap and let it chill in the fridge for at least 8 hours. (The dough will hold in the fridge for up to 5 days at this point.)

TO MAKE THE FILLING

Combine the chicken legs (skin, bones, and all), chicken broth, salt, and pepper in a large pot and bring it up to a simmer, uncovered, over high heat.

Cook the chicken for about 45 to 50 minutes at a very low simmer, so it poaches instead of boiling (the broth should be at 160° to 170°F).

When a knife goes into the chicken easily and it's more or less falling off the bone, use a slotted spoon to pull it out of the pot, pile it on a plate, and put it in the fridge to cool down until you're able to handle it. Don't dump out the broth! Instead, pour it into a bowl—it's the key to pot-pie goodness. Use a ladle to skim off any fat that rises to the top, so you don't end up with oily broth. You should have about 6 cups of broth.

Rinse the pot and put it back on the stove. Add the butter, and melt it over low heat.

When the butter has melted, add the flour and cook it over low heat, stirring constantly with a wooden spoon, for about 1 minute, so the butter and flour are completely combined.

Add the chicken broth back to the pot, whisking everything together. Turn the heat up to medium and bring the mixture to a low simmer.

Meanwhile, take the chicken out of the fridge, remove the skin, and pull out the bones. Use your hands to tear the meat into chunks.

Cook the broth for about 5 minutes, so that the taste of the raw flour disappears and the broth is thick and full of chickeny flavor. Use a ladle or spoon to skim off any white foam that rises to the top. Then add the carrots, onions, celery, mushrooms, potatoes, and thyme, and continue cooking for about 10 to 15 minutes, until the vegetables are cooked but not mushy.

Turn off the heat, and add the peas and chipotle Tabasco. Stir well to combine, and then stir in the chicken meat. You should have a thick, soupy mixture. (The filling can hold in the fridge for up to a day at this point.)

TO FINISH THE DISH

Take the dough out of the fridge an hour before you're ready to use it. The dough will be really tough, so you want to bring it to room temperature so it's easier to work with.

Preheat the oven to 425°F.

Here's the key to this dish: the filling has to be nice and hot, but not boiling. So if you've let the filling cool down, return it to the stove and heat it up gently.

Flour your work surface, and using either a rolling pin or a pasta roller, roll the dough out as thin as you can get it without tearing it.

Turn your casserole over so it's face-down on top of the dough. Use a sharp knife to cut the dough about 1 1/2 inches outside the edge of the casserole (so you have a piece of dough that fits the casserole and has an overhang). If you're making individual pot pies, make sure you cut out all your shapes at the same time.

Make an egg wash by whisking the egg, salt, pepper, and 2 tablespoons of water together in a small bowl.

Pour the filling into the casserole. (If you're using individual casseroles, ladle about 1 1/2 cups into each one.

Make sure you get chicken, vegetables, and broth into every casserole.)

Brush the outside edges and the top lip of the casserole with the egg wash, using a pastry brush (or, working very carefully, with a spoon). Do the same with the outside edges of the dough. Then flip the dough over on top of the casserole so it completely covers the top. You want to get it tight, like a drum, so it closes all the air in. Smooth and tap the edges to make sure it's all sealed.

Brush the entire surface of the dough with the egg wash, being sure to cover all of the edges (this will help the top of the pot pie come out nice and golden brown). Sprinkle the Parmesan on top.

Put the pot pie (or the individual pot pies) on a baking sheet, and put the sheet on the middle oven rack. Bake for 10 minutes. Then rotate the sheet and bake for another 15 minutes or so, until the pot pie is golden brown and crispy on top. When you cut into it, you'll see that the pastry is like a dome, with a hollow of air underneath it and the filling below that. Do this at the table for maximum chef drama.

RED CHICKEN

This is not Communist chicken. It's a take on a fish marinade that some of the Mexican guys we used to work with would make for family meal at the restaurant. Theirs had citrus, annato, and oregano. I played around with it, and what I ended up with was a perfect marinade for chicken.

Achiote (also called annato) is one of the coolest spices around. It has this tangy kind of citrus quality to it, so it's super-refreshing. It's used a lot in Mexican, Caribbean, and Asian cooking, and in southwestern Mexican-American food, too. (It's also the ingredient that makes cheddar cheese yellow.) You can buy the berries whole, but they're really really really hard, so they're tough to work with. I like to use ground achiote powder instead.

This recipe is super-simple, but it takes time: you really need to marinate the chicken overnight to bring the flavor out. And you'll want an apron for this one: it's messy and it stains everything. That's why it's called Red Chicken.

SERVES 4

10 cloves garlic, peeled
1/4 cup extra-virgin olive oil
1 cup orange juice
1/2 cup tequila
Juice of 4 limes (about 1/4 cup)
1/4 cup apple cider vinegar
1/3 cup guajillo or pasilla chile paste (from a jar; see sidebar, page 125)
1 tablespoon achiote powder (also called annato powder)
1/2 teaspoon ground allspice
1 teaspoon ground cumin
2 tablespoons dried oregano, preferably Mexican dried on the branch
2 teaspoons salt

1 teaspoon fresh-ground black pepper
Two 3-pound chickens, quartered

Put everything but the chicken in the blender.

Blend on medium speed for about 20 to 40 seconds, until you have a smooth, bubbling orange liquid and there are no big garlic chunks. It should look a lot like a smoothie.

Put the chicken in a large mixing bowl, pour the marinade over it, and mix everything around with your hands to make sure the chicken is completely coated on all sides.

Marinate the chicken in the fridge for at least 8 hours, but no more than 12 (there's a lot of acid in the marinade, so you don't want the meat to break down too much).

Take the chicken out of the fridge and let it marinate on the countertop for another half hour, so it comes up to room temperature. Meanwhile, preheat the oven to 425°F.

Take the chicken out of the bowl and lay it, skin side up, on a rack in a roasting pan. Hold on to the liquid in the marinating bowl. Put the pan on the middle oven rack, and bake for 15 minutes.

Pull the pan out of the oven and glaze the chicken with some of the leftover marinade, using a pastry brush or a spoon. Put the pan back into the oven, turning it so the chicken cooks evenly.

Repeat the glazing process every 15 minutes, until the chicken is springy to the touch when you poke it with a finger (about 45 minutes).

Pull the pan out of the oven and let the chicken rest for 10 minutes before you serve it.

FRIED CHICKEN

The great fried chicken debate is all about the inside versus the outside: is super-super-crispy skin key to killer fried chicken, or is super-juicy meat more important? Like the best pizza or burger, it's all about personal taste (personally, I'll go for succulent meat over crispiness every time). Fried chicken that hits the skin *and* the meat is about as easy to find as a unicorn or a four-leaf clovers, but I like to think this recipe is as close as you're going to get.

Fried chicken is really hot right now, but I've been doing it in my restaurants since way before the Great Comfort Food Revolution. Back when I was cooking uptown at Café Boulud, we were making fried chicken dinners to go, packaging them up with my buttermilk biscuits (page 239), A.C.'s collards (page 172), and Anthony's Slaw (page 170). (It made me very happy when we delivered one of those dinners to a fancy uptown doorman building.) So I can tell you for sure that this is the best fried chicken ever. Period. Ever. The key is the buttermilk soak.

SERVES 4

FOR THE BUTTERMILK MARINADE
1 quart (4 cups) buttermilk
1/4 teaspoon cayenne pepper
2 teaspoons Old Bay seasoning
2 teaspoons salt
1 teaspoon fresh-ground black pepper
2 teaspoons Tabasco sauce
2 tablespoons honey

FOR THE CHICKEN
2 chickens (2 pounds each—you don't want huge chickens for this), cut up into pieces
2 quarts corn oil
4 cups all-purpose flour
4 teaspoons paprika

2 teaspoons chili powder
2 teaspoons garlic powder
2 teaspoons onion powder
2 tablespoons Old Bay seasoning
2 teaspoons cayenne pepper
2 teaspoons ground celery seed
4 teaspoons salt
1 teaspoon fresh-ground black pepper

TO MAKE THE BUTTERMILK MARINADE
In a large mixing bowl, whisk the buttermilk together with the cayenne, Old Bay, salt, pepper, Tabasco, and honey.

Put the chicken pieces in the mixing bowl and submerge them in the buttermilk marinade. Cover the bowl with plastic wrap, put it in the fridge, and let the chicken marinate for at least 12 hours.

TO BREAD AND FRY THE CHICKEN
Pull the chicken out of the fridge and let it come up to room temperature, still in the marinade (this will take about 45 minutes).

Preheat the oven to 200°F.

Heat the oil in a deep pot or a deep-fryer over high heat. The oil should be 3 inches deep, and it should be so hot that it starts popping (about 350°F). A good rule of thumb: if you drop a pinch of flour into the oil and it fries up immediately, you're good to go.

While the oil is heating, combine the flour, paprika, chili powder, garlic powder, onion powder, Old Bay, cayenne pepper, celery seed, salt, and pepper in a large mixing bowl. Mix things around with your hands so everything is distributed evenly. Pour half of the mixture into a small bowl and set it aside.

>>>

Add the flour to the large bowl and mix well.

When the oil is hot, pull a piece of chicken out of the marinade. Put it right into the dredging flour bowl and heap flour on top of it; flip it around until the chicken is completely coated. Do the same with each piece until there's no more space in the bowl.

Pick up a piece of chicken, give it a light shake (just enough to get rid of the really loose bits of flour), and use your hands or a pair of tongs to drop it into the fry pot. Do the same with the rest of the chicken pieces. (You will definitely need to fry your chicken in batches, unless you've got some really big bowls and pots.)

Let the chicken fry for about 8 minutes, until it's golden brown. Pull the chicken pieces out of the fryer with tongs and put them on a rack set on a baking sheet.

Sprinkle each piece of chicken with the seasoning mixture, using the tongs to turn the piece so it's coated on all sides.

Put the baking sheet in the oven. The chicken pieces should rest in the oven for at least 10 minutes, so that the cooking process finishes. Meanwhile, fry up the next batch of chicken.

Hold the fried chicken in the oven until all the pieces are fried and rested and you're ready to serve it up. Then pile the chicken on a big plate, put it in the center of the table with biscuits, collards, and slaw, and let everybody start grabbing pieces. I guarantee it will disappear fast.

KITCHEN AIR CLEANER

You know I love the smell of great food cooking, but sometimes the aroma—of fried chicken, for example—sticks around a little longer than you'd like. Here's an easy way to get your place smelling pretty again.

Fill a big pot with a quart of water. Add a tablespoon of ground cinnamon, a couple of pieces of star anise, a handful of cardamom pods, and a couple tablespoons of honey. Set the pot on the stove, let it come up to a boil, and then just let it boil away. The aroma of the boiling spices will cut right through grease smells and other kitchen odors—and it smells a hell of a lot better than some perfume stick you plug into a wall.

FREE-RANGE TURKEYS IN THE BERKSHIRES

DUCK WITH PEACHES, GINGER, AND LEMON THYME

This is a shout-out to John D'Amico, chef-owner of Chez François in Vermilion, Ohio, the first serious restaurant I ever got the chance to cook at. Chez François is an old-school French restaurant to the core, but John could teach the locavore kids a thing or two: he's been cooking local and seasonal since way before anybody thought about pig tattoos and backyard beekeeping. In the summertime, there was always some kind of roast bird with fruit on his menu, and, this being Ohio, summer peaches were often his inspiration. This is my home version of a dish you might have seen on John's menu.

If you can't find lemon thyme, regular thyme will work fine here. Timing, on the other hand, is important. Make the peach syrup while the duck is cooking; cut the peaches and bake them while the duck is resting. Kitchen control is also important: watch out for the flame when you add the peach schnapps to the syrup, and keep long hair, kids, and pets out of the way!

FOR THE DUCK BREASTS

4 boned duck breasts (about 3 pounds total)

1 1/2 teaspoons salt

1 1/2 teaspoons fresh-ground black pepper

FOR THE PEACH SYRUP

1 tablespoon butter

One 2-inch piece of fresh ginger, peeled and chopped fine (2 tablespoons)

1 shallot, chopped fine (about 2 tablespoons)

3 tablespoons peach schnapps

1/3 cup peach preserves

Juice of 3 lemons (6 tablespoons)

TO FINISH THE DISH

4 to 6 ripe medium-sized peaches

2 tablespoons fresh lemon thyme leaves

TO PREPARE THE DUCK BREAST

Preheat the oven to 450°F.

Use a small sharp knife to score the fatty skin of the duck in a crosshatch pattern, scoring about 5 times in one direction, 5 in the other. (This will stop the skin from supercontracting, so it cooks right and protects the meat.)

Season the duck breasts well with the salt and pepper on all sides.

Put the duck breasts, skin side down, in a large ovenproof saucepan and render the fat over medium-high heat. (You'll want to open a window, and maybe disable your smoke alarm: this will definitely be smoky.) Use a pair of tongs to shake the duck breasts around every so often, so they don't stick. (If you don't have a big enough pan, you can do this in two pans at the same time.) The ducks will give off a lot of liquefied fat; it's a good idea to drain it off every so often by taking the pan over to the sink and tipping it out, holding the duck breasts back with a pair of tongs.

When the skin has crisped and turned a deep golden brown (about 8 to 10 minutes), turn the duck breasts over so they're skin side up, and put the pan on the middle oven rack. Roast the duck for 5 to 7 minutes, until the flesh springs back a little when you poke it. (You want your duck nice and medium-rare: if the skin is very loose, it's not cooked enough, but if it's completely taut, it's overcooked.) The internal temperature should be about 115°F.

TO MAKE THE PEACH SYRUP

While the duck is in the oven, melt the butter in a medium-sized saucepan over medium heat.

Add the ginger and shallots, and stir everything together. Cook for a minute or two, until the ginger aroma has come out and the ginger and shallots have softened.

Add the peach schnapps. Be careful! The alcohol is likely to flame up pretty high. Let it cook, stirring it (carefully) for about 30 seconds or so until the alcohol has burned off and the mixture has thickened up.

Stir in the peach preserves and squeeze the lemon juice into the saucepan, using a strainer to catch the seeds.

Bring the syrup up to a simmer, and let it cook for about 5 minutes, until it reduces a little and the flavors are blended into a sweet-and-sour mix.

TO FINISH THE DISH
Pull the pan out of the oven (leave the oven on) and move the duck breasts to a plate to rest.

While the duck is resting, cut the peaches in half, remove the pits, and lay the peaches, skin side down, in the same pan that you cooked the duck in.

Bake the peaches on the middle oven rack for about 5 minutes, until they start to soften and roast a little on the bottom.

Pull the peaches out of the oven and pour the glaze over them right in the pan. Sprinkle on the lemon thyme, and drizzle the resting liquid (the drippings) from the ducks over them.

Slice the duck into 1-inch-thick slices. Lay each breast, in slices, on an individual plate. Lay a couple of peaches next to each breast, and then spoon the glaze mixture over everything. Serve right away.

BEEF SHORT-RIB MOLE

Mole sauces are the hardest sauces in the world to make, period. I know a lot of French chefs who would throw a bowl of snails at me for saying that, but it's true: mole is way harder than any fancy French stuff. You've got to balance so many different flavors: bitter, sweet, savory, spicy spice, savory spice, and sour.

There are definitely a lot of steps involved in making a great mole: toasting the spices and nuts, toasting the chiles, browning the tortilla . . . it's all important if you're going to get the layers of flavor right. Usually I'm the king of kitchen multitasking, but you really can't do that with mole; if you try to do everything at once, you'll end up with a bitter-tasting mess. So go slow. This is a two-day job: you need to let the mole sit in the fridge overnight before you cook with it, so the flavors mellow and come together. If you take your time with this, you'll end up with rich, falling-off-the-bone ribs in a sauce that's thick and chocolatey, with just a little bit of spice.

Moles come in a couple of different varieties. This one's a black mole, with Oaxacan roots; you find lots of great versions of this stuff across the Southwest, especially around San Antonio. Here we actually cook the ribs right in the mole, but you can also leave the ribs out and use the mole as an accompaniment for grilled chicken or roast turkey.

SERVES 4 TO 6

FOR THE ROASTED CHILES
4 pasilla chiles
4 ancho chiles
2 chipotle chiles
4 guajillo chiles

FOR THE SPICE MIXTURE AND TORTILLAS
1/4 cup blanched almonds (whole or slivered)
1/4 cup sesame seeds
1/4 cup walnuts (pieces or whole)

1/4 cup pumpkin seeds
1/2 teaspoon fresh-ground black pepper
1/2 teaspoon ground allspice
1/2 teaspoon ground cinnamon
2 tortillas (flour or corn)

FOR THE SAUCE
1/4 cup pork lard (or butter—but lard really makes a difference here, and it's very traditional)
1 large onion, sliced (about 2 cups)
7 tomatillos (about 1/2 pound), husks removed, quartered (see page 219)
1 medium banana, chopped
2 whole cloves garlic, peeled
One 28-ounce can diced tomatoes with their juice
1/2 cup raisins
One 3.5-ounce bar bittersweet chocolate, chopped into medium-sized pieces

FOR THE RIBS AND TO FINISH THE DISH
2 1/2 pounds boneless beef short ribs
1/2 teaspoon salt
1 tablespoon sesame seeds
1 tablespoon slivered blanched almonds

TO ROAST THE CHILES
Combine all the chiles in a sauté pan (not nonstick, if possible) and dry-roast them slowly over medium heat for about 5 minutes, until they become very fragrant and char up a bit. Shake the pan around every so often to stop the chiles from burning and sticking.

Pull the chiles from the pan, put them in a large bowl, and add enough hot tap water to cover them. Place a pot lid or a plate directly on top of the chiles so they are submerged in the water. Leave the chiles in the water until they rehydrate, at least 2 hours, or up to 8 hours. (The longer you leave the chiles in the water, the softer and easier to work with they will be.)

Pull the stems off the chiles with your fingers and rinse out the seeds (you can do this right in the soaking water).

TO TOAST THE NUTS AND PREPARE THE TORTILLA

Combine all the nuts, seeds, and spices for the spice mixture in a medium-sized pan. Dry-roast the mixture over very low heat for about 5 minutes, shaking every-thing around occasionally to avoid burning, until the spices really release their aroma. The aroma should be a little deep and woody as the nuts toast. Set aside.

Put a tortilla in a dry skillet (or on the grill if it's hot), and let it char a bit on both sides. The whole operation should take about 3 minutes. Set it aside and repeat with the second tortilla.

TO MAKE THE SAUCE

Melt the lard in a large pot over medium heat. Add the onions and sauté them for about 2 minutes, until they soften.

Add the tomatillos, banana, garlic, tomatoes, raisins, the spice mix and the chiles. Stir in 6 cups of water. Break up the tortillas into large chunks and add them to the pot. Mix well to combine everything, and let the mixture cook at a low bubble over low to medium heat, stirring occasionally to keep things from sticking, for about 55 minutes.

Add the chocolate and mix it in well so it melts. Let the mole cook for another 5 minutes, until the tomatillos and chiles are soft and the flavors come together. The mole will be pretty strong-tasting and bitter at this point. Don't worry. We're not done yet.

In batches, fill a blender about halfway with the mole, blend on medium speed for about 10 seconds, until the mixture forms a thick paste. (Be sure to hold a towel over the lid to prevent hot-liquid accidents.) Pour each batch of the blended mole into another pot or a bowl as you go. Let the mole cool to room temperature.

Cover the mole and put it in the fridge overnight (at least 8 hours). (The mole will keep in the fridge for up to a week, or in the freezer until freezer burn sets in.)

TO ROAST THE RIBS AND FINISH THE DISH

Preheat the oven to 475°F.

Season the short ribs on all sides with the salt, and put them on a roasting rack set in a rimmed baking sheet, making sure that the pieces don't touch so they can roast evenly. Put the baking sheet on the middle oven rack, and roast the short ribs for about 30 minutes, until they're dark brown on each side and some of the fat has been rendered.

Meanwhile, pour 4 cups of the mole into a large oven-proof pot. Add 1 cup of water, mix to combine, and heat the mole slowly over low heat. The sauce will still have a kick to it, but the bitterness should be gone. If the kick is too strong or harsh for you, don't worry: when the mole cooks with the beef, it will keep mellowing out.

Tip the ribs into the mole pot, and mix everything around so the ribs are well coated. Cover the pot and bring the mixture up to a simmer.

Lower the oven heat to 350°F, and put the pot right in the oven. Bake the ribs, covered, for about 2 1/2 hours, or until they're fork-tender and a sharp knife goes through the meat easily.

Pull the pot out of the oven and let the ribs rest for about 5 minutes.

Using a ladle, carefully scoop some of the grease off the surface of the sauce. You can use a wooden spoon to hold back the non-greasy mole so you don't lose too much of it. (The grease will be easily visible: it's red and oily-looking instead of brown and smooth.)

Serve the dish right away, topped with sprinklings of the sesame seeds and almonds.

DRIED CHILES

Quite a few recipes in this book use Mexican chiles. Different regions and traditions use different kinds of chiles, and in different proportions. Here's a quick primer:

CHIPOTLE is a smoked and dried jalapeño; it gives food a smoky, spicy, earthy bite.

ANCHO is a dried poblano, which gives kind of a mild spiciness. *Ancho* means "wide" in Spanish; ancho chiles are usually the biggest ones.

PASILLA is a dried chilaca pepper—also known as *chile negro* because of its black color. I'd call it medium-hot.

GUAJILLO is more on the sweet side dried. Guajillos are easy to spot: they're very red.

Chiles are pretty easy to find: specialty food stores and spice stores carry them, but you can also usually snag them in the "Latin" section of your local supermarket.

When you're working with chiles, the most important step is to toast them before you use them. This really develops the flavors of moles and chili dishes. Toast chiles on a griddle or in a pan; let them dry-roast until they start to darken up a little, shaking them around in the pan every so often to make sure they toast on all sides. By the time you're done, the whole house will have that warm, spicy chile aroma.

Once the chiles have turned dark brown, put them in enough warm water to cover, and let them soak until they soften up (you can leave them in the water for up to 12 hours).

The last step is cleaning the chiles: you want to make sure you pull out all the seeds, because they have a more intense, sharp flavor than the meat of the chile. It's a good idea to wear rubber gloves you're while doing this, so you don't end up with chile oil on your hands (and be very careful about touching your eyes!). Cut or pull off the stems and any hard outside skins that are left, and then you're good to go.

If you don't want to mess around with dried chiles or you can't find them locally, you can always use premade chile paste. I've found that about 1 tablespoon of puree is equal to 1 chile.

BRAISED BEEF SHORT RIBS WITH GUINNESS

The inspiration for this dish came from the best meal I had in my trip through Ireland: bangers and mash and Guinness in a pub in Westport, a picture-perfect little place (it actually won an award for being a "tidy town") in the northwest of the Republic. So it's not exactly locally inspired—but come on, who doesn't love an Irish pub? In New York, there's a place serving bangers and mash on every other block—and when it comes to celebrating, everybody's Irish.

To make this right, try to find thick-cut, well-marbled beef: the better the meat, the better the ribs. I like to use bone-in short ribs: they make for a great presentation, and the flavor of the bones bumps up the flavor of the sauce. I marinate the meat overnight for maximum beef beeriness, but I toss the beer marinade down the sink the next day; if you actually cook with the beer, everything turns really bitter. Instead, I add some fresh beer at the end, to give the sauce that straight-from-the-bottle flavor.

The caramelized onion puree balances the beer out with a little bit of sweetness. The idea here is slow caramelization to bring out the sugar in the onions. I bang out the onion puree while the ribs are in the oven, but you can also make the puree the day before, when you marinate the ribs, and stick it in the fridge overnight.

The ribs are great with sour cream mashed potatoes. And beer, of course.

SERVES 6

FOR THE RIBS
5 1/2 pounds bone-in beef short ribs (or 4 pounds boneless short ribs)
Two 12-ounce bottles of Guinness, plus 1/2 cup for finishing the dish
1 tablespoon salt
1 teaspoon fresh-ground black pepper
2 tablespoons corn oil
2 tablespoons extra-virgin olive oil
1 medium onion, rough-chopped (about 1 cup)
2 celery stalks, cut into large chunks (about 1 cup)
1 large carrot, peeled and cut into large chunks (about 1 cup)
1 heaping tablespoon tomato paste
1 tablespoon all-purpose flour
2 cups cheap red wine (the cheaper the better)
2 fresh thyme sprigs
2 bay leaves
4 cups beef broth or low-sodium chicken broth

FOR THE ONION PUREE AND TO FINISH THE DISH
2 tablespoons corn oil
1 large Vidalia onion or other sweet onion, sliced (1 1/2 cups)
1/4 teaspoon salt
1/8 teaspoon fresh-ground black pepper
1/3 cup fresh celery leaves, for garnish

TO COOK THE RIBS
The day before you want to serve the ribs, put the meat in a baking dish or other large container and soak it with 2 bottles of the Guinness. Cover the ribs with plastic wrap, and let them marinate in the fridge for 12 to 24 hours, turning them over at the halfway mark to make sure everything gets evenly beered up. (The longer you marinate the meat, the beerier—and better—it will be.)

Take the ribs out of the fridge and let them sit on the countertop for about an hour, until they come up to room temperature.

Meanwhile, preheat the oven to 400°F.

>>>

Pull the ribs out of the beer, pat them dry with a paper towel, and season them generously on all sides with the salt and pepper.

Heat the corn oil in a very large ovenproof pot or casserole with a tight-fitting lid over medium-high heat. When the oil is smoking, put the short ribs in the pot. Let the meat cook, turning each piece every couple of minutes with a pair of tongs, for about 8 minutes, until the ribs are chocolate brown and caramelized on all sides, like a good steak (they should smell like a good steak, too). This is a smoky process, so you might want to open a window or two before you start (and maybe think about pulling the battery out of that smoke alarm).

Use a pair of tongs to pull the ribs out of the pot and put them on a plate. Then pour the oil out of the pot and use a paper towel to wipe down the insides, so the caramelized stuff doesn't burn and flavor everything.

Return the pot to the fire on medium heat. Pour in the olive oil, and then add the onions, celery, and carrots. Cook the vegetables, stirring regularly to stop them from sticking, for about 4 to 5 minutes, until they're roasted and caramelized; they should be soft, with some brown color.

Add the tomato paste and mix it in well, so the vegetables are coated in the paste. Let the mixture cook for about 30 seconds, until you can smell the tomato caramelizing.

Add the flour, mix it in, and let it toast for about 30 seconds, being careful not to let it burn on the bottom of the pot.

Add the red wine and scrape the bottom of the pot to release the *fond* (the base of the sauce—the good stuff that's caramelized down there). Then add the thyme and bay leaves.

Raise the heat to high and let the sauce cook for about 5 minutes, until it thickens up and the wine has reduced by three quarters. This is a good time to wipe down the sides of the pot above the cooking mixture with a wet cloth, so that anything that's splashed onto the sides doesn't burn and fall into the sauce, wrecking the flavor.

When the sauce is a thick chocolate color, pile the ribs back into the pot. Add the beef broth and 2 cups of water, so the short ribs are submerged in the liquid. Give everything a stir to bring it together, wipe down the sides of the pot again, and bring the mixture to a boil.

Cover the pot and put it on the middle oven rack. Cook the ribs for 2½ to 3 hours, turning them every hour. They're ready when they're fork-tender.

TO MAKE THE ONION PUREE

Heat the corn oil in a medium-sized saucepan over high heat. Add the onions, stirring them around and shaking the pan so they're coated in the oil. Cook the onions for about 1 minute, until you start to get a little caramelization. Then turn the heat down to medium and keep cooking for about 5 minutes, until the onions are golden brown.

Add the salt and pepper and 1½ cups of water. Stir to combine everything, and continue cooking for about 10 more minutes, until the onions are very soft and all the sharpness has gone out of their flavor.

Pour everything in the pan—onions and liquid—into a blender, and blend (starting on low speed and working your way up) for about 30 seconds, until everything's liquified. Pour the onion puree into a bowl and set it aside.

TO FINISH THE DISH

Pull the meat from the pot with tongs, and pile it on a serving platter.

Strain the cooking juices into a medium-sized saucepan. You'll end up with a thick mush in the strainer: take a spoon and push everything through so you get all the good stuff.

Add the last $1/2$ cup of Guinness and the onion puree to the saucepan, and stir everything together; if the sauce has cooled down, warm it up over medium heat.

Pour the sauce over the short ribs. Sprinkle the celery leaves on top, and serve the ribs right away—with more Guinness, of course.

JULIE'S TEXAS-STYLE CHILI WITH CHEDDAR AND BEER

Julie Farias worked with me as a cook at Café Boulud; now she's a chef herself. She's from San Antonio, where her aunt and uncle still run the grocery store and tortilla factory that her grandmother opened back when she moved to the States from Mexico. Food's a big deal in her family, and this chili is a serious family recipe. This is what Julie has to say about it:

"Chili is an old-school San Antonio dish: back in the 1930s or before, Mexican women used to sell chili from little carts right in Mercato Square, downtown. They were called the Chili Queens. In my family, though, the chili master is my great-uncle Fermin, and his chili isn't exactly traditional. He's a rancher, from the original Canary Islanders who founded San Antonio. On New Year's Eve, my uncle would host the whole family—at least seventy people—for a fireworks display. There was a lot of eating and drinking—all the usual stuff, tamales and everything, and there was also always a huge pot of venison chili going all night. My uncle hunted the venison himself. The other ingredients in the recipe all came from my aunt's store.

"My chili is a version of my uncle's. It has some things in common with a Texas-style chili, because it doesn't have any beans, but it's also a lot like *carne guisada*, a beef stew that's one of the fillings they put in tacos at my aunt's store. The garnish is totally San Antonio: Tex-Mex is really big there, and it's all about flour tortillas and yellow cheese and Fritos."

You want to make this chili the day before you eat it, so the flavors have a chance to mellow. You can find just about everything you need online—mexicangrocer .org has it all. (The sidebar on page 125 describes the various chiles here.) If you're cooking for a crowd (and you're not hunting your own meat, like Julie's uncle), chuck is the super-economical way to go in this recipe; if you want to go soigné, shell out for the short ribs

(they'll definitely make the chili a little richer). Either way, this chili is really smooth-tasting, rich, and meaty. It's best eaten with a beer on the side.

SERVES 6 TO 10,
DEPENDING ON PORTION SIZE

FOR THE CHILE PEPPER PASTE

2 ancho chiles

2 gaujillo chiles

2 pasilla chiles

2 canned chipotle peppers in adobo sauce (I like La Morena brand)

2 cups beer (one 12-ounce bottle ale or pilsner, but not an I.P.A., it's too bitter)

1 cup brewed coffee

FOR THE CHILI

2 tablespoons lard or corn oil

2 $1/2$ pounds boneless beef stew meat (chuck or short ribs), cut into 1-inch pieces

1 large onion, chopped (about 1 $1/2$ cups)

2 cloves garlic, minced

6 cups beef broth, low-sodium chicken broth, or water

$1/4$ teaspoon fresh-ground black pepper

$1/8$ teaspoon ground cinnamon

Pinch of ground cloves

$1/8$ teaspoon ground allspice

$3/4$ teaspoon ground coriander

$1/2$ teaspoon ground cumin

Pinch of cayenne pepper

1 teaspoon salt

TO FINISH THE DISH

$1/4$ cup masa harina (the stuff they make tortillas with; if you can't find this, you can substitute fine-ground cornmeal)

>>>

½ teaspoon chipotle-flavored Tabasco sauce
1 ounce bittersweet chocolate (one-third of a
    standard 3-ounce bar)

FOR THE GARNISH
1 small onion, diced superfine (about ½ cup)
1 cup grated very sharp cheddar cheese
2 corn tortillas per person, or a handful of Fritos
    per person

TO MAKE THE CHILE PEPPER PASTE

Combine all the chiles (but not the chipotle peppers)
in a sauté pan (not a nonstick pan) and dry-roast them
slowly over medium heat for about 5 minutes, until
they char up a little and become very fragrant. Shake
the pan around every so often to stop the chiles from
burning and sticking.

Pull the chiles from the pan, put them in a large bowl,
and add enough hot tap water to cover them. To keep
the chiles submerged, cover them directly with a pot
lid that fits inside the bowl. Let the chiles rehydrate
for at least 30 minutes (you can leave them like this
for up to 8 hours).

When the chiles are ready, clean them by pulling the
stems off with your fingers and rinsing out the seeds
(I like to do this right inside the soaking water). Make
sure you get all the seeds out, so they don't end up
floating around in the chili and overspicing it. (Be
careful not to touch your eyes while you're doing this,
and wash your hands when you're finished working
with the chiles!)

Transfer the chiles to a blender; add the chipotles, the
beer, and the coffee. Hold down the top of the blender
with a kitchen towel to avoid hot-liquid disasters, and
blend everything together on high speed for 30 sec-

onds, till you have a thick paste. The paste will be bitter, but don't worry about that: when you cook it with
the meat, it will mellow out.

TO MAKE THE CHILI

Melt half of the lard (or heat half the oil) in a large
saucepot over medium-high heat.

When the lard has completely melted (or the oil is
hot), add half of the meat to the pot. Mix it around well
so it's all coated in the fat, and then keep cooking for
4 minutes or so, until it's browned on all sides, shaking
or stirring the meat around every few seconds to keep
it from sticking.

Pull the meat out of the pot with a slotted spoon, pile
it on a plate, and then melt the rest of the lard and
brown the rest of the meat.

Add the first batch of meat back to the pot, along with the onions and garlic. Mix everything together well, and cook for 2 minutes or so until the onions have softened but not colored and the garlic has released its aroma. Make sure you stir regularly so the garlic doesn't burn.

Add the chile pepper paste, the broth, all the spices, and the salt. Mix everything together well. Scrape down the sides of the pot to make sure that nothing burns and falls into the chili: you don't want bitter burned bits inside. Bring the chili up to a simmer; then turn the heat down to low and cook it at a low simmer, uncovered, until the meat is really tender and shreds easily—about 2$\frac{1}{4}$ hours.

When the chili has cooked, pour the masa harina (or cornmeal) into a small bowl. Add 2 cups of the liquid from the chili pot, and whisk the mixture together until it forms a thick paste without any lumps. Stir this into the chili. (If you just add the masa harina directly to the chili pot, it will get lumpy.) Let the chili cook, uncovered, at a low simmer for another 15 minutes, stirring it every couple of minutes to make sure it doesn't stick as it thickens up.

When the chili looks rich and thick, turn the heat off and stir in the chipotle Tabasco.

Break the chocolate into the pot in small pieces, and stir it in gently with a wooden spoon until it has melted into the chili.

Spoon the chili up into individual bowls, and top it with the diced raw onions and grated cheddar. (Don't skip the onions: the contrast they give the dish is key!) Pile the corn tortillas or Fritos on the side. Serve the chili with a cold beer.

KOREAN STEAK, PAGE 137

KOREAN STEAK

Here's what I've learned from all the Korean cooks who've worked with us over the years: at the end of a long service, there's nothing better than Korean barbecue. We like to go to Hahm Ji Bach in Flushing, Queens (I like Park's in Los Angeles, too), but I wanted to learn how to make it myself. When I started asking Korean cooks about it, I learned that in every family recipe, there's always one key ingredient in the overnight marinade for sweetening and tenderizing. Sometimes it's ground-up Asian pears; sometimes it's kiwi. But the most popular ingredient? The ultimate American flavor: Coca-Cola.

This recipe is definitely not authentic *bulgogi*: it's my backyard version of that sweet-salty late-night flavor. I like rib-eyes for my version, but you can use any kind of steak that you grill—and you don't need a grill to do it. Even if you're using the broiler in your apartment oven, I guarantee it will come out seriously succulent and flavorful.

SERVES 4 TO 6

1 cup soy sauce
1 cup Coca-Cola
1/4 cup sesame oil
1/4 cup hoisin sauce
4 cloves garlic, chopped
4 green onions, minced
2 bone-in rib-eye steaks (2 1/2 pounds each)
1/2 cup kimchee (from a jar), for serving (optional)
1/2 cup peeled, grated daikon radish (from a 3-inch piece), for serving (optional)

In a small bowl, whisk together the soy sauce, Coke, sesame oil, and hoisin sauce. Add the garlic and green onions, and whisk well.

There are two ways to get the marinade on the steak. Do whichever of these floats your boat: (a) Put the steaks in a large deep dish and pour the marinade over them. Cover the dish tightly with tin foil and put it in the fridge. Or (b) pour the marinade into a gallon plastic bag, put in the steaks, seal the bag, and shake them around till they're coated in the marinade. Either way, the steaks should marinate in the fridge for 12 hours. (But don't let them marinate for longer than that: you don't want the meat to break down too much.)

Pull the steaks out of the marinade, pile them on a plate, and let them come up to room temperature (about 20 to 30 minutes).

Either fire up the grill or turn the broiler on high. If you're using the grill, you should also preheat the oven to 400°F.

If you're using the broiler, put the steaks on a rack set over a rimmed baking sheet, place the baking sheet on the middle or middle-high rack, and broil the steaks for about 6 minutes per side. *If you're using the grill,* lay the meat right on the rack so it gets a nice char, and let it grill for 4 to 6 minutes a side, depending on the thickness of the meat: you just want to get a nice char going. Then bring the meat back inside and finish it on a rack in a roasting pan in the oven at 400°F for 6 minutes, turning it over once so it cooks more evenly.

No matter how you're cooking the steak, it's done when the meat springs back to the touch (if you have a meat thermometer, the internal temperature should be 115°F).

Let the meat rest for 5 minutes; then slice it thin. If you want the full Korean experience, serve up a bowl of kimchee on the side. And even though it's not Korean at all, I really love to serve this with grated daikon, too.

SALT-BAKED BEEF TENDERLOIN

This is a party recipe—the kind of thing that's great for a tableful of big eaters. Beef tenderloin is the safe guy's meat: it's easy to just throw it on the grill, but it doesn't usually have as much flavor as sirloin or rib eye. That's why chefs don't like it. Well, this version may be a little more complicated, but it has plenty of flavor. That's because I rub the meat with herbs and mustard and then bake the whole thing in a salt crust. The crust keeps the meat tender like butter, and the flavors of the rub really come through—it doesn't need a sauce or any of that dress-up stuff tenderloin usually begs for. (It makes great next-day sandwiches, too.)

There are a couple of different ways to make a salt crust. This one looks like a really great bread crust when it's done. If you want to make like a culinary superstar, you can do a great dramatic tabletop presentation here: carry the tenderloin out to the table and cut into the crust right in front of everybody. The steam escapes; people go ooh and aah; you're the hero. Just don't let anybody at the table make the mistake of trying to eat the crust.

SERVES 8 TO 10

FOR THE TENDERLOIN AND RUB

1 beef tenderloin (5 to 6 pounds)
8 cloves garlic, peeled
1/4 cup corn oil
2 tablespoons white wine
1/4 cup Dijon mustard
1 tablespoon prepared horseradish
3/4 teaspoon fresh-ground black pepper
2 tablespoons fresh or dried thyme leaves
2 tablespoons fresh or dried rosemary leaves

FOR THE SALT CRUST

12 egg whites
4 cups kosher salt
6 cups all-purpose flour, plus 1/2 cup for flouring your work surface
2 tablespoons dried thyme leaves
2 tablespoons dried rosemary

TO PREP THE TENDERLOIN AND MAKE THE RUB

Cut the silverskin off the tenderloin: the silverskin (the membrane that runs along the top of the tenderloin) is tough to cut and to chew, so if your butcher hasn't gotten rid of it, make sure you do. Slide a long sharp-pointed knife under the membrane, saw along underneath it, and then pull the silverskin off.

Cut off the fat on the sides and bottom of the tenderloin. The fat lies in long, thick white ribbons along the meat. It's OK to leave a little bit, but you want to trim it up some, especially the hard pieces: they won't render and help the meat. Basically, if it's red, it stays; if it's white or silvery or light pink, take it off. When you're done, you should have a pretty clean-looking piece of raw red meat.

Put the tenderloin in a large baking dish.

Put the garlic, corn oil, white wine, Dijon mustard, horseradish, and pepper in a blender, and blend on low speed for 30 seconds. Then kick it up to high speed for another 45 seconds or so, blending until the garlic is pulverized and you have a smooth, thick paste.

Using your hands, rub the garlic paste all over the tenderloin, making sure all the meat is covered. Sprinkle the thyme and rosemary over the top.

>>>

Cover the baking dish with plastic wrap, making sure the wrap isn't right on the meat, and let it marinate in the fridge for 4 to 6 hours (don't leave it overnight—you don't want the meat to break down too much).

TO MAKE THE SALT CRUST

Put the egg whites in a stand mixer fitted with the whisk attachment, and whip them until they form a meringue, starting the mixer on low speed and going up to medium once the egg whites start to bubble. Take your time: meringue is better when you build it slowly, because it has a more stable structure. When the meringue is almost formed—when the egg whites have turned translucent and have begun to hold a structure—turn the mixer up to high for the last few seconds. The whites are done after about 8 minutes, when they hold a soft peak: when you scoop out a little bit, it won't stand straight up, but instead slumps over without breaking.

Take the bowl off the mixer, add the salt and the 6 cups of flour, and mix everything together well with a rubber spatula. Then add ½ cup of water and the dried thyme and rosemary, and use your hands to turn and knead the dough until it's combined and soft without crumbling. If the dough is too dry to come together well, add a little more water, bit by bit.

Flour your work surface well, turn the dough out, and knead and work it lightly, patting it into a thick patty. Then flour the top and roll the dough out with a rolling pin until it's a bit longer than the tenderloin, wider by about 6 inches, and about ½ inch thick. Be careful not to tear the dough; if you do, roll it up and then roll it out again.

TO WRAP AND BAKE THE TENDERLOIN IN THE SALT CRUST

Preheat the oven to 425°F.

Lay the tenderloin on top of the dough. There should be about 3 inches of extra dough on each side. Wrap the closest side over the tenderloin, and then gently roll the tenderloin and dough together to form a cylinder. Pinch the dough closed at the ends, cutting off any big extra pieces, and pat all the seams closed so there are no holes. If the dough tears, patch it with the extra pieces.

Use a metal spatula to flip the tenderloin over, so that the smoother side is on top, and lay it on a baking sheet. Insert a temperature probe, if you've got one, at the thickest point; then put the sheet on the middle oven rack.

After about 25 to 30 minutes, when the crust is golden-brown and looks like the outside of a loaf of bread, and the internal temperature has reached 115°F, pull the tenderloin out of the oven. This will give you a nice medium-rare piece of meat. (The meat will become a little less rare as it rests, so you really want to make sure you take it out as soon as it hits the right temperature.)

To impress your guests, carry the tenderloin out to the table and, using the tip of a sharp knife, cut all the way along the top of the crust, being careful not to cut into the meat inside.

Bring the meat back to the kitchen. Use the knife to peel the sides of the crust away from the meat, so that it doesn't overcook as it rests. Let it sit on the countertop for 10 minutes; then carve the meat into thin slices and serve it right away.

MAC-'N-CHEESE-STUFFED MEATLOAF

Meatloaf is the quintessential American home-cooked dish—the one that everybody's mom made. It's comfort food, diner food . . . the kind of thing you crave when you've had a really bad day. And mac and cheese? Well, that's the *other* basic of American home cooking. So I thought: why not put them together? What could be more American than that? OK—it's kind of over the top. But that's what America's all about, right?

Meatloaf is basically a giant meatball, and the key to making great meatballs is the bread crumbs: you need to make sure that you have enough bread crumbs, and it's crucial to soak them in milk before you add them to the meat. (The French call this a *panade* when they use it in terrines: it's what stops the meat from falling apart.) Here that process, plus freezing, is what holds everything together. This recipe takes time, patience, and higher-level use of plastic wrap—but I can tell you for sure that the payoff in diner reaction is definitely worth it.

SERVES THE WHOLE NEIGHBORHOOD

FOR THE MACARONI AND CHEESE
1/4 pound elbow pasta (about 1/4 box; I like De Cecco #81)
A little more than 1/2 a stick (4 tablespoons) butter
1/4 cup all-purpose flour
1 1/2 cups 2 percent or whole milk
2 cups grated sharp cheddar cheese
1 cup grated Parmesan cheese
1/2 teaspoon salt
1/4 teaspoon fresh-ground black pepper
Pinch of ground nutmeg
Pinch of cayenne pepper

FOR THE MEATLOAF
2 tablespoons extra-virgin olive oil
1 1/2 medium onions, diced (1 1/2 cups)

3 tablespoons ketchup
2 tablespoons Dijon mustard
1 1/2 cups fresh bread crumbs
1 cup whole milk
1/2 teaspoon ground cumin
1 teaspoon chili powder
1 teaspoon paprika
1 1/2 tablespoons salt
1 1/2 teaspoons fresh-ground black pepper
3 pounds ground beef
3 eggs

TO FINISH THE DISH
1 cup Greco's Barbecue Sauce (page 300), plus extra for dipping

TO MAKE THE MACARONI AND CHEESE
Bring a large pot of well-salted water to a boil. Add the pasta, and stir to stop it from sticking. Cook the pasta for 1 minute less than the directions on the box tell you to.

Drain the pasta, but don't rinse it (you want the sticky stuff so the sauce adheres). Return the pasta to its cooking pot.

Cover a rimmed baking sheet with a sheet of plastic wrap.

Melt the butter in a medium-sized pot over low heat, being careful that it doesn't color or burn.

Turn the heat to medium and add the flour. Mix well (to make what the French call a *roux*) and cook for 1 minute, stirring constantly, so the starch cooks out a little.

Add the milk to the roux and whisk everything together. Cook for about 3 minutes, whisking frequently to make sure solids don't form in the milk. It's ready when the

>>>

flour taste has cooked out and the mixture has a custardy texture.

Turn off the heat, and whisk in the grated cheddar and Parmesan so the cheeses melt into the milk-butter mixture.

Whisk in the salt, pepper, nutmeg, and cayenne.

Pour the cheese sauce over the drained pasta in the pot, and mix well.

Pour the macaroni out onto the plastic-wrap-covered baking sheet, spreading it out so it will cool evenly, and put it in the fridge for 5 minutes.

When the macaroni has cooled, take it out of the fridge and roll it up in the plastic wrap, forming a "sausage" about 8 to 9 inches long and 1½ inches in diameter. Squeeze each end to seal off your macaroni sausage.

Lay another large sheet of plastic wrap out on the counter, and roll the macaroni sausage up in that. Then, pinching the ends between your thumb and forefinger, press down and roll the whole thing (like you're rolling a rolling pin) to make a tight cylinder, so you have a double layer of plastic wrap.

Take the two ends of plastic wrap, twist them to make a "rope" on each end, fold them over, and turn the cylinder over so the plastic-wrap "rope" ends are on the bottom.

Put the macaroni roll on a plate, put it in the freezer, and freeze it for at least 2 hours, until it's hardened and holds its shape. (It will keep in the freezer at this point for up to a week.)

TO MAKE THE MEATLOAF MIXTURE
Heat the olive oil in a medium-sized pan over medium heat. Add the onions and sauté them, stirring regularly,
until they've softened but not colored: about 3 minutes.

Add the ketchup and Dijon mustard; then pull the pan off the fire and mix everything together well, so that the ketchup turns the onions red. Spoon the onions out onto a plate and put them in the freezer to cool for about 5 minutes.

Meanwhile, in a small bowl, mix the bread crumbs and milk together with your hands, using a scrunching motion to help the bread crumbs absorb the milk. Then add the cumin, chili powder, paprika, salt, and pepper, and mix the spices in with your hands.

Scoop the meat into a large bowl and add the bread crumb mixture.

Beat the eggs slightly and add them to the bowl.

When the onions have cooled, add them to the meat. Use your hands to knead everything together, like you're making bread dough.

TO STUFF THE MEATLOAF AND FINISH THE DISH
Preheat the oven to 375°F.

Cover a large cutting board with plastic wrap. Lay a piece of tin foil on a rack in a roasting pan, and pierce it all over with a sharp knife.

Turn the meat mixture out onto the plastic-wrap-covered cutting board. Spread it and pat it with your hands to form a flattish rectangle covering the whole board (about 15 by 10 inches and ¾ inch thick).

Remove the macaroni roll from the freezer, clip off the ends, and pull off the plastic wrap.

Lay the macaroni roll in the center of the meat, making sure there's no plastic wrap left anywhere.

Wrap the macaroni up in the meat in exactly the same way you wrapped the macaroni with the plastic wrap. Make sure you wrap the meat very tightly around the macaroni—otherwise, your log will fall apart.

When the macaroni is wrapped in the meat, pull the plastic wrap off the sides of the meat roll, leaving it underneath the meatloaf-macaroni log. Pat the meat all around to make sure you have a smooth cylinder with no holes.

Using the plastic wrap as a carrying sheet, pick up the meat roll and transfer it to the tin foil sheet on the roasting pan, turning it out off the plastic wrap. Pat the bottom—now the top—to smooth it out and make sure there are no holes.

Using a pastry brush or a spoon, brush some of the barbecue sauce over the meat, covering all the exposed parts. Then put the roasting pan on the middle oven rack.

Bake the meatloaf, glazing it with more barbecue sauce every 10 minutes, until the meat is well browned and the internal temperature is about 130°F (about 1 hour).

Let the meatloaf rest on the counter for 15 minutes. I like to cut it into big 1-inch-thick slices so everyone can see the cheesy, yummy macaroni and cheese inside. Serve it with more barbecue sauce on the side.

BACON-WRAPPED PORK LOIN WITH MAPLE AND VINEGAR

In my humble opinion, there's nothing more mid-western-American than maple syrup. (My Canadian wife thinks the Canucks have got some kind of national claim here, but what does she know?) When I was a kid, we drove down to Burton, Ohio, deep in the heart of Amish country, for the Maple Syrup Festival every year. We would eat maple candy, drink fresh-pressed cider, stick our tongues into thimble-sized syrup cups, and watch the old guys cook sap into maple syrup in a log cabin right in the middle of in the town square. It was like Norman Rockwell, only more delicious. So when the cold weather comes, I crave fresh maple syrup, and I love cooking with it. This pork loin has the deep dark sweetness of maple syrup, plus some smoke and a tiny bit of spice.

SERVES 4

FOR THE BRINE (BEST MADE THE DAY BEFORE)
2 1/2 cups kosher salt
1 cup sugar

FOR THE PORK
2 pork loins (about 2 pounds)
1/4 teaspoon cracked black pepper
10 fresh sage leaves, chopped
1/2 pound sliced bacon (one 8-ounce package)

FOR THE GLAZE
1/2 cup apple cider vinegar
1/2 cup maple syrup
2 tablespoons Dijon mustard
1 teaspoon chipotle chile powder
Pinch of salt
1 tablespoon cornstarch

TO MAKE THE BRINE
Pour 6 cups of water into a medium-sized saucepan, and stir in the salt and sugar.

Bring the mixture to a boil.

Pull the pan from the heat and put the brine in the refrigerator to cool. Use it only when it's completely cooled down. (It will keep in the fridge for up to 2 weeks.)

TO COOK THE PORK
Using a boning knife, remove the silverskin—the fatty, shiny, light-colored parts—from the pork loin: slide the knife under the end of each piece of silverskin, and cut and then pull it away from the meat. (If you leave it on, it will get tough and hard to chew when you cook the pork.)

Submerge the pork in the brine so it's completely covered. Brine the pork in the fridge, covered or not, for 25 minutes.

Preheat the oven to 425°F.

Pull the pork out of the brine, rinse it off to get rid of the excess salt, and lightly pat it dry with a paper towel.

Sprinkle the pepper over the pork loins. Then do the same with the sage, pressing on it so that it sticks to the meat.

Lay the pork loins out flat on a work surface. Take a piece of bacon, and starting at one end, wrap it around one of the loins, like you're putting on a bandage. Take the next piece of bacon and do the same, overlapping with the first piece to make sure there are no naked parts. Continue until the entire loin is wrapped. Do the same with the second loin.

Lay the pork loins directly on a rack in a roasting pan, and put the pan on the middle oven rack. Bake the pork loins for about 25 minutes, until the bacon crisps up and the pork has an internal temperature of 135°F. The loins should be springy to the touch.

WHILE THE PORK IS IN THE OVEN, MAKE THE GLAZE
Combine the ingredients except the cornstarch in a small pot. Mix well to combine. Then bring the mixture to a boil over medium-high heat.

Boil the mixture for about 2 minutes, until it reduces and thickens up a bit.

Dissolve the cornstarch in 2 tablespoons of warm tap water. Then whisk the cornstarch liquid into the glaze and cook everything together for 1 minute, until you've got a thick syrup.

TO FINISH THE DISH
Take the pork loins out of the oven and immediately drizzle 2 tablespoons of the glaze over each one.

Let the loins rest for 10 minutes.

Slice the pork into rounds with a sharp knife (a serrated one works well). There will be some red drippings left behind. Don't worry: the meat is cooked.

Arrange the slices on a serving plate and drizzle them with the rest of the glaze. Serve right away.

CIDER-GLAZED RACK OF PORK WITH SPICE RUB

Cider-glazed pork is really a Northeastern dish, but when I was down in Memphis doing a barbecue tour, I got the idea of pumping up the flavor by adding a spice rub. The mix is something else: the meat is tender and flavorful, with a rich mouthfeel; the glaze gives it sweetness and a little tang; and the rub brings the bite and the grit.

I use a rack of pork here because the pork chops stay moist—and because bringing a huge rack of pork to the table is a pretty great way to entertain. But if you have individual chops and you just want to grill them or sauté them, that works, too—just add the glaze and the spices before you bring the meat to the table.

The brine will make the pork much more tender, but if you really don't have time (and all of your dinner guests have strong teeth), you can skip this step.

SERVES 4

FOR THE BRINE (BEST MADE THE DAY BEFORE)
2 1/2 cups kosher salt
1 cup sugar

FOR THE PORK
One 5-bone rack of pork (4 to 5 pounds)
1/2 teaspoon salt
3/4 teaspoon fresh-ground black pepper
3 cups apple cider
2 teaspoons apple cider vinegar

FOR THE SPICE RUB
1/2 teaspoon paprika
1/4 teaspoon ground cumin
1/4 teaspoon fresh-ground black pepper
1/2 teaspoon chili powder

TO MAKE THE BRINE
Pour 6 cups of water into a medium-sized saucepan, and stir in the salt and sugar.

Bring the mixture to a boil.

Pull the pan off the heat and put it in the fridge to cool. Use the brine only when it's completely cooled down. (It will keep in the fridge for up to 2 weeks.)

TO COOK THE PORK
Put the pork in a large container, cover it with the brine, and let it marinate in the fridge for 45 minutes.

Meanwhile, preheat the oven to 425°F.

Remove the pork from the brine, rinse off the salt to get rid of the excess, and pat the meat dry with a paper towel.

Season the pork with the salt and pepper, being sure to cover all sides of the meat.

Place the meat on a rack in a roasting pan, put it on the middle oven rack, and roast until the meat reaches an internal temperature of at least 135°F (about 50 to 60 minutes, depending on your oven). When you poke the meat hard with a finger, it should bounce back, like a little trampoline; if your finger sinks in, it isn't done yet. I don't like my pork too well done. If you prefer it that way, keep cooking it—but please don't kill it. (If the meat has no bounce and no give at all, it's overdone.)

While the meat is in the oven, pour the cider into a medium-sized saucepan and let it reduce over medium-high heat for about 45 minutes, until you've got a loose, dark golden-brown syrup.

Pull the pan off the heat and stir in the apple cider vinegar.

>>>

Pour the glaze into a small bowl and put it in the fridge to cool down. As it cools, the syrup will thicken.

TO MAKE THE SPICE RUB
Combine all of the rub ingredients in a small bowl, and mix well.

TO FINISH THE DISH
Pull the pork out of the oven, but leave the oven on at 425°F.

Take the glaze out of the fridge. It should be sweet-tangy and will probably have formed a bouncy "shell" on top. Paint the pork all over with about half of the glaze, using a pastry brush (you can also do this by pouring and spreading it with your hands, but it's pretty messy).

Put the pork back in the oven and roast it for 2 more minutes so the glaze can set. Then take it out and let it rest for 15 minutes.

Paint the pork all over with the rest of the glaze.

Sprinkle the spice rub all over all sides of the pork.

Cut the rack into chops by cutting right down the middle between each pair of bones.

Arrange the meat on a platter, and serve it right away.

CHEF'S TIP

If there's any leftover glaze and spice mix, combine them and pour in some of the drippings from the pork. Mix it all together, and then spoon it over the chops.

PIGS IN THE BERKSHIRES

SLOW-ROASTED PORK BUTT

This is a really easy dish, but like the name says, it's not fast: you need to start at least one night ahead of time. If you don't have any brine hanging around in your freezer, you'll need to make that *two* nights before you plan on serving the pork. You marinate the meat overnight, and then on the day you're going to serve it, it's all about slow cooking. The advance work is worth it, though: the meat comes out soft and succulent, with a crispy edge and a smoky-sweet flavor.

The crucial secret ingredient in this dish, believe it or not, is fish sauce. You don't taste it in the dish (don't worry—this isn't fishy pork), but the natural gluta- mates in the sauce (the same stuff you find in MSG in chemical form) really bumps up the flavor.

You can serve the pork as it is, or you can top it with barbecue sauce (see the one on page 300) or a vin- egar sauce. I like it as a sandwich on a soft roll. It's good no matter what.

Pork butt varies in size from 6 to 9 pounds, so your weight measure may not be exact here, but that's OK: you'll have plenty of paste and rub.

SERVES THE WHOLE NEIGHBORHOOD

FOR THE BRINE AND THE PORK
1 1/2 cups kosher salt
1 1/3 cups sugar
One 7-pound boneless pork butt

FOR THE MUSTARD PASTE MARINADE
5 cloves garlic, peeled
1/2 cup whiskey or bourbon
1/2 cup Dijon mustard
2 teaspoons fish sauce (see page 72)

FOR THE SPICE RUB
1 tablespoon salt
1 1/2 tablespoons sugar
1 tablespoon light brown sugar
2 teaspoons paprika
1 teaspoon chipotle chile powder
1/2 teaspoon ground cumin
1/2 teaspoon chili powder
1/2 teaspoon fresh-ground black pepper

TO MAKE THE BRINE AND BRINE THE MEAT
Bring the salt, sugar, and 2 quarts of water to a boil in a medium-sized pot.

Pour the brine into a container with a lid, and cool it down in the fridge overnight before you use it. The brine should be completely cool before you start work- ing with it.

Put the pork in a deep container, and pour the brine over it, so the meat is well covered. Cover the con- tainer and brine the pork in the fridge for 4 to 5 hours, to soften up the proteins in the meat. (If you leave it for too long, the pork will be salty.)

TO MAKE THE MUSTARD PASTE MARINADE AND
MARINATE THE MEAT
Put the garlic, whiskey, Dijon mustard, and fish sauce in a blender, and blend on medium speed for 20 to 30 seconds, until you've got a smooth paste.

Pull the pork butt out of the brine, rinse it to get rid of the excess salt, and pat it dry with a paper towel.

Move the pork butt to a baking dish or other con- tainer, and spread the mustard paste over it, making sure you've coated it on all sides. Use your hands to smooth the paste on evenly: you don't want any naked

>>>

meat. Cover the dish with plastic wrap and marinate the meat in the fridge for at least 6 hours.

TO MAKE THE RUB AND COOK THE MEAT

Take the pork butt out of the fridge and let it come up to room temperature on the countertop, about half an hour. Meanwhile, preheat the oven to 225°F.

Combine all the spice rub ingredients in a small bowl and mix them together well.

Use your hands to sprinkle the rub generously all over the pork butt. Pat the rub down so it sticks, and turn the pork butt to make sure you cover all of the meat.

Lay the pork on a rack set in a rimmed baking sheet, put it on the middle oven rack, and bake it for about 7$\frac{1}{2}$ hours, until it's dark and crisped up on the outside, and the meat pulls apart really easily. (If you have a meat thermometer, the internal temperature should be 200°F).

Take the pork out of the oven and let it rest for 10 minutes, or until it's cool enough to handle.

Pull the pork: use a spoon to dig into the meat and pull pieces of it away. This is a messy process, the opposite of slicing, but you end up with big, delicious chunks of meat. Mix the charred bits, the skin, and the meat all together so you end up with a really great texture.

Season the pork with a little bit of salt, if you're feeling it. You can serve it right away.

WHITE-BOY ASIAN RIBS

I'm a big fan of late-night Chinese food, and ribs are one of my favorite menu items. But I've never been able to get the flavors exactly right at home. So I played around with the basics until I came up with something that's maybe sort of kind of on the same page. There's nothing traditional going on here: it's just my white-boy take on the thing.

These ribs are succulent and meaty, but they aren't "falling off the bone." I know a lot of people think that's the only way to do ribs, but barbecue masters don't cook their meat like that—they think if the meat is falling off the bone, it's overdone. And if the masters don't do it, then I don't either. You don't need a grill to cook these ribs: I make them in my New York City apartment kitchen all the time, and I don't even smoke out the neighbors. If you do have a grill, though, you should definitely char the ribs up at the end. Don't leave out the green onions and the sesame seeds—they really dress up your basic plate of great ribs with some crunch and sharp freshness. You won't be able to stop eating these.

This is an easy do-ahead party dish: bake the ribs off the day before, hold them in the fridge, then warm them up in a 200°F oven, lacquer them up with the sauce, and throw them back in the oven or on the grill just before you're ready to serve 'em. You'll probably have more sauce than you need. I like to serve the ribs with a bowl of extra sauce on the side for dipping.

SERVES 3 TO 4 AS AN APPETIZER

FOR THE RIBS

2 tablespoons five-spice powder
1/2 teaspoon garlic powder
1 teaspoon chipotle chile powder
1/8 teaspoon cayenne pepper
1/2 teaspoon salt
1 rack St. Louis ribs (spare ribs, trimmed, with the brisket bones removed)

FOR THE SAUCE

1/3 cup hoisin sauce
2 tablespoons black bean sauce
1/3 cup ketchup
1/3 cup rice vinegar

TO FINISH THE DISH

3 green onions, chopped fine (about 1/2 cup)
1 tablespoon sesame seeds

TO MAKE THE RUB AND COOK THE RIBS

Mix the spices and salt together in a small bowl.

Lay the ribs on a baking sheet. Use your hands to spread the rub over both sides of the ribs and rub it in (like the name says), so that all of the meat is coated.

Let the ribs rest in the fridge for 2 hours, uncovered, so the rub soaks in.

Preheat the oven to 250°F.

Cut a piece of tin foil a little longer than the rack of ribs. Transfer the ribs to the foil, and shake any loose bits of spice rub on the baking sheet over the meat. Fold the foil around the ribs so all the meat is covered, put the ribs on a baking sheet, and put the sheet on the middle oven rack.

>>>

At the three-hour mark or so, when a sharp knife can go through the meat without too much resistance, turn the heat down to 225°F.

Keep cooking the ribs for another 2 hours or so, until the meat is really tender and easily pulls away from the bone with a knife (or with your teeth).

TO MAKE THE SAUCE AND FINISH THE DISH

While the ribs are in the oven, whisk together the hoisin sauce, black bean sauce, ketchup, and rice vinegar with 2 tablespoons of water until you have a thick, smooth sauce.

When the ribs are ready, pull them out of the oven and set the baking sheet on the countertop. Open the foil, lift the ribs out, and put them right on the baking sheet. If there's liquid left inside the foil, whisk it into the sauce.

Use a pastry brush to generously brush the sauce onto both sides of the ribs.

If you don't have a grill, put the ribs back in the oven at 400°F for 5 minutes. If you have a grill, throw the ribs directly on the grill and cook each side for 1 to 2 minutes, so the meat caramelizes a little.

Pull the ribs out of the oven or off the grill, lacquer them up with more sauce, and sprinkle the green onions and sesame seeds on top. Serve the ribs up right away, while they're hot.

WELCOME TO NEW YORK

MY BUDDY D.C. IN THE ASTORIA APARTMENT (NOTE THE
CARDBOARD FURNITURE)

I was a weekend cook for Governor Cuomo at the mansion up in Albany while I was at school. But when I wasn't working for money, I staged in every restaurant that would take me. Back then, my goal was to work for David Bouley. He was the first American chef ever to get a four-star review from the *New York Times;* I spent a good chunk of my hard-earned cash on dinner at his restaurant one night, and I was absolutely blown away. So, like any red-blooded young cook, I volunteered to work for free. It was absolute madness. The crew showed up at 11 in the morning, and no one left till 2 a.m. They *moved* every second of the day. It was crazy and amazing and overwhelming: the energy and focus was like nothing I'd ever seen. It was exactly what I wanted.

So when I graduated in 1991, I moved right down to Manhattan. But it turned out I couldn't swing a job at Bouley: back in the day, getting a position at a really great restaurant in the city was tough. It's not like now, when there are tons of high-quality places around; back then, there were only a handful, and suddenly there were a lot of young cooks fighting for those gigs. So instead of signing on to the vanguard of the American food revolution, I ended up cooking at an old-school high-end Italian restaurant in midtown. Six days a week, fourteen hours a day, paying about 75 cents a month.

In the secret plan I'd been carrying around in my head, the great job was going to come with a great apartment, for almost no money, in Manhattan. But I figured out pretty fast that wasn't going to happen, either. Instead of a kick-ass bachelor pad in some tower in the sky, I ended up on the second floor of an old Greek lady's house in Astoria, Queens, with my buddies Dante and Perry. Dante was working at a high-end American restaurant in midtown; Perry had a gig at a Greek restaurant near our place. It was everybody's first apartment, and when we moved in, we didn't have any furniture. There was a sofa already in the living room, and there was a bed with a mattress in my room. I wasn't sure where it came from, but it looked like it had been around a long time. It was free, so—you know—nothing tastes better, right? But since Perry and Dante and I had about a dollar fifty between us, we couldn't afford to buy any other furniture. No problem. Dante and I went down to the King Kullen—America's First Supermarket!—and convinced the store manager to give us a bunch of old cardboard boxes from the produce section. We took them home and we duct-taped them together, and voilà! We had nightstands, dressers, a coffee table—everything you need to start out life in the big city.

GREEK LAMB STEW WITH OLD-SCHOOL MARINATED GREEK VEGETABLES

My first apartment in New York City, back in 1990, was in Astoria, Queens, the heart of Greek New York. My roommate, Perry, was Greek, and he had a gig cooking at a Greek restaurant in the neighborhood. The place was OK for a cheap NYC apartment, but there was a catch: Perry's landlady rented only to Greek people. If she found out I wasn't Greek, she'd freak out. Lucky for me she was pretty old—and kind of blind and deaf. I learned three words in Greek, and I'd use them all every time I saw her: I'd yell *"Yassou!"* (hello), *"Kalimera!"* (good morning), *"Ti kanete?"* (how are you?). I thought I could transfer my skills to the project of finding a nice Greek girl, but that never really worked out—my three words took me only so far.

Perry's restaurant had a pretty great traditional lamb stew on the menu. This is a souped-up version of that, with the classic Greek spice combo of coriander, fennel seed, and dill. Serve this with Orzo with Yogurt and Lemon (page 235) and the vegetables.

SERVES 4 TO 6

1/4 cup extra-virgin olive oil
2 pounds boneless lamb stew meat
1 large onion, sliced (1 1/2 cups)
1/8 teaspoon cayenne pepper
1/4 teaspoon ground coriander
1/2 teaspoon ground fennel seed
1/4 teaspoon dried dill
2 bay leaves
2 cloves garlic, peeled and crushed
One 15-ounce can chopped tomatoes with their juice (I like Jersey Fresh)
1 1/2 tablespoons all-purpose flour
1 cup white wine
3 cups chicken broth or water
2 small carrots, peeled and chopped (1 cup)
1 celery stalk, chopped (1/2 cup)

Preheat the oven to 350°F.

Heat the olive oil in a large ovenproof saucepot (one with a lid) over high heat.

When the oil starts to smoke, add the lamb. Sear the meat for about 2 minutes, until it browns on one side.

Stir in the onions, reduce the heat to medium, and cook, stirring every so often, for about 4 minutes, until the meat is browned on all sides.

Mix in the cayenne, coriander, fennel, dill, bay leaves, garlic, and tomatoes, and keep cooking for about 3 minutes, until the juice reduces and glazes the meat.

Sprinkle the flour over the meat and vegetables in the pot and then cook it out: stir the mixture, toasting and incorporating the flour, until you don't see any white and you've got a paste in the pot (about 30 seconds to a minute).

Deglaze the pot by adding the wine and stirring up any brown bits. Then let it reduce for about 1 minute, until there's no liquid left and the meat is glazed and shiny from the wine.

Add the chicken broth and bring the mixture to a simmer. Cover the pot, place it on the middle oven rack, and bake the stew for 1 hour.

Pull the pot out of the oven, and add the carrots and celery. Stir everything together and put the pot back in the oven.

Let the stew cook for another hour or so, until the lamb is tender and the liquid has thickened into a sauce. If the meat isn't tender but the mixture is starting to dry out, add 1/2 cup of water and keep cooking until the lamb softens up, checking it pretty frequently. Serve it up right away.

OLD-SCHOOL MARINATED GREEK VEGETABLES

You can serve this up on its own, or as a side with the Greek Stew.

SERVES 4 AS A SIDE DISH

2 cups sliced cucumbers
2 cups cherry tomatoes, cut in half
One 15-ounce can chickpeas, drained
$\frac{1}{4}$ cup crumbled Greek feta cheese
1 small red onion, sliced
10 fresh mint leaves, torn
2 tablespoons red wine vinegar
$\frac{1}{4}$ cup extra-virgin olive oil
1 teaspoon dried Greek oregano
$\frac{1}{4}$ teaspoon cracked black pepper
1 teaspoon salt
1 clove garlic, minced

Combine the cucumbers, tomatoes, chickpeas, feta, onions, and mint in a large bowl.

Sprinkle the vinegar, olive oil, oregano, black pepper, salt, and garlic on top.

Mix everything together well with your hands.

LAMB CHILI WITH CHICKPEAS AND RAITA

A while back, I lived in the Manhattan neighborhood known as Curry Hill. It's just what the name says: full of Indian restaurants and grocery stores. Our place was right next door to a pretty great Indian restaurant, so whenever we opened our windows, the apartment would be filled with the smells of ghee, curry spices, and fried pappadams. (What we got from the apartment on the other side was not so good: no aromas, just really bad electric guitar.) You know how just about every block in New York has some kind of corner deli? Well, ours was Kalustyan's, the city's best and craziest spice shop, selling everything from guajillo chiles to fresh curry leaves. Our kitchen was full of every kind of Indian spice, dahl, and condiment you can think of. Sometimes I cooked actual Indian food—but usually I just used Indian spices in whatever I happened to be making.

This dish is that kind of cooking. It's definitely not traditional Indian. We're talking America-meets-India fusion: a good ol' American chili, Indian-style. The chili's got a tiny bit of heat, but what we're really all about here is the layering of the Indian flavors. It's pretty great on its own, but I think the cucumber raita is key—leaving it out is like serving chile con carne without the sour cream or grated cheddar. Make the raita first, so it has time to chill down in the fridge; then serve the chili hot and the raita cool, with hot basmati rice and cold beer.

SERVES 4 TO 6

FOR THE RAITA
1 medium English cucumber
Juice of 1 lemon (about 2 tablespoons)
1 cup thick yogurt (I like Fage)
6 large fresh mint leaves, minced
$1/2$ teaspoon salt

$1/4$ teaspoon ground cumin
Pinch of cayenne pepper

FOR THE CHILI
1 tablespoon corn oil
2 pounds ground lamb
1 medium red onion, diced (about 1 cup)
One 1-inch piece of fresh ginger, peeled, sliced thin, and diced (1 tablespoon)
1 clove garlic, minced
3 teaspoons garam masala (or 2 teaspoons curry powder plus a pinch of cinnamon)
1 teaspoon chili powder
$1/2$ teaspoon salt
$1/2$ teaspoon fresh-ground black pepper
1 cup canned coconut milk
One 28-ounce can chopped tomatoes with their juice
3 cups low-sodium chicken broth, vegetable broth, or water
1 medium red bell pepper, diced (about 1 cup)
One 15-ounce can chickpeas, drained

TO FINISH THE DISH
$1/2$ cup torn fresh cilantro leaves

TO MAKE THE RAITA

Use a vegetable peeler to peel the cucumber. Cut the cucumber in half lengthwise, and then cut each piece in half widthwise. Use a small spoon to scrape out the seeds.

Using a box grater or a large flat grater, grate the cucumber into a bowl. Tip the bowl over the sink, holding the cucumber in with your hand or with a plate, and drain out the excess cucumber water.

Squeeze the lemon juice into the cucumber, using your hand as a filter to catch any seeds. Add the yogurt and mix everything together.

Add the mint, salt, cumin, and cayenne, and mix gently.

Cover the bowl and put it in the fridge. The raita should be served cold.

TO MAKE THE CHILI

Heat the corn oil in a large saucepot over medium-high heat. Use your hands to break the ground lamb into small pieces; then add the meat to the pot. Cook for about 2 to 3 minutes; use a wooden spoon to keep breaking the meat up, chopping it and stirring it constantly so that it browns evenly without clumping up.

Turn the heat down to medium. Add the red onion, ginger, garlic, garam masala, chili powder, salt, and pepper. Mix everything together so the meat is well coated in the spices and the oil, and then toast the mixture for a minute or so, until the spices release their flavor and aroma.

Add the coconut milk, tomatoes, broth, and bell pepper. Mix everything together, turn the heat up to medium-high, and bring the chili up to a simmer. Then let it cook, uncovered, at a low bubble, stirring occasionally to make sure it doesn't stick.

When the chili has been cooking for an hour and a half, stir in the chickpeas, and cook for another hour, until the chili has thickened and the flavors are rich and well combined.

TO FINISH THE DISH

Ladle the chili into individual bowls, and add a spoonful of the cold raita and a sprinkling of the fresh cilantro to each one. Serve the chili up right away, with basmati rice and cold beer.

LAMB CHILI WITH CHICKPEAS AND RAITA, PAGE 162

LAMB TAGINE WITH GREEN OLIVES, page 166

LAMB TAGINE WITH GREEN OLIVES

Bouchid Jehhar works as a runner at The Dutch; he's been with me and my team for ten years, through three restaurants. He's a great guy, a hardworking Moroccan immigrant. His wife, Sihane Bazi, is a really good Moroccan cook, and sometimes she sends some of her specialties to the restaurant for us to try. She makes unbelievable lamb bread and pastillas (savory meat pies with pigeon or chicken). When the *New York Times* gave us three stars at the Italian restaurant I used to work at, she stenciled "Carmellini" across the top of a pastilla, and drew three stars in powdered sugar. But my favorite dish of hers is tagine. It's one that I love to make, too. I've been doing this one for years—but because I love Sihane's version so much, here I've added the green olives she uses in hers. They give the dish a nice briny flavor that really balances out the richness of the tagine.

Sihane's tagines are the real deal, but mine don't exactly follow the rules. In traditional tagines, you don't brown the meat—but that's how I like it, so that's how we're doing it here. And you usually serve lamb tagine with couscous, but I think it's pretty delicious with rice—my Citrus Rice (page 220), to be exact.

Tagine is best when it's made in a tagine (no surprise there), but if you don't have one, a big stewpot will work fine.

SERVES 4

FOR THE SPICE MIX
3/4 teaspoon ground coriander
1/2 teaspoon ground cumin
1/8 teaspoon ground cinnamon
1/2 teaspoon paprika
Generous pinch of cayenne pepper
Pinch of saffron threads

FOR THE TAGINE
1/4 cup extra-virgin olive oil
1/2 teaspoon salt
1/4 teaspoon fresh-ground black pepper
2 pounds boneless lamb stew meat, cut into chunks
1 medium onion, sliced (about 1 cup)
1 clove garlic, peeled
One 1-inch piece of fresh ginger, peeled and diced (1 tablespoon)
Juice of 1 orange (1/3 cup)
One 14-ounce can diced or chopped tomatoes
One 2-inch-long, 1-inch-wide strip of orange peel, white pith removed
2 cups chicken broth
1 teaspoon honey
1 medium carrot, peeled and sliced 1/2-inch thick (1 cup)
2 celery stalks, sliced 1/2-inch thick (1 cup)
1/4 cup sliced almonds
1 1/2 tablespoons sesame seeds
8 green olives, pitted and quartered (1/4 cup)

TO MAKE THE SPICE MIX
In a small bowl, mix together the coriander, cumin, cinnamon, paprika, cayenne, and saffron.

TO MAKE THE LAMB TAGINE
Preheat the oven to 350°F.

Heat the olive oil in a large ovenproof tagine or stewpot over medium-high heat.

Sprinkle the salt and pepper over the stew meat. Add the meat to the tagine, being sure to break up the pieces as you put them in. Stir to coat the meat in the oil. Then cook it for about 5 minutes, stirring occasionally, until the meat has browned evenly on all sides.

Use a slotted spoon to pull the meat out of the pot and pile it in a bowl. Set it aside.

Turn the heat down to medium, add the sliced onions to the tagine or pot, and stir to coat them in the olive oil and pan juices. Sauté the onions for about a minute, until they start to soften.

Stir in the garlic and ginger, and then add the meat back to the pot. Stir everything together to combine the flavors.

Squeeze the orange juice into the pot through a strainer (to keep the seeds out) and mix it in well.

Add the tomatoes, orange peel, spice mix, chicken broth, and the honey. Mix well to combine everything.

Turn the heat to medium-high and bring the mixture up to a simmer. Then cover the pot, put it on the middle oven rack, and bake for about 1 hour, until the meat is about halfway cooked.

Add the carrots and celery, return the pot to the oven, and cook for another 30 to 45 minutes, until the sauce is thick and reduced and the lamb is tender. The tagine should smell—and taste—rich, citrusy, and spicy.

While the tagine is baking, toast the almonds and sesame seeds in a small dry pan over low heat for about 5 minutes, tossing or shaking things around regularly to make sure the nuts don't burn, until the almonds are golden brown.

Pull the garlic clove and orange peel out of the tagine. Add the olives, stir, and spoon the tagine onto a large serving plate.

Sprinkle the almonds and sesame seeds on top of the tagine, and serve it up while it's hot.

VEGETABLES, BEANS, RICE, GRAINS, AND PASTA

ANTHONY'S SLAW

COLLARD GREENS A.C.-STYLE

SWISS CHARD WITH DRIED APRICOTS AND SUNFLOWER SEEDS

UTICA GREENS

CORN ON THE COB OKONOMIYAKI-STYLE

SUCCOTASH OF CORN, ZUCCHINI, VIDALIA ONIONS, AND COTIJA

SUGAR SNAP PEAS WITH SUN-DRIED TOMATOES, RADISHES, AND HERBS

WAX BEANS WITH POPCORN AND PARMESAN

SMOKED POTATO SALAD WITH VIDALIA ONIONS, HORSERADISH, AND MUSTARD

HEIRLOOM ZUCCHINI BAKE WITH FRESH TOMATO, MOZZ, AND BASIL

RUTABAGA-TURNIP GRATIN WITH MAPLE SYRUP

ROASTED BRUSSELS SPROUTS WITH BACON AND CHEDDAR

OVEN-ROASTED VEGETABLES GLAZED WITH APPLE CIDER, DRIED CRANBERRIES, AND PUMPKIN SEEDS

PAUL'S BAKED SQUASH DINNER WITH A SALAD OF RADICCHIO, WALNUTS, AND PARMESAN

WINTER COLESLAW

PIEROGIES

HOPPIN' JOHN

SUSIE'S BEANS

BLACK-EYED PEA AND KALE CHILI WITH MONTEREY JACK CHEESE

SPAM MUSUBI

STRAIGHT-UP ARROZ VERDE

CITRUS RICE

DIRTY RICE

WILD RICE AND QUINOA PILAF WITH PECANS, GREEN ONIONS, AND CRANBERRIES

SAUSAGE AND SHRIMP PILAU

GREEN GRITS

RIGATONI WITH SUNDAY NIGHT RAGU

ORZO WITH YOGURT AND LEMON

ANTHONY'S SLAW

Coleslaw might be the most American dish ever created, but it wasn't something I ever thought about much . . . until my first trip to New Orleans. Our very first meal in that crazy food city was lunch at Uglesich's, an only-in-New-Orleans kind of place. It was a divey joint in kind of a rough neighborhood—tables scattered around in no particular pattern, cases of beer piled against the walls—but there was a line out the door, and all around us, members of New Orleanian high society and captains of industry were chowing down on fried catfish, fried okra, and gumbo. We were in the 'hood, and we were underdressed.

Everything we ate at Uglesich's was great, but the coleslaw was a real surprise. We couldn't figure out why it was so good: rich, smooth, savory, and spicy, all at once. Finally, I got Anthony Uglesich to spill about the secret ingredient. The little bits of green in the coleslaw? Pickled jalapeños.

Pickled jalapeños are pretty widely available, but if you can't find any in your local grocery, you're going to have to use my recipe, which definitely makes this slaw a plan-in-advance two-step process.

I haven't used cup measurements for the vegetables here: coleslaw is one of those things where exact amounts just don't matter. And since cabbage grows big, you're definitely going to have a lot of slaw, so plan on feeding a crowd.

SERVES 6 TO 8

FOR THE SLAW
1 medium head green cabbage (about 3 ½ pounds)
2 or 3 small carrots, peeled
1 medium red onion, quartered and sliced thin
6 pickled jalapeños (page 305) or from the jar

FOR THE DRESSING
1 cup mayonnaise
1 cup sour cream
¼ teaspoon ground celery seed
½ cup juice from pickled jalapeños
2 tablespoons Dijon mustard
½ teaspoon Tabasco sauce
1 teaspoon salt
½ teaspoon fresh-ground black pepper

TO FINISH THE DISH
½ teaspoon salt
¼ teaspoon fresh-ground black pepper

TO MAKE THE SLAW
Cut off the stem of the cabbage and peel off the outside leaves, removing any brown pieces. Using a large knife, slice the cabbage into quarters. Cut away the thick core on the inside of each quarter. Then slice each quarter right through the layers, so you end up with thin ribbons. Pile the sliced cabbage in a (very) large bowl.

Slice the carrots as thin as possible. (Some people like to shred them, and you can do that if you have strong feelings about it, but I like slicing better—the bigger pieces make for better eating.) Add the carrots and red onions to the bowl.

Cut the ends off the jalapeños; slice each jalapeño lengthwise, cut away the core, and remove the seeds. Then slice each jalapeño crosswise into small thin pieces. Add them to the bowl.

TO MAKE THE DRESSING
In a medium-sized bowl, combine the mayonnaise, sour cream, celery seed, jalapeño juice, mustard, Tabasco, salt, and pepper. Whisk all the ingredients together until they form a smooth liquid.

TO FINISH THE SLAW

Season the slaw with the salt and pepper, mixing it in with your hands. Then pour the dressing over the slaw right away, and mix everything together well with your hands, so all of the vegetables are coated. (Don't season the slaw with the salt and pepper too early: the salt will start to draw the liquid out of the cabbage, so that it goes limp and the sharpness gets pulled out.)

Serve the coleslaw immediately. You don't want to keep this around too long; it's a same-day serve-it-right-away recipe.

COLLARD GREENS A.C.–STYLE

I learned how to make great collard greens from my mom. When I was growing up, she used to buy collards at West Side Market, the great farmers' market in downtown Cleveland. I can pretty much guarantee she was the only Polish woman in town cooking up collards soul-food-style, with bacon and onions, back in the '70s. My mom? She's got soul.

When I grew up and started eating collards in restaurants, I found that they were usually pretty bland and mushy. I wanted to pump them up a bit, so I added honey, vinegar, and Frank's RedHot (the classic Buffalo hot sauce) to round the dish out and give it a great hot-sweet-sour taste. True collards should taste earthy, smoky, vinegary—like these. Serve them with Cider-Glazed Rack of Pork (page 149) or Fried Chicken (page 117).

SERVES 4 AS A SIDE DISH

1 tablespoon vegetable oil
5 slices bacon, cut into 1-inch pieces
1 medium onion, sliced (about 1 cup)
3 bunches collard greens (about 3 pounds total), stems removed, leaves sliced into 1-inch-wide pieces
$1/2$ teaspoon salt
$1/4$ teaspoon fresh-ground black pepper
2 teaspoons honey
2 tablespoons white wine vinegar
1 tablespoon Frank's RedHot or your favorite hot sauce

Heat the vegetable oil in a large soup pot over medium heat. Add the bacon and let it fry up a little, stirring occasionally to keep it from sticking.

When some of the bacon fat has rendered and the meat has started to brown (about 3 minutes), add the onions and mix them in well, so they're coated in the bacon fat. Keep cooking for another 2 minutes or so, until the onions have softened.

Add the collard greens, salt, and pepper, and toss everything together as well as possible, so the leaves are really coated and shiny.

Add $1^1/2$ cups of water. Bring the mixture to a low boil, cover the pot, and let the greens cook for about 45 minutes, until they're really tender and most of the liquid has evaporated.

Add the honey, vinegar, and Frank's RedHot, and stir it all together. Serve these right away.

NOTE

When I'm working with collard greens, I like to lay each leaf flat on a cutting board and cut the stem out by running the point of a sharp knife along either side of the big inner stem; then I just slice it across the top to pull it out. When all the stems are removed, I pile the greens up and slice them at 1-inch intervals from top to bottom, right through the pile.

SWISS CHARD WITH DRIED APRICOTS AND SUNFLOWER SEEDS

People don't give chard enough respect, in my humble opinion. They think it's health food. This dish may look healthy, but it's really all about the flavors: it's earthy, savory, sweet, salty, and spicy, all at the same time, with a nice little bit of crunch from the sunflower seeds.

Swiss chard comes in lots of varieties. The big leafy green stuff is the most common, but I like organic rainbow chard. If you have the big leaves, you should throw away the stems, but if you happen to find the really delicate small stuff, you can cut up the stems and cook them up with the greens: they'll be tender and delicious.

I've just rediscovered sunflower seeds. I always thought of them as '70s health food, but in fact they're salty, buttery, and crunchy: completely addictive. They're my new favorite snack.

SERVES 4 AS A SIDE DISH

2 tablespoons extra-virgin olive oil

1 small onion, sliced (about 1 cup)

$1/4$ teaspoon salt plus a pinch

2 cloves garlic, peeled and slightly crushed

$1/4$ teaspoon crushed red pepper flakes

2 large bunches Swiss chard (about 1 pound total), washed, stemmed, leaves cut into thirds

12 dried apricots, sliced into slivers ($1/2$ cup)

1 tablespoon unsalted butter

1 tablespoon red wine vinegar

3 tablespoons shelled, toasted salted sunflower seeds

Heat the olive oil in a large pot over medium-low heat.

Add the onions and the pinch of salt. (The salt will help the onions soften without browning: it pulls the liquid out of the onions so they steam instead of frying.) Cook the onions slowly, stirring occasionally, for about 5 minutes, until they're nice and soft.

Add the garlic cloves and keep cooking for about 1 minute, until the garlic softens up.

Add the red pepper flakes and Swiss chard. (The chard will take up a lot of space in the pot, but don't worry about that; it will reduce to almost nothing in a few minutes.) Add $1/4$ cup of water, so the chard starts to steam, and turn the heat up to medium-high.

After $2 1/2$ minutes or so, when the chard has shrunk by about $1/4$, mix in the dried apricots and the $1/4$ teaspoon salt. Keep cooking for another $2 1/2$ minutes, or until the apricots soften up and the chard is tender.

Pull the pot off the heat and stir in the butter and vinegar, mixing until the butter has completely melted into the chard.

Spoon the chard mixture into a serving bowl, and top with the sunflower seeds. Serve it right away.

UTICA GREENS

My buddy Dean Nole is a chef and restaurateur up in Utica, New York. He's the king of 'scarole—in fact, he and his brother are now selling a microwave-friendly supermarket version of their famous Italian-style escarole dish under the name Scarola Incorporated. Here's what he has to say about Utica Greens:

"Escarole is delicious, healthy peasant food. In Utica, a lot of people with roots in southern Italy and Sicily grow their own in their gardens, so we eat a lot of 'scarole. Sautéed greens the way we make them, with the bread crumbs and the cherry peppers, are a real local specialty. This dish has a nice familiar Italian flavor, but when visitors come over from Italy, they feel like they're eating something a little different from what they get back home. I've never had anything exactly like it anywhere but Utica. That's why we call it Utica Greens. A lot of restaurants in town will serve a dish like this as an appetizer, but you can also make a meal out of it, with a nice glass of wine; if someone's putting together the menu for an event, they'll say, 'Give me a pan of Utica Greens' like you'd say, 'Give me a pan of pasta.'

"My brother Jason and I make a version of Utica Greens that's a little more refined, but still has the flavor we're familiar with. In our restaurants, we serve it as an appetizer, and we put it inside stromboli and calzone; we're experimenting with ravioli, and with Utica Green sausage."

I'm not from Utica, but take it from me: this dish is spicy, salty, cheesy, bitter-green yumminess.

SERVES 4 AS A SIDE DISH

2 heads escarole
¼ cup grated Pecorino Romano, plus a sprinkling to finish the dish
¼ cup dry bread crumbs
4 tablespoons extra-virgin olive oil
½ medium onion, chopped (½ cup)
¼ cup diced pancetta or bacon (about 2 ounces)
2 cloves garlic, sliced superfine
¼ cup halved and sliced hot Italian peppers (about 8 to 10 peppers)

Put a large pot of water on to boil.

Pull the brown-edged outer leaves off the escarole. Then cut the bottom off each head and use a big, very sharp knife to cut the escarole into thirds crosswise. Wash and drain the leaves well, since escarole can hide a lot of dirt inside.

Pile 2 handfuls of ice into a big bowl and fill it with cold water to make an ice bath.

When the water boils, add the escarole to the pot and let it cook for about 30 seconds. You want it to soften up a little; the color will intensify and deepen. (If you cook escarole too long, it gets slimy.) Use a sieve or a pair of tongs to pull the escarole out of the pot and put it right into the ice bath.

While the escarole is cooling down, pour the water out of the cooking pot and rinse the pot.

You don't want the escarole to sit around in the ice water getting soggy, so as soon as it's cool, drain it in a colander, and then squeeze the greens with your hands, a handful at a time, to get the rest of the water out—like you're squeezing water out of a sponge. Break the squeezed-up bunches apart into individual leaves. When you're finished, the volume of the escarole should be reduced to about a heaping plateful. Set this aside.

Mix the Pecorino Romano and bread crumbs together in a small bowl. Add 2 tablespoons of the olive oil and use your hands to mix everything together well until the liquid is soaked up.

Heat the remaining 2 tablespoons of olive oil in the large pot over medium-high heat. Add the onions and pancetta and cook them together for about 3 to 4 minutes, stirring until the onions are soft and just starting to turn a little bit brown and the pancetta has started to render and bubble.

Mix in the garlic and keep cooking for another 2 minutes or so, stirring regularly, until the garlic starts to brown.

Add the peppers, stir them around quickly, and then add the escarole. Stir everything together well, so the leaves are coated in the mixture, and cook, stirring constantly, for another minute and a half or so, until the escarole is heated through.

Pull the pot off the flame and stir in the bread crumb mixture. Then spoon the 'scarole into a serving dish, top it off with more cheese, and serve it right away.

CORN ON THE COB OKONOMIYAKI-STYLE

This is a total fusion street-cooking dish, combining the flavors of *elotes* (Mexican-style corn on the cob, covered with mayonnaise, Cotija cheese, a squeeze of lime, and chili powder) and *okonomiyaki* (a Japanese pancake with cabbage, bean sprouts, a flour-egg batter, and maybe shrimp or bacon, all mixed together and served up hot). When you put these two together, the combo is super-*umami*—that famous Japanese "fifth flavor." (Like some other things, you'll know it when you hit it.) Basically, this dish rocks.

You can get Japanese mayonnaise and the other Asian ingredients at any Asian supermarket. Kewpie is the name for the most popular Japanese mayonnaise (the one in the squeeze bottle with the drawing of the baby doll on the front). Japanese mayonnaise has different flavorings than the American version, and it tastes a little sharper, so you don't want to sub it out.

SERVES 8 AS A SIDE DISH

8 ears fresh corn
1/4 cup Kewpie brand Japanese mayonnaise
3 tablespoons yakisoba sauce
3 tablespoons furikake seasoning (see page 63)
1/3 cup bonito flakes
2 green onions, chopped

Shuck the corn, put it in a large pot, add water to cover, and bring it up to a boil.

When the water comes to a boil, cover the pot with a tight-fitting lid, pull it off the heat, and let the corn sit in the pot for 10 minutes.

Remove the corn from the water with tongs, shaking each ear well to get rid of any excess water.

Squeeze the mayonnaise into a bowl. Using a pastry brush or a table knife, spread the mayonnaise very generously over each ear of corn, so that it's coated on all sides.

Drizzle 1 teaspoon of the yakisoba sauce over each ear of corn; roll the corn in any sauce that drips onto the plate.

Sprinkle the furikake generously over each ear; then do the same with the bonito flakes and the green onions. Eat it while it's hot!

SUCCOTASH OF CORN, ZUCCHINI, VIDALIA ONIONS, AND COTIJA

My all-time number-one favorite summertime food is simple grilled fresh corn. I used to say I could eat it every night—but one August, I tried that, and I have to admit that I can get tired of eating even the best thing in the world. So I went to the next-best way to eat corn: succotash. It's old-school American for sure (*succotash* comes from a Native American word meaning "boiled corn"). Here I mix it up with the flavors of Mexican corn on the cob: chiles, lime, and Cotija, the white Mexican cheese. (If you can't find Cotija in your neighborhood market, feta works just fine.) This is a really easy summertime recipe, and it's got everything: crunch, freshness, sweetness, smoke, heat. You may not want to eat it every single night . . . but I bet you could eat it every other night and be pretty damn happy.

SERVES 6 AS A SIDE DISH

2 ripe beefsteak tomatoes
2 tablespoons butter, plus 1 tablespoon for finishing
   the dish (optional)
1 Vidalia onion, chopped (about 1 1/2 cups)
Kernels from 7 ears fresh corn (about 6 cups)
1 medium zucchini, chopped (1 1/2 cups)
1/2 teaspoon salt
1/4 teaspoon fresh-ground black pepper
One 4-ounce can Hatch diced green chiles (about
   1/3 cup)
Grated zest of 1 lime
1/4 cup fresh cilantro leaves, chopped
1 cup *queso Cotija* (white Mexican cheese, a lot like
   Monterey Jack)

Roast the tomatoes: If you have a gas stove, turn on the flame to high and roast the whole tomatoes directly over the fire for about 2 minutes, moving them around with tongs, until the skin blisters and peels back. (It will blacken in some parts—that's OK.) If you don't have a gas stove, you can do this under the broiler or on a grill. Don't skip this step: you want that smoky fire-roasted flavor.

Let the tomatoes cool just until you're able to handle them. Then use your fingers to pull the skins off.

Cut the tomatoes in half; throw away the cores. Then chop the tomatoes up and scoop the flesh, juice, and seeds into a bowl. You should have about 2 cups total. (The juice will make the succotash a little watery, but the trade-off is a really good strong tomato flavor.)

Melt 2 tablespoons of the butter in a large pot over low heat. Stir the onions in so they're coated in the butter, and let them cook for about 4 minutes, until they soften up, stirring them every once in a while so they don't stick or color.

Add the corn, zucchini, and tomatoes and their juices to the pot, and stir everything together.

Raise the heat to medium-high and add the salt, pepper, and chiles. Stir everything together and let the succotash stew for about 5 minutes.

When the corn is just cooked through and the zucchini has softened but still has some crunch to it, pull the pot off the heat and grate in the lime zest.

Add the cilantro and the last tablespoon of butter if you're using it, and stir everything together so the butter melts. (The butter makes everything a little thicker and richer, but you can leave it out if you like.)

Pour the succotash into a serving bowl, and sprinkle the *queso Cotija* on top. Serve this up while it's hot.

SUGAR SNAP PEAS WITH SUN-DRIED TOMATOES, RADISHES, AND HERBS

This cold dish is all about texture and contrast: the crunch of the peas and the thick smoothness of the sauce, the sharpness of the citrus, the green mint freshness, and the sauce's savory tangy sweetness. The sauce is thick, because that's what you need for snap peas; if you try topping 'em with a vinaigrette or some other wimpy liquid, it'll slide right off.

Any hard, salty cheese will work with this recipe. I've used Parmesan here, but if you happen to be at the Union Square Greenmarket in New York on a Wednesday or a Saturday (or at their store on Spring Street in SoHo right down the street from The Dutch), buy the smoked sheep pecorino from Valley Shepherd Creamery in New Jersey and grate that in instead. It's the best.

SERVES 4 AS A SIDE DISH

FOR THE PEAS
1 pound sugar snap peas

FOR THE SAUCE
1 cup sun-dried tomatoes, packed in oil
1 clove garlic
1 tablespoon pine nuts
$1/3$ cup extra-virgin olive oil
1 tablespoon tomato paste
1 teaspoon Sriracha (Thai hot sauce; see page 85)
    or Tabasco sauce

FOR DRESSING THE SNAP PEAS
4 radishes, sliced thin
8 fresh basil leaves, chopped into small pieces
8 fresh mint leaves, chopped into small pieces
$1/4$ teaspoon salt
$1/4$ teaspoon fresh-ground black pepper
$1/4$ cup extra-virgin olive oil
Grated zest of 1 lemon
Juice of 1 lemon (2 tablespoons)

FOR FINISHING THE DISH
$1/4$ cup grated Parmesan cheese

TO PREP THE SNAP PEAS
Put a large pot of salted water on to boil.

Clean the sugar snap peas by snapping off one hard tip, grabbing the edge of the "string" that runs across the top, and pulling it off, then snapping off the other end.

When the water is boiling hard, plunge the snap peas into the pot. (Make sure the water is really boiling when you add the peas—you want them to be bright and crisp and crunchy, so they need to cook fast.) Blanch the snap peas for about a minute and a half, until they turn emerald green and their flavor has mellowed a little bit (they should still taste pretty fresh). If you let the snap peas sit in the water too long, the outsides will turn slimy.

While the peas are blanching, make a "bath" of ice and water.

When the peas are ready, pull them out of the pot with a strainer and plunge them right into the ice water bath, to stop the cooking process. Leave them in the ice water to cool completely.

TO MAKE THE SAUCE
While the snap peas are cooling, put the sun-dried tomatoes in a blender. Add 1 $3/4$ cups of hot tap water, the garlic, pine nuts, olive oil, tomato paste, and Sriracha. Blend everything together on high speed for about 1 minute, until you have a smooth, sun-dried-tomato-tasting orange paste. (You'll have a little more sauce than you need for the dish, but this is the best way to get the right proportions.)

>>>

Cool the sauce down in the fridge for 15 minutes or so: you don't want to pour hot sauce on your cold snap peas. (The sauce will keep in the fridge for up to 4 days, and in the freezer for up to a month.)

TO MAKE THE DRESSING

Drain the water from the snap peas. Add the radishes to the bowl and mix the vegetables with your hands, so you've got an even mix of radishes and snap peas.

Add the basil, mint, salt, pepper, and olive oil to the bowl.

Zest and squeeze in the lemon zest and juice, and then mix everything together well, so that all the radishes and snap peas are coated evenly.

TO FINISH THE DISH

Pull the sauce out of the fridge, and use a spoon to spread it thickly over the bottom of a serving plate.

Pile the snap peas and radishes on top of the sauce.

Sprinkle the Parmesan cheese generously over the top, and serve this up right away.

WAX BEANS WITH POPCORN AND PARMESAN

In July and August, the tables at the farmers' markets in the Northeast are piled high with yellow wax beans. When they're fresh and tender, these beans rock; tossed with butter and salt, they're meaty, creamy, and delicious. And what else is really good tossed in butter and salt? And also totally American? Yep: popcorn. So I thought: why not put them together? The result is pretty damn good: you've got sweet onions, meaty beans, and that irresistible buttered-popcorn flavor. Serve this as a summer side with something grilled.

SERVES 4 TO 6 AS A SIDE DISH

One 3-ounce bag unsalted, unbuttered, un-golden-toppinged microwave popcorn
1 1/2 pounds yellow wax beans, ends snapped off
2/3 stick (5 tablespoons) unsalted butter, at room temperature
1 tablespoon extra-virgin olive oil
1 medium Vidalia onion, diced (about 1 cup)
2 cloves garlic, halved and sliced superfine
1/2 teaspoon salt
1/4 teaspoon fresh-ground black pepper
1 teaspoon Tabasco sauce
1/4 cup chopped fresh parsley
1/3 cup grated Parmesan cheese

Put a large pot of well-salted water on to boil.

Pop the popcorn, following the directions on the bag.

When the water boils, pile in the wax beans and let them cook for about 5 minutes, until they soften up a little. When you bite into one, it shouldn't bounce back between your teeth, but it shouldn't be mushy, either.

While the beans are cooking, make an ice-water bath by filling a big bowl with ice and cold water.

Use a slotted spoon or a strainer to pull the beans out of the pot and put them right into in the ice-water bath so they stop cooking.

When the beans have cooled completely, drain off the water and set them aside.

Put 3 cups of the popcorn and all of the butter in a food processor fitted with the metal blade. Process the mixture until you have a grainy butter-and-popcorn paste.

Heat the olive oil in a large saucepan over a medium flame. Add the onions and sauté them, stirring regularly to keep them from sticking, for about 3 to 4 minutes, until they're soft but not colored.

Add the garlic, stir everything together so the garlic is coated in the fat, and cook for about a minute, stirring all the time, until the garlic softens and releases its fragrance. Be careful: garlic burns fast.

Add the beans to the saucepan, mix everything together, and then add 1/4 cup of water.

Cook the mix over medium heat for a minute or two, until the beans are heated through, tossing everything with a spoon so the beans are coated in the onions and garlic.

Season the beans with the salt, pepper, and Tabasco.

Add the popcorn butter and stir everything together so the beans are coated.

Pull the pan off the heat and mix in the parsley.

Pour the beans out into a serving bowl. Make sure you scrape down the pot with a spatula, so you get all the good stuff on the bottom.

Crumble 2 more cups of the popcorn over the top (you'll have some left over for snacking), and then sprinkle the Parmesan over everything. Serve it while it's hot.

SMOKED POTATO SALAD WITH VIDALIA ONIONS, HORSERADISH, AND MUSTARD

This is not your average potato salad: it's tangy and clean-tasting, without that thick gumminess you get in mayo-based potato salads. The vegetables and the watercress give it a little bit of crunch and freshness, and the horseradish sauce makes it rich and a little bit sharp at the same time. It's great with slow-roasted pork butt.

I love smoked potatoes, but I definitely don't have a smoker in my New York City apartment kitchen. So I fake it: I use bacon to give the potatoes that smoky taste, with the added bonus of some extra lusciousness from the fat.

SERVES 4 TO 6 AS A SIDE DISH

FOR THE POTATO SALAD
2 pounds yellow-fleshed potatoes (Yukon Gold or German Butterball) or new potatoes
4 slices bacon, diced (1/2 cup)
1 small Vidalia onion, diced (about 1 cup)
1/2 cup red wine vinegar
1/2 cup beef broth or chicken broth
1/4 cup extra-virgin olive oil
1 tablespoon Dijon mustard
1/4 teaspoon dry English mustard (I like Colman's)
Pinch of cayenne pepper
1/8 teaspoon ground celery seed
1/4 teaspoon salt
1/4 teaspoon fresh-ground black pepper

FOR THE HORSERADISH CREAM TOPPING
1 cup yogurt (whole-milk or low-fat)
1 tablespoon prepared white horseradish
1 teaspoon red wine vinegar
1 tablespoon extra-virgin olive oil
1/4 teaspoon salt
1/4 teaspoon fresh-ground black pepper

TO FINISH THE DISH
2 celery stalks, chopped fine (about 1 cup)
3 green onions, chopped (about 1/2 cup)
Salt to taste
Fresh-ground black pepper to taste
Red wine vinegar to taste
1 bunch watercress, washed, leaves only

TO MAKE THE POTATO SALAD
Wash the potatoes really well; then cut them into 1/2-inch cubes (depending on the size of your potatoes, you'll probably be quartering them).

Scoop the potatoes into a medium-sized pot, and add enough cold water to cover them by about 1 inch. Bring the water up to a boil and then cook the potatoes, uncovered, for about half an hour over medium heat, until they're very soft but not falling apart.

Meanwhile, cook the diced bacon in a large nonstick pan over medium heat for 2 to 3 minutes, stirring it every 30 seconds or so.

When the bacon is just crisped, add the onions to the pan. Shake or stir everything around so that the onions are coated in the bacon fat.

Let the onions caramelize for about 4 minutes, so that they're just colored but not blackened, and they still have some crunch to them. Keep stirring every once in a while to make sure nothing sticks or burns.

Pull the pan from the heat and pour the vinegar, broth, and olive oil right into the pan.

Stir in the Dijon mustard, dry mustard, cayenne, celery seed, salt, and pepper; mix everything together well. Then set the sauce aside on the countertop. (At this stage, the sauce will be very vinegar-y and bacon-y.)

When the potatoes are cooked, strain them, being careful not to smush them. Make sure you get all the water out.

I like to put the potatoes in a big Pyrex baking dish instead of a bowl, so they can really soak up the sauce. Lay them out in as thin a layer as possible, and pour the bacon-onion sauce on top. Put the baking dish in the fridge, uncovered, and let the potatoes cool and absorb the sauce for at least 2 hours, so they soak up all the flavors.

TO MAKE THE HORSERADISH CREAM TOPPING
Combine the yogurt, horseradish, vinegar, olive oil, salt, and pepper in a small bowl. Mix everything together well until it's smooth; it should taste like very creamy horseradish.

Hold the horseradish cream in the fridge until you're ready to serve the potato salad.

TO FINISH THE DISH
Pull the potato salad out of the fridge and add the celery and green onions. Mix everything together well, so the greens get into every part of the salad.

Taste the potato salad: depending on your potatoes, you may want to add a little more salt or pepper or a splash of vinegar.

Transfer the potato salad to a serving bowl. Top it with some of the horseradish sauce, and scatter the watercress over the top. Serve this cold with more sauce on the side.

HEIRLOOM ZUCCHINI BAKE WITH FRESH TOMATO, MOZZ, AND BASIL

Our local greenmarket has great summer zucchini in all kinds of crazy shapes, sizes, and colors, with really intense flavors. (Some that I like a lot: golden zucchini, Black Beauty, and the best name ever, Italian vegetable marrow.) Zucchini have a long season around here: the stalls at the market are piled high with 'em all the way through the summer, and you can get some good stuff right into October. But if you can't find zucchini in your farmers' market or if they're not looking too good, the regular green and yellow grocery store zucchini will do just fine.

SERVES 4 TO 6 AS A SIDE DISH

2 large beefsteak tomatoes (a little bit more than a pound)

$^1/_4$ cup extra-virgin olive oil

1 Vidalia onion, sliced (about 2 cups)

$^1/_2$ teaspoon crushed red pepper flakes

2 cloves garlic, sliced superfine

$^3/_4$ teaspoon salt

$^1/_2$ teaspoon fresh-ground black pepper

2 pounds mixed heirloom zucchini (about 4 zucchini, depending on size), cut into $^1/_2$-inch chunks

1 tablespoon dried oregano

$^1/_4$ cup fresh basil leaves (about 8 leaves), torn

4 tablespoons grated Parmesan cheese

$^1/_4$ cup fresh mozzarella, cut into chunks

Preheat the oven to 400°F. Put a medium-sized pot of water on to boil. Fill a large bowl with ice and cold water, and set it aside.

Use the tip of a sharp knife to cut out the core of each tomato. Score the bottom of each tomato, using the tip of your knife to make an X in the skin.

When the water is boiling hard, plunge in the tomatoes and blanch them until the skins loosen (about 15 to 30 seconds—you don't want to actually cook the tomatoes).

Pull the tomatoes out of the water with a strainer and put them right into the ice water to stop the cooking process. When they've cooled enough to handle, use your hands or a knife to strip away the skins. Cut the tomatoes in half, squeeze out the juice and discard it, and then roughly chop the tomatoes.

Heat the olive oil in a large pot over a medium flame. Add the onions, stirring to coat them in the oil, and sauté for about 2 minutes, until they soften, being careful to make sure they don't stick or color.

Add the red pepper flakes and garlic, and cook, stirring constantly, for about 30 seconds, until their aroma is released. Then add the chopped tomatoes, $^1/_2$ teaspoon of the salt, and $^1/_8$ teaspoon of the pepper, and stir everything together. Turn the heat up to high and cook until most of the liquid has evaporated (about 12 to 15 minutes), stirring regularly so nothing sticks to the bottom.

Add the zucchini, seasoning it in the pot with the remaining $1/4$ teaspoon salt and $3/8$ teaspoon pepper, and stir everything together so the zucchini is coated in the sauce. Cook the mixture for about 3 minutes, until the zucchini has just started to absorb some liquid but is still pretty firm; you don't want to let it get too soft at this point.

Pull the pot off the heat and add the oregano, basil, and 2 tablespoons of the Parmesan cheese.

Pour the mixture into a 5 x 8-inch baking dish, using a wooden spoon to spread everything out nice and evenly. Put the baking dish on the middle oven rack.

After about 15 minutes, when the zucchini is cooked through but not mushy, pull the pan out of the oven. Turn on the broiler.

Sprinkle the remaining 2 tablespoons of Parmesan and the mozzarella over the baked zucchini. Put the dish back on the middle oven rack and broil for about 2 minutes, until the cheese browns and bubbles. Serve it right away.

SALTING VEGETABLES

Salt is really, really, really important in cooking. If you want real American flavor—if you want pretty much *any* flavor—you can't be afraid of using salt. Here's how to do it right when you're cooking vegetables:

If you're roasting or caramelizing vegetables, or if you want to pull the sugar out of vegetables and use it as a base for a sauce, put the salt in at the end. If you put it in too early, it starts to leach the water out of the vegetables, so that they steam instead of caramelize. It's basically the same principle as putting salt on your driveway to get rid of ice: salt draws the water out.

If, on the other hand, you don't want caramelization on your veggies, add your salt—plus some pepper—at the beginning. That will draw the liquid out of the vegetables and help them to cook faster. If you're making pasta sauce, for instance, it's crucial to salt your tomatoes well so that the water gets drawn out and the tomatoes cook down fast, before they lose their freshness.

RUTABAGA-TURNIP GRATIN WITH MAPLE SYRUP

The title might sound like health food, but don't be fooled: this is just about the richest dish in the book, meant to be eaten on a cold winter night. It's all about Midwestern fall flavors: maple syrup, late-picked vegetables, cream. It's sweet, savory, harvesty—the perfect Thanksgiving dish, especially if you can get fresh maple syrup where you live.

Don't be afraid of rutabagas—they're the ugly yellow waxy turnipy-looking things that are in the vegetable section all year round, the ones you look at and think, "What would I do with *that*?" They're actually really sweet-and-bitter delicious. But if you can't find rutabagas in your local grocery store, you can always do an all-turnip version. It's just as good.

SERVES 6 TO 8 AS A SIDE DISH

2 medium-sized rutabagas
2 medium-sized turnips (about 3 pounds total of
     rutabagas and turnips together)
3 cups heavy cream
1/4 cup maple syrup
Pinch of cayenne pepper
Pinch of ground nutmeg
1 tablespoon unsalted butter
1/2 teaspoon salt
1/4 teaspoon fresh-ground black pepper
2 fresh rosemary sprigs, leaves chopped
     (about 2 teaspoons)
Leaves of 9 fresh thyme sprigs
     (about 2 teaspoons)
1/3 cup grated Parmesan cheese

Preheat the oven to 400°F.

Cut the ends off the rutabagas and turnips, and peel them with a knife. Then slice them as thin as possible, using a mandoline if you've got one. The slices don't all need to be perfect: if you end up with some nice pieces and some weird shapes, just save the good-looking ones for the top of the gratin and bury the others.

Combine the cream, maple syrup, cayenne, and nutmeg in a medium-sized pot, and heat over a medium flame.

While the cream-maple syrup mixture is heating, grease the bottom and sides of an 8 x 8-inch baking dish with the butter.

Pile the root vegetables into a large bowl and toss them with the salt, pepper, rosemary, and thyme.

When the cream mixture comes to a boil, arrange one-third of the root vegetables in the baking dish. Pour a third of the cream mixture over the vegetables, and sprinkle with a third of the Parmesan (about 2 tablespoons). Then add another third of the root vegetables, and so on. Remember to save the best-looking vegetables for the top layer. And don't overfill the dish: the cream should stop just below the top, so it doesn't bubble over in the oven.

Cover the baking dish with tin foil and put it on the middle oven rack.

After half an hour, uncover the dish, then let it keep baking for another hour or so, until the top is browned and there's only a little bit of liquid left inside.

You can serve the gratin as soon as it's cool enough to handle, but it's better to let it settle for a while, so the turnips absorb a little more of the liquid.

ROASTED BRUSSELS SPROUTS WITH BACON AND CHEDDAR

People think they hate Brussels sprouts, but what they really hate is *bad* Brussels sprouts: overcooked, mushy, cabbagy-tasting. Good Brussels sprouts like these, on the other hand, are just another example of how bacon makes everything better. Of course, it also helps that we blanch the Brussels sprouts to soften them up and then roast them in the pan, instead of boiling them to death. The caramelized vegetables combined with the smokiness of the bacon and the sharpness of the cheddar give the dish a kick-ass flavor: these ain't the Brussels sprouts your grandma made you finish.

To make this recipe really rock, use good sharp English farmhouse cheddar and the smokiest bacon you can find.

SERVES 4 TO 6 AS A SIDE DISH

1 1/2 pounds (about 1 1/2 pints) Brussels sprouts
1 heaping cup diced bacon (5 to 7 slices)
1 medium onion, diced (1 cup)
1/4 teaspoon salt
1/4 teaspoon coarse-ground black pepper
1/2 cup grated sharp cheddar

Put a large pot of water on to boil.

Prep the Brussels sprouts: cut the stem end off each sprout, pull off any brown leaves, and cut it in half lengthwise.

When the water boils, blanch the Brussels sprouts for 2 to 3 minutes, until they're bright green but still have some good crunch on 'em. Remember: they're going in the pan, so don't overdo them here.

While the Brussels sprouts blanch, put together an ice-water bath: a big bowl of ice cubes and cold water.

Pull the Brussels sprouts out of the pot with a spider or a slotted spoon, and plunge them right into the ice-water bath, to stop the cooking process. Once they've cooled down, drain them and lay them out on a paper towel to dry out a little.

Meanwhile, cook the bacon in a large saucepan over medium-high heat for about 2 minutes, stirring it every 30 seconds or so to stop it from sticking, until it begins to render and crisp up.

Stir in the onions and keep cooking, stirring and shaking the pan to keep things from sticking, for another 2 1/2 minutes or so, until the onions start to caramelize and color.

Pour the bacon and onions into a bowl, leaving a little of the bacon fat in the pan (make sure there are no onions left). Put the pan back on the heat, add the Brussels sprouts, and cook them in the bacon fat for about 2 1/2 minutes, until they start browning up, moving them around with a wooden spoon every so often so they cook evenly.

Add the onions and bacon back to the pan, season everything with the salt and pepper, and let it all cook together for about 2 minutes, stirring things up and shaking the pan so nothing sticks or burns, until the Brussels sprouts and the bacon have caramelized and the flavors have come together.

Pile everything onto a big serving plate and scatter the grated cheese on top. Serve this right away.

OVEN-ROASTED VEGETABLES GLAZED WITH APPLE CIDER, DRIED CRANBERRIES, AND PUMPKIN SEEDS

When we opened Café Boulud in 1998, I spent the first couple of months working with Alex Lee, a great chef who was then the chef de cuisine at Daniel. This dish is inspired by a vegetable side dish that he put together with pumpkin seeds, which I thought was a brilliant move. Even though we were cooking in a French restaurant, the dish was inherently American—and it's really seasonal. So I've adapted Alex's dish, adding apple cider and dried cranberries to make it feel even more like fall.

This recipe is all about contrasting flavors: you get bitterness from the celery leaves, crunchy spiciness from the nuts, sweet-tartness from the cranberries, and sweet-sourness from the cider—and every single root vegetable has its own flavor, too. If you put a little of everything in your mouth at once, it's pretty incredible. You can use any kind of winter root vegetable you're feeling—just follow the same basic method.

SERVES 4 TO 6 AS A SIDE DISH

FOR THE SAUCE
2 cups apple cider

FOR THE VEGETABLES
1 butternut squash, skinny top half only, peeled and cut into 1-inch chunks (about 2 cups)
2 small white turnips, peeled and sliced into 1-inch chunks (about 2 cups)
1 small rutabaga, peeled and sliced into 1-inch chunks (about 2 cups)
(or any combination of root vegetables: about 3 pounds total)
2 tablespoons extra-virgin olive oil

1/2 teaspoon salt
1/4 teaspoon fresh-ground black pepper

FOR THE ROASTED PUMPKIN SEEDS
2 teaspoons butter
1/2 cup pumpkin seeds
Pinch of salt
Pinch of cayenne pepper

TO FINISH THE DISH
2 tablespoons dried cranberries
Salt to taste
Fresh-ground black pepper to taste
A handful of fresh celery leaves

TO MAKE THE SAUCE
Cook the apple cider in a small sauté pan over high heat for 15 to 20 minutes, until it reduces down to about 1/3 cup and thickens up into a syrup.

TO ROAST THE VEGETABLES
Preheat the oven to 450°F.

Lay the squash, turnips, and rutabagas on a rimmed baking sheet, and pour the olive oil over them. Shake the salt and pepper over the vegetables, and then use your hands to turn and mix the vegetables so that they're coated with oil all over.

Roast the vegetables on the middle oven rack. At the 8-minute mark, pull the baking sheet out and turn the vegetables over to make sure they roast evenly on all sides, then put the sheet back in the oven.

Keep roasting the vegetables for another 7 to 9 minutes or so, until they've browned up and softened and a knife can go through them easily.

TO ROAST THE PUMPKIN SEEDS

Melt the butter in a small pan over medium heat.

Add the pumpkin seeds, reduce the heat to medium, shake the pumpkin seeds around to coat them in the butter, and let them toast for a couple of minutes, until they start to puff up and make sharp cracking sounds. Shake the pan every so often so nothing sticks or burns.

Add the salt and cayenne, and shake the pan to coat the seeds with the spices. Then pull the pan off the heat, but leave the seeds in the pan. They should be buttery, salty, and a little bit chewy—like really, really good popcorn.

TO FINISH THE DISH

Pull the roasted vegetables out of the oven and pile them into a large bowl.

Add the dried cranberries to the reduced cider.

Spoon the cider glaze over the vegetables, and toss everything together, so the vegetables are coated and shiny. Season with more salt and pepper if you're feeling that.

Spoon the vegetables into a serving bowl, and top them off with the toasted pumpkin seeds and the celery leaves.

CHEF'S TIP

It's easiest to cut root vegetables with a serrated knife.

OVEN-ROASTED VEGATABLED GLAZED WITH APPLE CIDER, DRIED CRANBERRIES, AND PUMPKIN SEEDS, PAGE 194

PAUL'S BAKED SQUASH DINNER WITH A SALAD OF
RADICCHIO, WALNUTS, AND PARMESANS, page 198

PAUL'S BAKED SQUASH DINNER WITH A SALAD OF RADICCHIO, WALNUTS, AND PARMESAN

In my parents' house, my mom is the serious cook: she clips recipes, she keeps files, she annotates and modifies and plans menus. My dad doesn't cook much, but when he does, it's usually something simple and really good. He doesn't work from recipes. When something's in season and tasting really good and he wants to eat it, he always knows exactly what to do to make it delicious, so he kicks my mom out of the kitchen. This is a classic Paul Carmellini fall dish: something he makes every year when the butternut squash is fat and sweet.

My dad usually serves this as a side dish with roast pork or chicken, but it's so filling on its own that a half-squash per person, with a little bit of radicchio salad to balance the sweetness out, makes a perfect vegetarian meal. If you don't see butternut squash in your local market, acorn squash will work just as well.

SERVES 4 AS A MAIN DISH

FOR THE SQUASH

1/2 cup dried cherries or raisins
2 large butternut squash (about 6 pounds total), split in half lengthwise, seeds and guts removed
1/2 stick (4 tablespoons) unsalted butter
1 medium apple, cored and diced large (about 1 1/4 cups)
1/8 teaspoon ground cinnamon
1 tablespoon light brown sugar
1 teaspoon salt
1/2 teaspoon fresh ground black pepper

FOR THE SALAD

1 medium head radicchio, bottom cut off, chopped
3/4 cup chopped walnuts
1/4 cup grated Parmesan cheese, plus a little extra for sprinkling (optional)
1/4 cup extra-virgin olive oil
1 tablespoon red wine vinegar
1 tablespoon balsamic vinegar
1/4 teaspoon salt
1/4 teaspoon fresh-ground black pepper

TO MAKE THE SQUASH

Preheat the oven to 425°F.

Sprinkle the cherries or raisins in the cavities of the squash halves, distributing them more or less evenly.

Cut the butter into 1-tablespoon pieces and put 1 piece in the cavity of each squash half.

Distribute the apple pieces in the squash cavities.

Sprinkle the cinnamon over the squash cavities.

Spoon the brown sugar into the squash cavities.

Sprinkle the salt and pepper all over the squash—cavities and flesh.

Place the squash, cavity side up, on a large rimmed baking sheet. Pour 1/4 cup of water onto the bottom of the sheet (to help the squash steam a bit). Cover the baking sheet fully with tin foil, set it on the middle oven rack, and bake for about 1 hour, until you can stick a fork in 'em.

TO MAKE THE SALAD

Pull the radicchio leaves apart and distribute them in a large bowl.

Mix the walnuts in with the radicchio, tossing with your hands.

Add the Parmesan, olive oil, both vinegars, salt, and pepper, and mix everything well with your hands, so that all the leaves are coated.

TO FINISH THE DISH

Pick up a squash half with both hands (so you don't lose any of the good stuff) and place it on a plate. Put the salad on the side.

Use a spoon to scoop out about half of the mixture inside the cavity and spoon it over the rest of the squash. If you'd like, sprinkle some more Parmesan over the top.

Put a scoop of squash and some of the radicchio salad in your mouth at the same time. The sweetness of the squash, the texture of the cherries, the tartness and texture of the radicchio . . . awesome.

WINTER COLESLAW

People think of coleslaw as a summertime, eating-outdoors kind of dish, but as far as I'm concerned, slaw is definitely not just for hot weather. This winter slaw is great as a side with stews, with roast goose, as a new dish for Thanksgiving or Christmas—and, you know, if your neighbor gives you a deer that he killed and you don't know what to do with it, the slaw is perfect with roast venison, too. There's no mayo in here: the red wine binds everything together and gives the slaw a really satisfying mouthfeel, along with deep flavor.

SERVES 4 TO 8 AS A SIDE DISH

$3/4$ cup dried cranberries
1 head red cabbage
2 cups dry red wine
1 tablespoon maple syrup
2 tablespoons red wine vinegar
2 teaspoons grainy mustard
$1/4$ cup extra-virgin olive oil
$1/4$ cup corn oil
$1/2$ teaspoon salt
$1/4$ teaspoon fresh-ground black pepper
$1/4$ teaspoon ground caraway seed
1 cup walnuts, toasted and chopped
$1/4$ cup fresh parsley, rough-chopped
2 tablespoons fresh celery leaves, rough-chopped

Rehydrate the cranberries in $1/2$ cup hot water in a small bowl.

Meanwhile, cut off the stem of the cabbage and peel off the outside leaves, so there are no brown pieces. Using a large knife, slice the cabbage into quarters. Cut away the thick core on the inside of each quarter. Then slice each quarter: you should end up with thin slices that fall apart into ribbons. Put the cabbage in a large bowl and set it aside on the countertop.

Combine the wine and maple syrup in a saucepan, and bring to a boil over medium-high heat. Let the mixture boil for about 10 to 15 minutes, until it has reduced by three-fourths, so you've got a thick syrup.

Pour the syrup into a small mixing bowl. Add the vinegar, mustard, olive oil, corn oil, salt, pepper, and ground caraway, and whisk everything together. The dressing should be sweet, winey, and a little bit tangy.

Pour the dressing over the cabbage and toss it well with your hands, making sure all the leaves are coated.

Drain the water from the cranberries and add them to the slaw, along with the walnuts, parsley, and celery leaves. Toss everything together with your hands.

Let the slaw sit on the countertop or in the fridge for an hour or so before you serve it, so that the everything really marinates. It will keep in the fridge, covered, for at least a couple of days.

PIEROGIES

My mom's family is Polish, so pierogies were really important in our house when I was a kid. But this was one thing my mom didn't make from scratch. Instead, we would buy them from the Pokrova Ukrainian Parish Hall in south Cleveland—otherwise known as the Pierogi Church. Twice a week, women from the church sold pierogies to a long line of Clevelanders. To get to the pierogies, you would walk through the empty church banquet hall and right into the catering kitchen at the back. When it was our turn, a woman in a white chef's apron would plant her hands on the steel counter and ask us what we wanted in a thick Eastern European accent. There were three choices: potato, mushroom, and cheese. She would sling a bag of preboiled pierogies across the counter at us, and we would take them home and pour them out of the bag and fry them up with onions. My mom served them with applesauce on the side. They were the best.

There are Pierogi Churches all over New York, but none of them are as good as the Cleveland branch, so I learned how to make my own. The good news? My pierogi dough is stupid-easy. I like the cheese filling the best, so that's what you get here. It's a good plan to make the dough and the filling the day before and store them in the fridge, since the filling is easier to handle when it's really cold. On the day you want to cook the pierogies, all you have to do is cut out the dough, fill in the dumplings, and cook 'em up. They're great with homemade applesauce (page 298) and caramelized onions.

MAKES ABOUT 50 PIEROGIES

FOR THE DOUGH
8 cups all-purpose flour, plus extra for flouring your work surface
1 teaspoon salt
3/4 stick (6 tablespoons) salted butter, melted
2 cups sour cream
1/4 cup corn oil
4 whole eggs
1 egg yolk

FOR THE CHEESE FILLING
1 pound farmer's cheese or ricotta cheese
1 egg
Pinch of ground nutmeg
1/2 teaspoon sugar
A few drops of vanilla extract

FOR MAKING THE PIEROGIES
2 eggs
All-purpose flour for sprinkling and flouring work surfaces and dough

FOR FRYING (OPTIONAL)
1 stick (8 tablespoons) butter
2 tablespoons poppy seeds

TO MAKE THE DOUGH
Combine the flour and salt in the bowl of a stand mixer fitted with the dough hook.

In a separate large bowl, combine the melted butter, sour cream, and corn oil.

Beat the eggs and egg yolk together, and add them to the sour cream mixture. Whisk everything together well, so it forms a smooth, thick liquid.

Add the wet mixture to the flour in the mixer bowl, and mix on low speed (#1 on a KitchenAid) for about a minute and a half, until you've got a thick dough.

>>>

Sprinkle some flour on your work surface, and knead the dough by hand, forming it into a ball. Then use a rolling pin to roll the dough out into a thick disk about the size of a Frisbee, or push it into this shape with your hands. (This will make the dough easier to work with when it's cold.) Wrap the dough well in plastic wrap and chill it in the fridge for at least 6 hours.

TO MAKE THE CHEESE FILLING

In the bowl of a tabletop mixer fitted with the paddle attachment, combine the cheese, egg, nutmeg, sugar, and vanilla.

Mix on medium-low speed (#2 on a KitchenAid) for about 10 to 15 seconds to bring everything together.

Turn the filling out into a bowl, cover it, and chill it down in the fridge for at least an hour. (You can keep it in the fridge for a couple of days at this point.)

TO MAKE THE PIEROGIES

Preheat the oven to 175°F.

Take the dough out of the fridge and let it come up to room temperature on the countertop until it's soft enough to work with (about 20 minutes).

Whisk the eggs together in a small bowl.

Flour a work surface well. Using a rolling pin, roll out the dough in batches, turning it and rolling in every direction, including diagonally, until it's basically the same thickness as one of the cookies in an Oreo. Use a round pastry cutter (or the bottom of a can) to cut out as many rounds as possible from each piece of dough.

Using a pastry brush, lightly brush the top of each round of dough with the egg (so it will stick together when you close it up).

Take the filling out of the fridge just before you're ready to use it.

Put 1 tablespoon of the filling on the middle of each round. Then fold the round in half around the filling, so you've got a half-moon with the filling inside. Use your fingers to pinch the open sides closed all the way around, making little pinches all the way along the edges (so you have those little indentations you always see on pierogies).

Put a large pot of well-salted water on to boil.

While the water is heating, put the pierogies on a tray in the fridge so they cool down a little and the dough sets.

When the water comes to a boil, put the first batch of pierogies in the pot—about 15 to 20 at a time. (They won't cook well if you put too many in at once.) The pierogies will take about 7 minutes to cook, depending on your stove and the thickness of your dough. They're definitely not done until they float up to the top, and then they probably need another minute or two. The best way to know if they're ready? Take one out, cut it open, and taste it. If you want boiled pierogies, you're done—serve 'em up right away.

TO FRY THE PIEROGIES

If you're making fried pierogies, melt a pat of butter in a nonstick saucepan (about 1 tablespoon or a little more for every batch of 8 pierogies). Put a batch of pierogies in the pan, but don't crowd them or they won't cook right.

Fry the pierogies, turning them every couple of minutes, until they crisp up (about 4 minutes total). The butter will brown a little bit as the milk solids start to caramelize, and that will give the pierogies a nice nutty flavor.

Sprinkle some poppy seeds over the tops of the pierogies, and then pull them out of the pan, put them on a plate or tray, and hold them in the oven while you fry up the remaining batches. Serve these hot as soon as they're all done, with applesauce on the side.

CHEF'S TIP

Pierogies freeze really well, so you can boil these ahead of time, like the Pierogi Church ladies do, and fry them up when you're ready.

HOPPIN' JOHN

Hoppin' John is basically rice and beans—except that, instead of beans, it's made with black-eyed peas. It's a traditional Low Country or Gullah dish, made by African Americans since slavery times. It's supposed to bring good luck if it's eaten first thing in the New Year, and in some African-American traditions, a bowl of hoppin' John gets handed out with the champagne at midnight. My Floridian grandmother used to make this dish all the time; my Midwestern mother adopted it; and I grew up eating it in suburban Cleveland. American flavor, right?

Traditional hoppin' John is just rice, beans, and meat. My version is a little bit tricked-out—and a little bit hurried up, too, since if you really want to do this the old-fashioned way, you'd start with dried beans. I don't have time for that. Traditionally you use ham hocks, but my mom used this great smoked bacon from the Polish butcher in town, so I use bacon, too. Hoppin' John is also not usually super-spicy, but I like to give it some action. You can control the spice by adding (or subtracting) hot sauce.

SERVES 6 TO 8 AS A SIDE DISH,
OR 4 AS A MAIN COURSE

FOR THE RICE
1 cup long-grain white rice or Cajun Grain
   (see Note)
2 cups chicken broth or water
1 tablespoon butter
1 fresh bay leaf

FOR THE BLACK-EYED PEAS
1 tablespoon corn oil
3 slices bacon, diced ($\frac{1}{2}$ cup)
1 small onion, diced ($\frac{1}{2}$ cup)

3 celery stalks, diced (1 $\frac{1}{2}$ cups)
1 small green bell pepper, diced ($\frac{1}{2}$ cup)
One 15-ounce can black-eyed peas, drained
1 cup chicken broth
$\frac{1}{2}$ teaspoon Cajun seasoning mix
A dash or two of your favorite hot sauce
1 fresh thyme sprig

TO FINISH THE DISH
2 small ripe tomatoes, diced large (1 cup)
3 green onions, sliced thin ($\frac{1}{2}$ cup)
1 tablespoon apple cider vinegar
$\frac{1}{4}$ teaspoon salt

TO MAKE THE RICE
Combine the rice, broth, butter, and bay leaf in a small pot, and bring to a boil over high heat.

Cover the pot, reduce the heat to low, and let the rice cook for about 20 minutes, until all the water has been absorbed.

TO MAKE THE BLACK-EYED PEAS
Heat the corn oil in a medium-sized pot over high heat.

Add the bacon and let it cook for about 3$\frac{1}{2}$ minutes, so the fat renders and the bacon is crispy. Stir the bacon every few seconds to keep it from sticking.

Add the onions, celery, and bell peppers. Lower the flame to medium-low and continue cooking, stirring regularly, for about 4 minutes, until the vegetables are soft.

Add the black-eyed peas, chicken broth, Cajun seasoning, hot sauce, and thyme sprig. Stir everything together well, and cook for about 15 minutes, until the flavors come together, the vegetables are really soft, and the mixture has thickened up a little.

TO FINISH THE DISH

Pull the pot of black-eyed peas off the heat, and pull out the thyme sprig.

Add the rice, tomatoes, green onions, vinegar, and salt to the pot and stir to bring everything together. Serve this up family-style, in a big bowl at the center of the table.

NOTE

I call for white rice in this recipe because that's traditional, but my favorite rice for hoppin' John is actually brown. It's called Cajun Grain, and I discovered it because of a piece Christine Muhlke wrote in the *New York Times Magazine* a while back. It's Cajun (from Kinder, Louisiana); it's organic, which is always good (for flavor, for the planet, for your health, whatever); and because it's brown rice, it hasn't had all the vitamin B and yummy stuff processed out. But most important, it has an amazing deep flavor. You can order Cajun Grain on Amazon; if you get your hands on some, just follow the cooking directions on the package.

HOPPIN' JOHN, PAGE 208

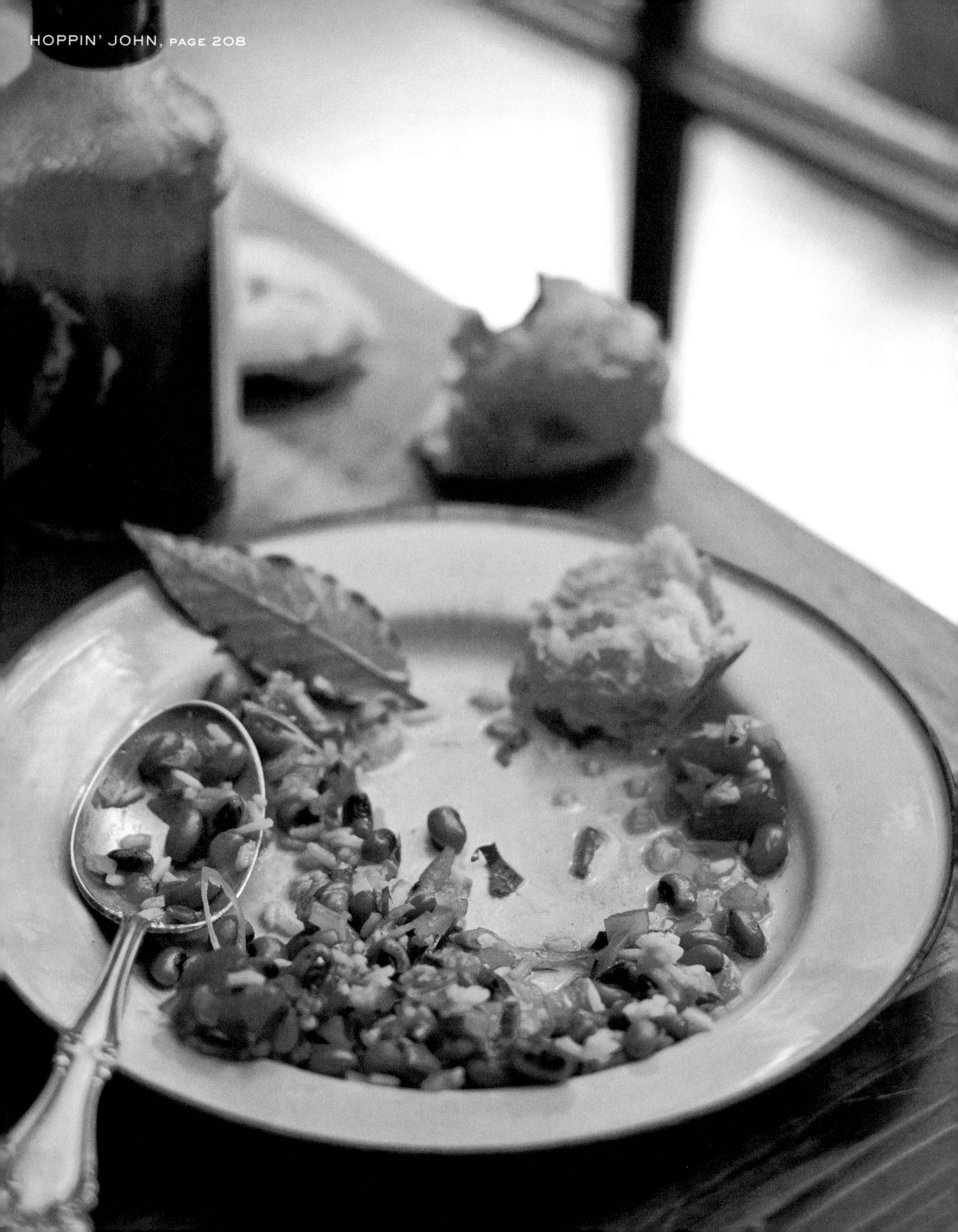

SUSIE'S BEANS, PAGE 212

SUSIE'S BEANS

This recipe comes from Michael Oliver, sous-chef at Locanda Verde. He's been working with us for the past eight years, and he's an expert on and booster of all things Maine. Here's what he says about baked beans:

"My mom used to make baked beans on the weekends when I was a kid. She'd get them in the oven really early in the morning: by the time I woke up at 6 a.m. or so, you could already smell the rich, savory-sweet aroma of baking beans all over the house. She'd bake them really slowly, until about 4 in the afternoon. Traditional New England–style baked beans are really simple: they're made with brown sugar, molasses, mustard powder, salt pork, and onion. There are lots of different variations. Up in Maine, where I grew up, and all through the Nova Scotia area, we like our beans sweet (I think this dates back to a surplus of rum in the Boston area way back when, which led to a whole lot of surplus molasses). In my mom's original recipe, she had 1/2 cup of molasses (plus brown sugar) for a pound of beans—and there was always molasses on the dinner table for drizzling on top. But she's toned it down some over the years. She's changed the pork up, too: when I was really little, we raised pigs, and we made our own salt pork, but my mom switched to bacon years ago. She likes the smoky flavor, and so do I.

"The saltine crust is optional: some people like to dress their beans up like this, but the Oliver family classic is just the beans.

"People feel pretty strongly about their bean choices where I'm from, but it's really all about family tradition and personal preference. Our neighbors used to use little tiny beans, but in my house, we like the bigger ones, so that's what I use. Jacob's cattle beans are grown at York's Farm, right near where I grew up. But you can use navy beans or soldier beans—they'll work just fine."

SERVES THE WHOLE DAMN NEIGHBORHOOD

FOR THE BEANS
1/2 pound Jacob's cattle beans, navy beans, or soldier beans (about 4 cups)
6 ounces smoked slab bacon, cut into large chunks (1 heaping cup)
1 tablespoon butter
1/2 large onion, diced (1/2 cup)
1 teaspoon salt
1/4 teaspoon fresh-ground black pepper
1 teaspoon dry mustard
1 1/2 teaspoons light brown sugar
1 tablespoon molasses

FOR THE SALTINE CRUST (OPTIONAL)
1 sleeve saltine crackers (about 2 cups)
1/4 teaspoon garlic powder
2 teaspoons light brown sugar
1/2 teaspoon salt
1 tablespoon fresh thyme leaves
3 tablespoons cold unsalted butter

TO FINISH THE DISH
2 tablespoons sherry vinegar
2 tablespoons Dijon mustard

TO COOK THE BEANS
Sort the beans: with dried beans, especially the locally grown small-farm variety, you're likely to find stones in the mix, and we're not making stone soup here.

Soak the beans in a large bowl or pot on the countertop, uncovered, for at least 12 hours. You should have enough water to cover the beans, with another 3 to 4 inches of water above them (so they don't soak up all the water and dry out).

Preheat the oven to 250°F.

Heat the bacon and butter slowly in a large oven-proof pot over medium-low heat for about 4 minutes, until you've got enough rendered fat in the pot to coat the onions. Watch the heat: you don't want the bacon to dry out.

Add the onions, salt, and pepper to the pot, mix everything together well, and cook for about 3 minutes, until the onions are tender, stirring regularly to keep them from sticking or coloring.

Add the dry mustard and stir everything together so the mustard blooms a little in the fat—you should smell it if you lean over the pot.

Add the brown sugar and mix everything together well. Keep stirring the mixture for a minute or two to break down the sugar crystals, so there aren't any lumps of sugar left.

Stir in the molasses (make sure you get it all out of the measuring spoon).

Drain the beans well and add them to the pot. Stir everything well, reaching the spoon down to the bottom of the pot and stirring up so that the beans are coated in the sugar-molasses-bacon-fat mix.

Add enough water to cover the beans, but as Mom says, "Don't drown them!" You'll need about 2½ cups of water.

Turn the heat up to high and bring the mixture up to a simmer.

Pull the pot off the stove, cover it with a tight-fitting lid, and put it on the middle oven rack. Bake the beans for about 2 hours. The beans shouldn't be boiling when they're in the oven: the top will foam up a bit, but there shouldn't be any action. If there is, turn your oven heat down.

Check to make sure there's enough liquid in the pot. If the beans are floating up to the top and cracking, pour in ¼ cup of water or so. Let the beans cook for another 3 hours (about 5 hours total baking time). They're done when the liquid's all gone and the beans are coated and shiny and brown.

TO MAKE THE SALTINE CRUST (OPTIONAL)

While the beans are baking, grind up the crackers, garlic powder, brown sugar, salt, and thyme leaves in a food processor fitted with the metal blade for about 30 seconds, until the crackers are reduced to fine crumbs.

Add the butter and process for another 20 to 30 seconds or so, until the butter is completely integrated into the mix and you've got a fine powder.

Scrape the crust into a bowl and hold it in the fridge till the beans are ready.

TO FINISH THE BEANS

Pull the pot out of the oven. If you're making a crust, turn on the broiler.

Mix the sherry vinegar and Dijon mustard into the pot.

If you've made a crust, sprinkle it over the beans and put the pot under the broiler. Broil the beans for about 5 minutes, until the crust crisps up and turns golden brown.

Serve the beans right away.

BLACK-EYED PEA AND KALE CHILI WITH MONTEREY JACK CHEESE

This might read like a dish that belongs on the menu of some vegetarian restaurant in California–but actually, it's a secret carnivore special: hidden inside is a whole cup of bacon. (If you want it veg, you can always just leave the bacon out: the chili will still have lots of flavor and smokiness from the peppers.) The black-eyed peas and kale both have a really good earthiness that makes this what you might call an *umami* chili. Toss a piece of cornbread on the side and you've got a perfect winter-day dish.

Don't go to the cheesemonger for fancy high-quality Monterey Jack for this one: believe it or not, the regular supermarket stuff gives you the best melting texture.

SERVES 6 TO 8 AS A MAIN DISH

2 tablespoons extra-virgin olive oil
8 slices bacon, diced (1 cup)
1 small onion, diced (1 cup)
2 celery stalks, diced (1 cup)
1 clove garlic, crushed
One 28-ounce can diced tomatoes, with their juice
One 15-ounce can black-eyed peas, drained
2 cups chicken broth
1 or 2 canned chipotle peppers in adobo sauce, depending on how spicy you like your chili (I like La Morena brand), including seeds, chopped fine (1 to 2 tablespoons)

¼ teaspoon ground cumin
¼ teaspoon ground coriander
1 tablespoon honey
1 tablespoon Dijon mustard
1 bunch Tuscan or green kale (about ½ pound), stems removed, leaves washed and cut into 1-inch pieces
½ cup grated Monterey Jack cheese

Heat the olive oil in a large soup pot over a medium flame. Add the bacon, and allow it to render a bit (about 2 minutes), stirring regularly to stop it from sticking.

Add the onions, celery, and garlic. Stir well to coat everything in the fat, and keep cooking for about 2 minutes, until the vegetables start to soften.

Add the tomatoes, black-eyed peas, chicken broth, 1 cup of water, and the chipotle peppers, cumin, and coriander. Stir to mix everything together well; then let the chili cook, uncovered, over medium heat for about 10 minutes, until the flavors come together.

Stir in the honey and mustard.

Stir in the kale and cook for 10 minutes or so, until the kale is soft.

Serve the chili in large bowls, with the Monterey Jack cheese grated right on top.

SPAM MUSUBI

Emily Iguchi is the sous-chef at The Dutch; we've worked together, on and off, for the past six years. She lived in Hawaii with her family for a while, and she was the first person who introduced me to Hawaiian food. This recipe is hers. Here's what she has to say about it:

"When you think about great food, Spam is probably not the first thing that comes to mind. But give Spam a chance: it's been a Hawaiian staple since World War II (when it was hard to get fresh meat) and it's *ono* (delicious)! *Musubi*, or rice balls, are a Japanese basic. I've eaten them all my life, and because there's such a big Japanese population in Hawaii, they're also a major part of Hawaiian cuisine. Put Spam and rice together and you have Spam musubi—my favorite way to eat Spam. It's meaty, sweet, salty, and comforting—like a little *umami* sandwich. In Hawaii, it's so popular you can even find it at the local 7-Eleven.

"When I moved from Hawaii to New York and started working with A.C., it was my secret goal to get everybody into Spam musubi. The cooks I worked with were willing to try anything, but Spam was a challenge. Once they finally tasted it, though, everyone loved it—except the French guy. 'Eh, what is dis?' he cried. 'Dis is disgusting: seared pâté!' I guess it takes an American to really appreciate Spam musubi."

SERVES 4 TO 8 AS AN APPETIZER,
DEPENDING ON HOW HUNGRY YOU ARE

FOR THE RICE
3 cups Japanese short-grain rice
1/2 teaspoon fine sea salt

FOR THE SPAM
1 can Spam
2 tablespoons sugar
2 tablespoons soy sauce (I like Yamasa brand)

FOR FINISHING THE MUSUBI
1 tablespoon furikake seasoning (see page 63)
2 sheets nori (flat sheets of dried seaweed; I like Nagai's Roasted Seaweed Sushi Nori)

TO MAKE THE RICE
Rinse the rice in a strainer under cold running water until the water runs clear.

Pour the rice into a pot with a tight-fitting lid (or into a rice cooker), add 3 1/4 cups of water, and bring it up to a boil. Then cover the pot, turn the heat to low, and cook the rice for about 25 to 30 minutes, until all the liquid has been absorbed.

Take the rice off the heat and let it rest, covered, for 5 minutes.

Fluff the rice with a fork so it's nice and light, and sprinkle the salt over the top.

TO COOK THE SPAM
Slice the Spam as you would a loaf of bread, in 1/4-inch-thick slices. You should have about 8 slices.

In a small bowl, mix together the sugar and soy sauce.

Heat a large nonstick pan over medium-high heat. (If your pan isn't big enough, you can sear the Spam in batches.)

Lay the Spam slices in the pan and let them sear on one side for about 2 to 3 minutes, until they turn golden brown on the bottom.

Turn the slices, let them sear for 10 seconds or so, and then glaze them with the soy-sugar mix. Let the liquid reduce in the pan for 10 to 15 seconds, stirring everything around, just until the glaze bubbles and sticks to the meat. (Be careful not to let the glaze cook in the hot pan for too long—if you leave it for more than 15 seconds or so, the sugar will burn.)

Pull the Spam out of the pan and pile it on a plate. If you're doing this in 2 batches, make sure you wash the pan so there's no glaze left over before you start the second batch.

TO FINISH THE DISH

If you have a Spam musubi mold, put about $3/4$ cup of the cooked rice inside. If you don't have a Spam musubi mold (and I'm betting you don't), you can mold the rice with your hands: Keep a small bowl of water beside you for dipping your fingers. Wet your hands so the rice doesn't stick to them, and roll the rice between your hands, squeezing and molding it into a thick rectangle the shape of a Spam slice, about $1^1/2$ inches thick. You can use the bottom of the Spam can to measure.

Sprinkle some of the furikake evenly over the rice; then lay a slice of Spam on top. If you're using the mold, press the Spam down with the top of the mold. If you're doing this with your hands, you don't have to press down: the rice will already be dense from the way you shaped it.

Fold or cut a $1^1/2$-inch-wide strip off a nori sheet.

If you're using the mold, pull it away from the rice. Either way, wrap the nori strip around the musubi widthwise, like you're wrapping a ribbon around a present.

Repeat until you've used up all the rice and Spam, dipping your fingers in the water as you go to make sure the rice doesn't stick to your hands.

You can eat the Spam musubi hot or at room temperature. It's great finger food.

NOTE

....

Everybody in Hawaii has a Spam musubi mold, and you can get one online if you want perfectly shaped Hawaiian-style musubi. But you can just as easily make like a sushi chef and do these by hand, using the bottom of the can as a measure.

STRAIGHT-UP ARROZ VERDE

There wasn't exactly a big local Hispanic community around when I was growing up in south Cleveland. The Mexican food I grew up with? That was mostly Chi-Chi's, cheese nachos, and the occasional Corona. But after high school graduation, a friend and I took off on a cross-country trip, and we happened to stop at a diner in Albuquerque. On the menu: something called *arroz verde*. That was the start of my obsession with Mexican food, one of my favorite kinds of American cooking.

This dish has two variations: straight-up green rice, and the "baked rice" version with cheese. The regular rice is good with fish, chicken, eggs—just about anything that could use a side dish, really.

The cheesy version is inspired by a dish at one of the best restaurants in my neighborhood: Mercadito, on Avenue B. It's just a simple little East Village spot, but my buddy Patricio Sandoval does some amazing casual Mexican cooking there: great tacos—the best in Manhattan—amazing guacamoles, crazy cocktails. His *arroz verde a honcho* is one of my favorite things on the menu. This dish is my homage to him.

SERVES 6 TO 8 AS A SIDE DISH

1 medium onion, sliced (about 1 cup)
1 clove garlic, peeled and smashed
1 pound tomatillos (see page 219),
   husks removed
2 whole poblano chiles, or 2 tablespoons
   roasted poblano paste
1 1/2 cups fresh cilantro leaves
1 teaspoon ground cumin
1 teaspoon salt
2 cups long-grain white rice

Combine the onions, garlic, tomatillos, and 2 1/2 cups of water in a medium-sized pot. Bring the mixture to a boil.

While you're waiting for the mixture to come up to a boil, roast the poblanos. If you have a gas stove, do this fast-and-dirty chef-style: Turn the flame on, use a pair of tongs to lay the peppers right on the burner, and let them blister and blacken, turning them occasionally with the tongs. The skins will pop a little as they roast (and watch out for flying sparks!). When the peppers are black on all sides (about 5 minutes), pull them off the flame, put them in a bowl, cover them with plastic wrap, and put them in the fridge to cool. If you don't have a gas stove, you can roast the poblanos on the grill or under the broiler in the same way. You can also substitute roasted poblano chile paste.

When the tomatillo mixture comes to a boil, adjust the heat so that things stay at a rolling boil and continue cooking, uncovered, stirring occasionally, for about 15 minutes, until the tomatillos are khaki-colored and you can crush them against the side of the pot with the back of a spoon.

Meanwhile, when the roasted poblanos have cooled, use the back of a sharp knife to scrape off the really burnt parts. Cut the end off each pepper, slice it lengthwise, and scrape out all the seeds. Make sure you rinse the peppers under running water so none of the seeds end up in the rice.

Put the contents of the tomatillo pot, the poblanos, the cilantro, and cumin in a blender, and blend until you have a smooth green puree (about 30 seconds, depending on your blender). I like to start on low speed and work up, so the blender doesn't explode; you also want to hold down the top of the blender with a towel to avoid ugly hot-liquid accidents. If your blender isn't big enough, it's better to do the puree in two batches than to fill it up to the top.

Pour the puree back into the pot. Mix the salt in well.

Add the rice, turn the heat to medium-high, mix everything together, cover the pot, and bring it up to a simmer. Then give it a stir, turn the heat to low, and cover the pot again.

When the rice has absorbed all the liquid and is nice and fluffy (about 20 minutes), it's ready to rock.

TOMATILLOS

The tomatillo is a fruit, related to the ordinary tomato, that's used widely in Mexican and Latin American cooking. Tomatillos come in a range of colors in Mexico, but in most places in the States you only see the green ones. They're a prime ingredient in *arroz verde*, but they're also great, boiled or roasted, in sauces. To prep them, just slip off the papery husks.

ARROZ VERDE PATRICIO-STYLE

If you want to make this the traditional way, use *queso Oaxaca*—the real Mexican deal. But Monterey Jack works pretty well, too. I like to put Manchego on top; that's how Patricio's grandma does it.

SERVES 6 TO 8 AS A SIDE DISH

1 cup half-and-half
1 recipe Straight-Up Arroz Verde (page 218), still hot and in the pot
1 cup grated queso Oaxaca or Monterey Jack cheese
1 cup grated Manchego cheese

Preheat the oven to 400°F.

Stir the half-and-half into the *arroz verde* in the pot and mix it in well.

Add the queso Oaxaca or Monterey Jack and mix well.

Pour the rice into a large ovenproof, broiler-proof baking dish. Sprinkle the Manchego cheese on top, and put the dish on the middle oven rack.

Bake for 15 minutes, or until the cheese has melted and baked.

Turn on the broiler and broil for about 5 minutes, until the cheese starts to brown and the top crisps up. Serve this right away.

CITRUS RICE

This recipe turns citrus into a side-dish version of sweet-and-sour candy. I use Valencia or navel oranges because they're the sweetest—their flavor is perfect with buttery, floral basmati rice and the crunch of the green onions. I guarantee you won't be able to stop eating this once you start. It's perfect with the lamb tagine on page 166.

SERVES 4 TO 6 AS A SIDE DISH

1 ½ cups basmati rice
1 fresh bay leaf
Grated zest of 1 lemon
½ teaspoon salt
¼ teaspoon crushed red pepper flakes
1 tablespoon butter
Juice of 1 lemon (about 2 tablespoons)
2 small Valencia or navel oranges, sectioned (see page 68) and chopped (about ½ cup)
2 green onions, sliced (about 2 tablespoons)

Wash the rice to get rid of the excess starch: Pour the rice into a bowl, and cover it with cold water. Shake the rice around with your hands to loosen the starch; then use a fine sieve to drain the water out. Repeat this 3 times.

In a large pot, combine the drained rice with 2 cups of water. Add the bay leaf, lemon zest, salt, red pepper flakes, and butter. Turn the heat to high.

When the mixture comes to a boil, turn the heat down to low and cover the pot with a tight-fitting lid. Let the rice cook for about 12 minutes, until all the liquid has been absorbed.

Pull the pot off the heat, pull out the bay leaf, and stir in the lemon juice, orange pieces, and green onions. Then pile the rice into a big bowl and serve it while it's hot.

DIRTY RICE

This dish looks exactly the way it sounds: the chicken livers and sausage make the rice look a little . . . dirty. And it tastes kind of dirty, too, because of the earthiness of the liver. But it's the vegetables that are the key here. Green bell peppers, celery, and onions sautéed together form the "holy trinity": the cornerstone of Creole and Cajun cooking, kind of like a Louisiana version of Italian sofrito.

I was obsessed with this dish from the first time I tasted it, down in New Orleans. I've done a hundred versions of it over the years; this one is my all-time best. In my restaurants, we've served this with a whole bunch of different dishes; it's great with roast duck. (It's nice with a fried egg the next morning, too.)

SERVES 8 TO 10 AS A SIDE DISH

FOR THE RICE
2 tablespoons corn oil
1 small onion, diced ($^1/_2$ cup)
$^1/_2$ green bell pepper, diced ($^1/_2$ cup)
2 celery stalks, diced (1 cup)
1 link fresh andouille sausage, diced ($^1/_2$ cup)
$^1/_4$ teaspoon celery seeds
$^1/_4$ teaspoon chili powder
1 bay leaf
1 clove garlic, peeled
1 $^1/_2$ cups long-grain rice
2 $^1/_2$ cups chicken broth, vegetable broth, or water
$^1/_2$ teaspoon salt

TO FINISH THE RICE
1 tablespoon canola oil
$^1/_2$ pound chicken livers (about 7 livers), cleaned (see page 223) and cut into small pieces ($^1/_2$ cup)
$^1/_4$ teaspoon salt
$^1/_4$ teaspoon chili powder
3 green onions, sliced thin ($^1/_2$ cup)

TO MAKE THE RICE
Heat the corn oil in a large pot (one that has a tight-fitting lid: you'll need this later) over medium heat.

Add the onions, peppers, celery, and sausage, and stir everything well, so the vegetables and sausage are coated in the oil.

Let the vegetables cook for about 4 minutes, until they soften up; stir the mixture regularly to stop the onions from sticking and coloring.

Add the celery seeds, chili powder, bay leaf, and garlic clove, and mix well to coat the vegetables and sausage in the spices.

Add the rice and stir everything together well.

Add the chicken broth and salt; then bring the mixture up to a simmer.

Cover the pot tightly, turn the heat to low, and let the rice cook for about 20 minutes, until it has absorbed all of the liquid.

Pull the pot off the fire, and scoop out the garlic clove and bay leaf.

TO FINISH THE RICE
Heat the canola oil in a medium-sized nonstick pan over high heat.

When the oil begins to smoke, add the chicken livers and sauté them quickly, shaking the pan to coat them in the oil, for about 1 minute, until they have browned.

Add the salt and chili powder. Then stir the rice into the chicken livers and cook for 10 seconds. Pull the pot off the heat, and stir in most of the green onions (hold some back for garnish).

Spoon the rice into a big serving bowl. Sprinkle the remaining green onions on top, and serve it up hot.

HOW TO CLEAN CHICKEN LIVERS

....

Chicken livers, which are often sold in tubs, usually arrive as two lobes connected by a central vein. Pinch the middle vein with one hand, and with the other, use a sharp knife to scrape one lobe of the liver away from the vein. You may have to scrape out some of the leftover vein once the lobes are separated: you want to get rid of as much of it as possible.

SANTA CLAUS IN VANGROOVY

On our first night in Vancouver, after our cross-country search for the Great American Breakfast, Gwen, Mitchell, and I found ourselves in a vegetarian restaurant called The Naam.

Gwen was super-excited. "It's the oldest whole food restaurant in North America!" she trilled, practically dancing up to the door.

Did I mention Gwen was a vegetarian back then?

All the way across the country, I'd watched her tell servers, "I don't eat meat, poultry, fish, or seafood. Nothing with eyes, basically." And all the way across the country, she'd eaten Main Course Vegetables—a medley of all the side dishes that came with the actual main courses.

No surprise: she was very excited to be at The Naam.

Also no surprise: Mitchell and I—less excited!

But what was I going to do? It was her car. Her apartment in Vancouver. And anyway, she was cute.

So there I was, sitting on what looked like a handmade chair (carved by a pretty shaky hand) at a rough wooden table (same shaky hand) in a little candlelit cave of a restaurant. The menu, on stained heavy brown paper: quesadillas and burritos; salads with sprouts and shaved carrots; stuffed chapatis; soup; chili; a sandwich optimistically called the "Naam Burger," which definitely didn't look anything like any burger I'd ever seen. Plus something called "grilled sambits," which were flat, fried, brown, and mysterious. It was like time-traveling straight back to 1975.

I looked across the table. Gwen smiled at me. She was still cute. "I want to try everything on the menu!" she practically sang.

So I ordered up a stuffed chapati, a side of tofu bacon, and a big bottle of local beer. I took a deep breath. I pictured in my mind the thick, juicy, non-Naam burger I would eat as soon as I got the chance. Next to me, Mitchell tried to look enthusiastic as he ordered his bean-and-tofu-cheese burrito.

But then, just as the food arrived, I saw a vision, and it told me that vegetarian restaurants in Vancouver were . . . good.

I saw Santa Claus.

He walked in the door with his beard down nearly to his waist and his eyes sparkling. He didn't appear to be wearing the official ho-ho-ho outfit, but then again, it was the off-season. And in case you had any doubts (the sandals, maybe?), he pulled presents for all out of his sack: a foot-long joint, a good 3 inches in diameter. Santa lit up, right in the middle of the restaurant, and then he went from table to table, offering comfort and joy to each and every one. When that spliff had burned down to a stub of its former self, he wished all a good night and disappeared out the door. I was pretty sure I heard the ringing of sleigh bells, but at that point I was not a reliable witness.

Nobody blinked an eye; nobody said, "Sir, you can't smoke that in here"; nobody said, "I'm calling the police"; nobody turned down Santa Claus. The West Coast, I thought, was an enchanted and magical place. Maybe I would stay forever.

And my tofu-spinach chapati? Delicious! I ate three.

WILD RICE AND QUINOA PILAF WITH PECANS, GREEN ONIONS, AND CRANBERRIES

A lot of great stuff came out of the '70s in America: Trans-Ams, beanbag chairs, the Sugarhill Gang, Steely Dan, the Doobie Brothers, *Convoy*, *Airplane!*, and quinoa-rice pilaf. This dish is like '70s America updated.

Quinoa has the whole '70s health food thing going on: it's a supergrain that's actually a seed; it's related to spinach (and to tumbleweed); it's high in magnesium, iron, and protein; and it's gluten-free. But that doesn't mean it has to taste bad. In this pilaf, the quinoa lightens things up a little bit, since wild rice is pretty heavy. The mix is a little bit sweet and a little bit nutty. The Earl Grey tea lends the cranberries a floral flavor, and the whiskey makes them sweet and smoky (and gives you a chance to take a swig in the kitchen). The green onions give the dish a fresh greenness that's a little unexpected.

This is great with big-holiday-dinner dishes with wings: roast goose, roast turkey, quail, chicken. If it's too healthy for you, throw in the butter at the end.

SERVES 6 TO 8 AS A SIDE

1 cup wild rice
3 cups chicken broth, vegetable broth, or water
$^{1}/_{4}$ large red onion, diced small ($^{1}/_{3}$ cup)
1 bay leaf
1 cup quinoa
$^{1}/_{2}$ cup pecans
1 Earl Grey tea bag (or 1 teaspoon loose Earl Grey tea in a tea ball)
$^{1}/_{2}$ cup dried cranberries
2 tablespoons whiskey
2 green onions, chopped fine (about $^{1}/_{2}$ cup)
$^{1}/_{2}$ teaspoon salt
$^{1}/_{4}$ teaspoon fresh-ground black pepper
1 tablespoon butter (optional)

Combine the wild rice, $1^{1}/_{2}$ cups of the broth, the red onion, and bay leaf in a large pot, and bring to a simmer over medium-high heat (just about 2 minutes). Then cover the pot and turn the heat to low. Cook the rice-broth mix for about 20 minutes, until the rice soaks up all the liquid, checking it and stirring it every so often to make sure the rice doesn't burn. Then pull the pot off the heat and let it sit, tightly covered, for 5 minutes.

While the rice is cooking, combine the quinoa with the remaining $1^{1}/_{2}$ cups broth in a small pot, and cook it in the same way you cooked the rice: bring it to a boil, cover, reduce the heat to low, and let it sit. The quinoa will cook faster: it only needs about 10 minutes to soak up all the broth.

While the rice and the quinoa are cooking, toast the pecans in a small dry pan over very low heat, tossing or mixing them around occasionally, for about 10 minutes, until they brown and crisp up, releasing their aroma. Make sure you keep the heat very low so the nuts don't burn. When they're toasted, rough-chop them using a large kitchen knife.

Put some water on to boil in a small pot or a tea kettle.

Put the tea bag and the cranberries in a bowl, and pour $^{1}/_{2}$ cup of the boiling water over them. Add the whiskey and let the mixture steep for 4 minutes, so the tea brews. Then pull the tea bag out and keep steeping the cranberries until they plump up (about 15 minutes).

When the rice is ready, pull the bay leaf out and throw it away. Add the cranberries and half their liquid ($^{1}/_{4}$ cup) to the rice, along with the nuts, green onions, salt, pepper, and quinoa. If you're using the butter, throw it in here, too. Stir everything together well (if you're using the butter, make sure melts in completely). Pour the pilaf into a large serving dish and serve it right away.

SAUSAGE AND SHRIMP PILAU

Pilau is a Southern thing: you see it in Florida and the Carolinas, places where they used to grow a lot of rice. A pilau is basically just a kind of pilaf—a straight-up one-pot rice meal—except that it uses Carolina rice, which has a shorter grain than the standard stuff in pilafs, so it doesn't come out fluffy. (I like to use Anson Mills Carolina Gold, because it's delicate and kind of buttery; you can find it online.) Basically, a pilau is what my dad would call an American risotto.

You can make pilau with just about any kind of protein, but my favorite is this combination of sausage and shrimp. And pilaus come with a million different kinds of vegetables, but I really like to use fresh peas, so I make this dish in the spring and summertime, when they're easy to get.

SERVES 4 TO 6 AS A MAIN DISH

2 tablespoons corn oil
$^1/_2$ medium Vidalia onion, diced ($^1/_2$ cup)
1 green bell pepper, diced (about $^3/_4$ cup)
$^1/_3$ pound andouille sausage, cut into $^1/_2$-inch slices
3 cups Carolina rice (I like Anson Mills Carolina Gold)
5 cups chicken broth
$^3/_4$ teaspoon Old Bay seasoning
$^1/_2$ teaspoon Worcestershire sauce
1 cup fresh peas
1 pound shrimp, shelled, cleaned, and cut into thirds
2 green onions, chopped (about $^1/_3$ cup)
1 tablespoon fresh thyme leaves

Heat the oil in a large pot over medium-low heat. Add the onions and bell peppers, and sauté for a minute or two, until the vegetables start to soften.

Add the sausage and cook everything together slowly for about 2 minutes, until the sausage starts to render.

Add the rice and keep cooking, stirring constantly, for about 2 minutes, until the rice begins to toast a little bit. (If you don't stir the rice, it will burn.)

Stir in the chicken broth, Old Bay, and Worcestershire sauce, and turn the heat up to medium-high. Use your stirring spoon to push anything that's splashed up on the sides back down into the pot: you don't want pieces of the pilau to burn and drop in, flavoring the whole pot.

When the pilau comes up to a boil, turn the heat to medium-low, cover the pot with a tight-fitting lid, and keep cooking for another 15 minutes or so, until the rice is mostly cooked through but still steaming and soaking up liquid.

Stir the peas and shrimp very gently into the rice. Then cover the pot and keep cooking the pilau for another 5 minutes, until all the liquid has been absorbed (the rice will be glazed and wet-looking).

Pull the pot off the heat. If your shrimp aren't cooked all the way through yet (they'll be a little translucent if they're underdone), cover the pot again and let the shrimp keep steaming in the heat inside the pot—off the flame—for a couple of minutes.

Add the green onions and thyme, and use your spoon to fluff the mixture very gently from underneath—you don't want to break up the rice grains too much. Serve this up while it's hot.

GREEN GRITS

Grits are one of the most iconic Southern foods around—so, being a red-blooded Northern boy, I thought I'd mess with them. I'm not totally unqualified, since grits aren't all that different from Italian dishes like risotto and polenta—but when I started thinking about how to brighten them up and make them a little more lively, I ended up over in the American Southwest. Go figure.

Cooking time and liquid-to-grits ratios will be different depending on the type of grits you use, so make sure you check the directions on the box for that. These amounts are for Anson Mills Carolina Whole Hominy Quick Grits, which I like a lot.

SERVES 6 TO 8 AS A SIDE DISH

1 1/2 cups whole milk
1 teaspoon salt
1/2 teaspoon fresh-ground black pepper
1 cup grits
1 heaping cup fresh cilantro leaves
One 4-ounce can diced green chiles (preferably Hatch brand, fire-roasted)
6 green onions, chopped (about 1/2 cup)
3 tablespoons unsalted butter
1/2 cup grated sharp cheddar cheese
1/4 cup grated Parmesan cheese

Combine the milk and 2 1/2 cups of water in a medium-sized pot, and bring the mixture up to a simmer over medium-high heat.

Mix in the salt and pepper. Then whisk in the grits, pouring them in slowly and whisking continuously until they're smooth, with no lumps. The grits should look a little like oatmeal, only finer.

Turn the heat down to medium-low and keep cooking, whisking regularly so nothing sticks.

Meanwhile, combine the cilantro leaves, diced green chiles, and green onions in a food processor and pulse for 30 seconds or so, until everything is finely chopped.

When the grits have cooked through and thickened, pull the pot off the heat and add the cilantro mixture. Whisk everything together so the grits turn green. Then add the butter and whisk again, so the butter melts in.

Whisk in the grated cheddar and Parmesan cheeses. Serve it up hot.

RIGATONI WITH SUNDAY NIGHT RAGU

As anybody with a TV knows, every mythical Italian-American family spends Sunday night around a big table, eating unbelievably huge servings of pasta with Grandma's Special Sunday Night Sauce, which has been simmering in a gargantuan pot in Grandma's kitchen all day long. And it's full of meat—really *meaty* meat—to keep all those big Italian men going: sausages, meatballs, *braciole*. This is my version of that TV classic. I use all pork: the sauce has pork butt and ribs inside it, so it's still super-meaty, but it's also rich and thick and really well flavored. On a cold winter night, this is the best Sunday-night pasta ever. Serve it up with a great big red wine.

SERVES 6

FOR THE RAGU

1 pound St. Louis ribs (spare ribs, trimmed, with the brisket bones removed)
1 teaspoon salt
1/2 teaspoon fresh-ground black pepper
3 tablespoons extra-virgin olive oil
1 1/2 pounds boneless pork shoulder, cut into 1-inch chunks
1 large onion, diced (1 1/2 cups)
3 cloves garlic, sliced superfine
3/4 teaspoon crushed red pepper flakes
1 1/4 teaspoons dried oregano (preferably Calabrian, dried on the branch)
Two 28-ounce cans chopped plum tomatoes with their juice (I like Jersey Fresh)

FOR THE PASTA AND TO FINISH THE DISH

1 pound dried rigatoni
1/2 cup grated Parmesan cheese
2 tablespoons extra-virgin olive oil
1/4 cup chopped fresh parsley

TO MAKE THE RAGU

Preheat the oven to 425°F.

Sprinkle both sides of the pork ribs generously with 1/2 teaspoon of the salt and 1/4 teaspoon of the black pepper.

Lay the ribs on a rack in a roasting pan, put it on the middle oven rack, and roast for 30 minutes.

When the ribs have been in the oven for 15 minutes or so, heat the olive oil in a large pot over medium-high heat.

Add the pork shoulder to the pot and let it cook for about 7 minutes, until it's well browned. Stir the meat every few minutes so nothing sticks.

Stir in the onions, turn the flame down to medium, and keep cooking for about 3 minutes, until the onions have started to soften and color up a little.

Stir in the garlic and let everything cook for another minute or so, until the garlic has released its aroma. Make sure you keep stirring during this portion of the proceedings, so the garlic doesn't burn and wreck everything. Then stir in the remaining 1/2 teaspoon salt and 1/4 teaspoon pepper, the red pepper flakes, and the oregano.

When the ribs have started to brown and caramelize, pull them out of the oven and add them to the pot, along with the canned tomatoes and 2 cups of water. (Don't worry too much about how perfectly done the ribs may or may not be—this is just to give them a head start. They're going to cook in the ragu for another 3 1/2 hours, so they're definitely going to be done.)

Bring the sauce up to a simmer; then turn the flame down to low and let the ragu keep cooking for about 3 1/2 hours, checking it every so often and giving it a stir

>>>

to make sure nothing's sticking or burning on the sides of the pot.

When the rib meat is falling off the bone and the pork shoulder is nice and tender, pull the pot off the flame and use a slotted spoon to pull the chunks of pork and the ribs from the pot. Pile them on a big plate and let them cool down on the countertop (or in the fridge, if you're in a hurry).

Use a ladle to skim the fat off the top of the sauce, so it doesn't get greasy.

When the meat is cool enough to handle, rip the pieces of shoulder apart, turning it into chunks, by digging in your thumbs and pulling. Do the same with the ribs, but be careful not to mush up the meat. Pile the pulled meat in a bowl; throw the bones away, but pour any sauce that's left on the plate over the pulled meat.

TO FINISH THE DISH
Put a large pot of well-salted water on to boil for the pasta.

When the water boils, add the rigatoni to the pot and let it cook for the time specified on the box minus 1 minute.

If the sauce has cooled, heat it up on the stove over a low flame.

Mix the meat back into the sauce.

When the pasta is just al dente, drain it (but don't rinse it) and add it to the pot on the stove.

Turn the heat to medium and cook the pasta in the sauce for about 1 to 2 minutes, stirring it every few seconds. You want the pasta to soak up the flavors of the sauce. If the sauce seems dry, add a little bit of water.

Turn the flame off; then add $1/4$ cup of the Parmesan and the olive oil to the pot and mix everything together really well. The Italians call this process *mantecare*, which means "to make creamy."

Scoop the ragu into individual bowls, sprinkle the rest of the Parmesan and the chopped parsley on top, and serve this right away.

ORZO WITH YOGURT AND LEMON

The Greek word for orzo is *kritharaki*, which means "little barley," and that's how it's usually treated: you mostly see it served as a salad or in a casserole. But no matter what the Greeks call it, orzo isn't barley: it's a type of pasta made from semolina. So that's how I like to use it. This dish—definitely an A.C. invention, authentic in no way at all—is kind of like a Greek risotto. I like to serve this with the Greek Lamb Stew on page 160; it cools down the spice and the vinegar and balances out the feta.

SERVES 4 TO 6 AS A SIDE DISH

2 tablespoons butter
$1/2$ medium onion, diced ($1/2$ cup)
1 bay leaf
$1\,1/2$ cups orzo
3 green onions, sliced thin ($1/2$ cup)
$1/4$ cup Greek yogurt (I like Fage brand)
1 teaspoon salt
Juice of 2 lemons ($1/4$ cup)

Melt the butter in a medium saucepan over medium-high heat.

Add the onions and let them cook for a minute or so, until they start to soften up, stirring them regularly so they don't stick or color.

Add $4\,1/2$ cups of water and the bay leaf. Turn the heat to high and bring the mix to a boil.

Add the orzo and stir it in really well, so that the water gets in between the grains and stops the orzo from sticking.

Bring the orzo back up to a simmer, cover the pot, and let it cook for about 10 to 12 minutes, until the orzo is soft and fluffy and the water has been absorbed.

Pull the pot off the heat. Pull out the bay leaf, then add the green onions, yogurt, salt, and lemon juice, and stir everything together until it's creamy. Serve it right away.

BREADS AND BREAKFAST

THE WORLD'S BEST BISCUITS—
END OF STORY

That's all I've got to say about these. The best. In the world. Period. Eat 'em while they're hot.

MAKES 8 TO 10 BISCUITS

FOR THE HONEY-BUTTER TOPPING

3 tablespoons unsalted butter, cut into small pieces

3 tablespoons honey

1/4 teaspoon salt

FOR THE BISCUITS

4 1/2 cups all-purpose flour, plus extra for flouring your work surface and rolling pin

1 teaspoon baking soda

1 tablespoon plus 2 teaspoons baking powder

1 teaspoon salt

2 teaspoons sugar

1 cup solid vegetable shortening

2 1/2 cups buttermilk

TO MAKE THE HONEY BUTTER

Bring 2 tablespoons of water to a boil in a small pot.

Slowly whisk in the butter, piece by piece, letting each piece melt completely into the water before adding the next one. Add the honey and salt, and whisk everything together until you have a shiny, well-combined liquid.

Let the honey butter sit in a warm area of the kitchen, or over the lowest possible flame on the stove, until you're ready to use it. It's important to keep it warm so it will spread easily—and the longer you let it sit, the better the honey butter will be.

TO MAKE THE BISCUITS

Preheat the oven to 425°F.

In a large bowl, sift together the flour, baking soda, baking powder, salt, and sugar. (If you don't have a sifter, you can use a whisk.)

Add the vegetable shortening. Using a pastry cutter, or holding a butter knife in each hand, cut through the shortening and flour in an X-shaped motion until the shortening is mixed in. Be careful to break up any large pieces. You should end up with lots of little pebbles.

Add the buttermilk and use your hands to mix everything together, turning the mixture until it forms a dough. Then keep turning and kneading until you've got a roughly shaped ball of dough. If things get sticky, add a little bit of flour.

Flour a board or countertop well, and turn the dough out on it.

Flour your rolling pin, and then roll the dough out until it forms a round about 1/2 inch thick. Fold the dough round into thirds, like you're folding a business letter. Slap the dough down hard with the palms of your hands to really bring it together, and then roll it out and fold it in again. Do this 7 times in all, skipping the folding step the seventh time. Reflour the work surface, the dough, and the rolling pin as you go.

Flour a 3 1/2-inch round pastry cutter, and cut out as many rounds of dough as possible (you should have 8 to 10 or so). Reflour the cutter as you go. (When we make these at the restaurant, we usually bake off the leftover pieces and eat them ourselves.)

Cover a baking sheet with parchment paper, lay the biscuits on it, and put it on the middle oven rack. At about the 10-minute mark, turn the baking sheet so that all the biscuits bake evenly.

When the biscuits are baked through and the tops are golden-brown (about 20 minutes), pull them out of the oven. Using a big pastry brush, coat the tops of the biscuits with the honey butter. The biscuits will be very soft and flaky inside, with just a little bit of crispness on the outside. Serve them while they're hot.

BUTTERNUT BISCUITS WITH CHIPOTLE GLAZE

People forget that Miami is part of the South—they sort of think of it as a party town in its own special category. But once upon a time, it really was a sleepy Southern burg. So when my grandma immigrated there from Italy, she learned to cook Southern: meringue pies, black-eyed peas, blackened fish, biscuits. One of my favorite family dishes is my Aunt Sylvia's sweet potato biscuits: they're really something special. Here I've adapted them and added some extra geography: I bring a little bit of the North and a little bit of the Southwest, with roasted butternut squash instead of the sweet potatoes and a glaze made of chipotle and maple syrup. The heat from the glaze is a really nice contrast to the warm, savory-sweet biscuits.

MAKES 1 DOZEN 2-INCH BISCUITS

FOR THE GLAZE
$1/2$ stick (4 tablespoons) unsalted butter, cut into small pieces
$1/2$ cup maple syrup
$1/2$ teaspoon salt
$1/4$ teaspoon chipotle chile powder

FOR THE BISCUITS
$1/3$ cup roasted butternut squash (see Chef's Tip, page 241)
1 cup buttermilk
$1 3/4$ cups all-purpose flour, plus extra for flouring your work surface
$1/4$ cup whole wheat flour
1 tablespoon baking powder
$1/2$ teaspoon baking soda
2 teaspoons kosher salt
$1/4$ teaspoon fresh-ground black pepper
$1/2$ teaspoon cayenne pepper

2 tablespoons sugar
$3/4$ stick (6 tablespoons) unsalted cold butter

TO MAKE THE GLAZE
Bring 2 tablespoons of water to a boil in a small pot.

Slowly whisk in the butter, piece by piece, letting each piece melt completely into the water before adding the next one.

Add the maple syrup, salt, and chipotle powder, and whisk everything together until you have a shiny, well-combined liquid.

Let the glaze sit in a warm area of the kitchen, or over the lowest possible flame on the stove, until you're ready to use it. It's important to keep it warm so it will spread easily—but the longer you let it sit, the better the glaze will be.

TO MAKE THE BISCUITS
Preheat the oven to 400°F.

Place the cooked squash in a large bowl, add the buttermilk, and mash everything together with a fork or a pastry cutter so the buttermilk is really well combined with the squash. Then set the bowl aside on the countertop.

Combine the all-purpose flour, whole wheat flour, baking powder, baking soda, salt, black pepper, cayenne pepper, and sugar in a medium-sized mixing bowl, and mix everything together well.

Cut the butter into $1/4$-inch cubes and add them to the flour mixture.

Using a pastry cutter or a fork, cut the butter into the dry ingredients until the butter is broken down to the size of small pebbles. If you don't break the butter down enough, the texture will be gummy. (Don't do this too early: once you cut in the butter, it will react with the flour, and the texture of your biscuits will change. You want to add the butter right before you bake off the biscuits.)

Make a well in the flour mixture—a hollowed-out space in the middle—and pour the squash mixture into it.

Using a spatula, gently combine the ingredients. Then use your hands to gently fold everything together, turning and pressing the mixture until it starts to come together as a dough.

Flour a countertop or a wooden board, and turn the dough out onto your work surface. Form the dough into a rough round with your hands, and then press it down so it flattens out a little.

Using a well-floured rolling pin, roll the dough out until it's about 1 inch thick.

Use a 2$\frac{1}{2}$-inch pastry cutter (or the top of a water glass) to cut out as many biscuits as possible.

Line a baking sheet with parchment paper, and then transfer the biscuits to the sheet, making sure every biscuit has some space around it.

Place the baking sheet on the middle oven rack, towards the center of the oven. Bake the biscuits for 5 minutes. Then turn the baking sheet around (so the biscuits bake evenly), and bake them for another 5 to 7 minutes, until the biscuits are light gold on the top, pretty firm to the touch (with a little bit of bounce), and golden brown on the bottom.

TO FINISH THE BISCUITS

Pull the biscuits out of the oven and brush them generously with the glaze. (If you don't have a pastry brush, you can just spoon the glaze over them.) Serve the biscuits while they're warm.

CHEF'S TIP

....

TO ROAST BUTTERNUT SQUASH

Preheat the oven to 400°F.

Cut the squash in half, scoop out the seeds, and lay the halves face up on a baking sheet. Bake the squash on the middle oven rack for about 45 minutes, until it's fork-tender (just like you're baking a potato).

Pull the squash out of the oven and let it cool. Then scrape off any burnt parts on the top and scoop the meat out into a big bowl. Mash the meat with a fork so that it smooths out a little.

DUTCH BABY

When I was a kid, my dad would sometimes work in Toledo, Ohio. That was about two hours away from home, so he would stay out there most nights. On Fridays after school, my mom would drive my brother and me out to Toledo to visit him. In the morning we'd go to this place called The Original Pancake House, where the specialty was a German pancake, also called a Dutch Baby. I thought about that Dutch Baby all the time. It was crispy on the outside, soft on the inside, airy and puffy; you could put butter or syrup on it or squeeze a lemon over it. When I was eight years old, it was about as big as my head. It was the coolest thing ever.

The key to a good Dutch Baby is making the batter the night before. It needs to rest in the fridge for at least 6 hours; otherwise, it will be too eggy. That's good news for your Sunday morning, though: you can bake off your Dutch Baby while you're making coffee.

SERVES 2 (YOU CAN EASILY DOUBLE THIS RECIPE TO SERVE 4)

FOR THE BATTER
$2/3$ cup milk
$1/4$ teaspoon vanilla extract
4 eggs
$2/3$ cup all-purpose flour
2 teaspoons granulated sugar
$1/4$ teaspoon kosher salt
$1 1/2$ tablespoons butter, melted

FOR COOKING THE DISH
Butter, for the skillet
Powdered sugar, for dusting

OPTIONAL GARNISH CHOICES
Lemon wedges
Fruit compote
Butter
Maple syrup

TO MAKE THE BATTER
Combine the milk, vanilla extract, and eggs in a blender, and blend on medium-high for about 15 seconds, until everything is combined.

In a mixing bowl, whisk together the flour, sugar, and salt.

Add the dry mixture to the wet mixture and blend again; then add the melted butter and keep blending until everything is smooth (about 30 seconds).

Pour the batter into a bowl, cover it tightly with plastic wrap, and let it rest in the refrigerator for at least 6 hours. The longer the batter rests, the better the Dutch Baby will be.

TO MAKE THE DUTCH BABY
Preheat the oven to 400°F.

Butter a 10-inch ovenproof skillet (preferably cast iron) and heat it on the middle oven rack for about 5 minutes, so it gets pretty hot.

When the skillet has heated up, pull it out of the oven, pour in the batter, and put it back in the oven. Let the batter bake for 15 minutes, then turn the skillet around, and bake for another 10 minutes or so, until the batter has risen high on the sides and a little bit in the center, and has turned golden brown right in the middle (the edges can get a little dark—that's OK).

Pull the Dutch Baby out of the oven and slide it right out of the skillet onto a plate (it won't stick). It will deflate a bit as it cools down—that's not a problem. Fill a small sieve with powdered sugar, and shake it over the Dutch Baby so the surface is thickly covered.

Put the Dutch Baby in the middle of the table with some little bowls of toppings: lemon wedges, fruit compote, pats of soft butter, maple syrup. You don't need a knife and a cake lifter for this: just let everybody pull pieces off with their fingers. I guarantee it will disappear fast.

KIERIN'S BACON-CHIPOTLE CORNBREAD

Kierin Baldwin, pastry chef at the Dutch, says she found the basics for this cornbread in an old cookbook in her mom's house when she was fifteen years old. It's been her go-to recipe, with a little bit of tweaking, ever since. She came up with this version—with the filling added and fluffiness upped—when she was in college. It's great with any simple homemade dinner; it's super-fast to put together, and if you serve it up hot, it's a big crowd-pleaser. The cornbread is savory and a little bit cheesy, but it also gets an unexpected bite from the chipotle peppers. Kierin says it's everybody's hands-down favorite.

The trick with this recipe is to make the bacon mixture first. Once you combine the wet and dry ingredients, the baking soda will start to react, so you'll want to get the cornbread in the oven as fast as you can—you can't let it sit around while you mix up the filling.

SERVES 6 TO 8

4 slices bacon

2 tablespoons butter, or a spray of vegetable cooking spray

3 ounces cheddar cheese, cut into 1/4-inch chunks (about 1/2 cup)

1 1/2 canned chipotle peppers in adobo, chopped fine

3 tablespoons honey

1 cup stone-ground cornmeal

1 cup all-purpose flour

1 tablespoon baking powder

1/2 teaspoon baking soda

1 teaspoon salt

1 egg

3 tablespoons sugar

1/4 cup grapeseed oil or corn oil

1 1/4 cups buttermilk

Preheat the oven to 350°F.

Cook the bacon in a sauté pan over medium-high heat until it's crispy. Pull the pan off the heat and pile the bacon on a plate. Let it cool down (so it doesn't melt the cheese when you combine it), and then dice it very fine.

If you're using butter to grease the loaf pan, melt the butter in a small pan over medium heat.

In a small bowl, combine the cheese, chipotle peppers, bacon, and honey. Mix together with a rubber spatula so the honey coats everything.

In a large bowl, mix together the cornmeal, flour, baking powder, baking soda, and salt.

In another small bowl, whisk together the egg and sugar. Once they're combined, whisk in the oil and then the buttermilk. The mixture should be thick and milky.

Pour the egg mixture into the cornmeal-flour mixture. Using a rubber spatula, fold the wet and dry ingredients together for about 20 seconds, just until everything combines. (It's OK if there are little bits of unmixed wet and dry—better to mix too little than too much. If you overmix, you'll end up with a lot of big holes in your bread, and less fluffiness.)

Pour in the chipotle-honey-bacon mix, and use the spatula to mix everything together, so you end up with ribbons and pockets of honey and bacon. Again, don't spend too long on this: fold everything together no more than 3 or 4 times.

Use vegetable cooking spray or the browned butter to grease a standard loaf pan, and then pour the cornbread mixture into the pan. Bake the cornbread on the middle oven rack for 15 minutes.

BISCUIT & JAM 3
FRUIT LOAF 2
BROWNIE 4
BUCKWHEAT CREPE
WITH MAPLE 4
GRANOLA & YOGURT 4
DONUTS 2 COOKIES 1
SLICE OF PIE 4

HOME MADE ALWAYS

EGG SAUSAG
PAN CON TOM
GRANGE 7 HO
5 FOIE GRAS
PICKLEDTON
CUBANO 76 C
BACON EGG
9 MAPLE SYR
HOT DOG 33
01 FRIES

Turn the loaf pan around so that everything bakes evenly, and bake the cornbread for another 40 to 50 minutes, until the top is really golden brown and bounces back when you touch it, and a sharp knife poked into the center comes out clean.

Pop the loaf right out of the loaf pan and let it cool on a baking rack, so the sides stay nice and crispy. Kierin usually lets it cool for about 10 minutes, so it firms up. But if you can't wait, you can cut into it while it's warm—if it doesn't rest, it will just be a little bit crumbly.

MUSH MY WAY

I may have been a precocious kid when it came to food, but when we stopped at local joints on road trips through the South, my favorite thing to order was . . . mush. I mean, come on: what could be better, when you're eight years old, than looking up at a grown-up and saying, "I'd like mush, please," without your dad whacking you upside the head? And–score!–it also tasted really good. Mush is usually just cooked cornmeal, sweetened and thick. It's served either as a porridge, kind of like grits, or fried up on the outside, the way I do it here. Either way, it rocks as kid food–and as grown-up comfort food, too.

Fried mush is easy to make, but getting the ratio of cornmeal to liquid right and really cooling it down are both key: otherwise, your mush won't be mushy. If the liquid ratio is off, the mush will be hard and dry; if the mush isn't cold enough, it will be too soft, and it'll fall apart in the pan when you heat it up. It's a good idea to chill it overnight, or to make the mush in the morning and fry it up at the end of the day. What do you get if you do it right? Crispy on the outside, like butter on the inside, yummy all the way through.

SERVES 4 TO 6

FOR THE MUSH
3 cups whole milk
$^1/_2$ teaspoon salt
3 tablespoons maple syrup
$^1/_2$ teaspoon vanilla extract
$^1/_4$ teaspoon ground cinnamon
Small pinch of cayenne pepper
2 cups cornmeal
1 cup raisins
1 cup farmer's cheese (you can also use ricotta)

TO FINISH THE DISH
$^1/_2$ cup cornmeal
$^1/_2$ stick (4 tablespoons) butter

OPTIONAL TOPPINGS
Powdered sugar
More raisins or dried currants
A little maple syrup drizzled on top
A scoop of farmer's cheese

TO MAKE THE MUSH
Combine the milk with $3^1/_2$ cups of water in a medium-sized saucepan over medium-high heat. Add the salt, maple syrup, vanilla extract, cinnamon, and cayenne. Whisk everything together and bring it up to a boil.

Turn the heat to low and whisk in the cornmeal, adding it bit by bit and making sure each batch is whisked in well (just like you're making polenta). When all the cornmeal is in the pot, you should have a thick porridge. Keep cooking the mush on low heat, whisking it periodically so it doesn't stick, for about 15 minutes, until the cornmeal's pretty soft.

Stir in the raisins and cook for about 5 minutes more, until the raisins plump up and the cornmeal is very soft.

Pull the pan off the heat. Add the farmer's cheese and mix it in well.

Pour the mush into a 9 x 13-inch baking dish and put it in the fridge, uncovered, to cool. You want the mush to be really cool before you work with it, so let it sit for at least 3 hours. It will hold in the fridge at this point for up to 2 days.

TO FINISH THE DISH
Turn the baking dish over on a cutting board and tap the mush out. Cut it into 4 x 2-inch rectangles (the easi-

est way to do this: cut the whole thing in half lengthwise and then cut out 2-inch rectangles). Lay the pieces on a baking sheet with the side that was on the bottom of the baking dish facing up.

Put the baking sheet in the fridge and chill the mush pieces for about 30 minutes, until the tops dry out.

Preheat the oven to 175°F.

Shake the cornmeal onto a dinner plate. Roll each mush rectangle around on the plate so you have a dusting of cornmeal on both sides of every piece.

Heat 1 tablespoon of the butter in a nonstick sauté pan over medium-low heat. Add 4 cornmeal-coated mush pieces, and fry them up slowly, turning them every 30 seconds or so, until they're golden brown on both sides (about 2 to 3 minutes a side).

Pull the finished mush pieces out of the pan, lay them on a baking sheet, and hold them in the oven.

Add more butter to the pan, and fry up the next batch.

When all the mush has been fried, serve it up piled on a plate. It's great with powdered sugar, with more raisins or dried currants, with a little maple syrup drizzled on top, with a scoop of farmer's cheese . . . or all by itself.

BAKED EGGS WITH ASPARAGUS AND RAMPS

There's a famous t-shirt that reads "BRUNCH IS FOR ASS-HOLES." Lots of times, it's easy to see why a person might want a shirt like that: in my experience, brunch can mean long waits, lousy service from hungover waiters, cold rubbery eggs, undercooked pancakes, and bad coffee. I always said that if I ever did brunch in one of my restaurants, it would be game-changing. When we opened Locanda Verde, we spent a good two weeks just testing brunch recipes—all day, every day—to make sure they were right on. Brunch there isn't "dinner lite": we cook hard for brunch, the way we do for every other meal. And we have exactly the same philosophy at The Dutch, where we treat brunch like the great American tradition that it is.

One of my favorite brunch menu items is baked eggs. This one's all about springtime. Ramps and aspara-gus are in season at the same time, and together they give the dish a green, fresh taste; the eggs and cheese are fluffy and rich; and the marinated tomatoes give it all a bounce of tartness. The dish is hearty enough to soak up your sins from the night before, but light enough to let you get going on the rest of your Sun-day. Serve it with toast.

SERVES 4 TO 6

FOR THE MARINATED TOMATOES
1 cup cherry tomatoes, sliced in half lengthwise
¼ teaspoon salt
Pinch of fresh-ground black pepper
½ teaspoon dried oregano
1 teaspoon balsamic vinegar
1 tablespoon extra-virgin olive oil
1 tablespoon chopped fresh parsley

FOR THE EGGS
1 large bunch asparagus (about 1 pound), washed
1 tablespoon butter, at room temperature

2 tablespoons extra-virgin olive oil
¼ pound ramps, leaves and stems sliced thin (about 3 cups sliced)
1 teaspoon salt, plus some for salting the water and for sprinkling over the ramps in the pan
½ teaspoon fresh-ground black pepper, plus a pinch for sprinkling over the ramps in the pan
8 to 10 eggs, depending on size (organic eggs are usually smaller but much more delicious; I like the ones from Flying Pigs Farm)
1 cup whole milk
⅓ cup grated Parmesan cheese

TO MARINATE THE TOMATOES
Combine the tomatoes, salt, pepper, oregano, vinegar, olive oil, and parsley in a medium-sized bowl.

Mix well with a spoon, so the tomatoes are coated with dressing. Set the tomatoes aside on the counter to marinate.

TO MAKE THE BAKED EGGS
Put a large pot of well-salted water on the stove to boil, and preheat the oven to 375°F. Fill a large bowl with ice and cold water, and set it aside.

Cut the bottom quarter off each asparagus spear so they will fit crosswise in a 9 x 13-inch baking dish.

When the water boils, drop in the asparagus and cook it for 1½ to 2 minutes (depending on the size and thick-ness of the spears), until the asparagus is just softened and the color has brightened. (You don't want to over-cook it—remember that it's going in the oven with the eggs, and you want to have some bounceback when you bite down into it at the end.) Then pull the aspara-gus out of the pot with tongs and put it right into the ice water to stop the cooking process.

Generously grease the inside of the 9 x 13-inch baking dish with the butter.

Heat the olive oil in a medium-sized sauté pan over medium heat.

While the oil is heating, pull the asparagus out of the ice water and pat them dry with a clean cloth or a paper towel.

Add the ramps to the hot oil in the sauté pan, and season them with the pinch of salt and pinch of pepper. Sauté the ramps for about 30 seconds, until they start to soften and brighten and their garlicky smell is released.

Spoon the ramps directly into the baking dish, spreading them out in an even layer covering the bottom of the dish.

Lay the asparagus over the ramps, making sure they're covering the ramps completely and evenly, and with the spears all pointing in the same direction (otherwise your presentation is not going to look pro).

Crack the eggs into a large bowl. Add the milk, 1 teaspoon salt, and 1/2 teaspoon pepper, and whisk everything together vigorously until the mixture is frothy. This is important: you want to get enough air into the eggs so that they bake up light and airy. Nobody likes flat baked eggs.

Pour the egg mixture over the asparagus, sprinkle the grated cheese on top, and put the baking dish on the middle oven rack. Bake for about 15 minutes, until the eggs are yellow on top and brown on the bottom.

Spoon the marinated tomatoes over the eggs, scoop the baked eggs onto individual plates, and serve them up hot.

DESSERTS

TEQUILA-LIME-BERRY CRISP WITH
PUMPKIN-SEED STREUSEL

RUSTIC PEACH AND CORNMEAL TART
WITH LEMON VERBENA CREAM

SOUR CHERRY PIE

SOUR ORANGE PIE

STRAWBERRY-RHUBARB FOOL

MEXICAN BAKED APPLES WITH
ANCHO CARAMEL

PINEAPPLE-GINGER ICE

TOASTED COCONUT CAKE

POTICA

ROOT BEER CAKE

PEANUT-BUTTER-OATMEAL-
CHOCOLATE-CHIP COOKIES

JASMINE RICE PUDDING

MOCHA PUDDING

TEQUILA-LIME-BERRY CRISP WITH PUMPKIN-SEED STREUSEL

When I was a kid, come June and July, when the berry bushes behind our house plumped up with fruit, we would pick big bowlfuls of blackberries and raspberries, and my mom would bake all that fresh fruit up into sweet, homey pies and cobblers. They were the definition of kid-friendly food. But my folks are strong believers in the idea that, for grown-ups, all desserts are better with a little bit of booze—and I don't think they're wrong. It's definitely true for this crisp. It's basically a berry margarita under a crust.

This dessert is all about ripe and delicious berries: don't try to make it in the middle of winter with sad supermarket leftovers! If you're really craving a hit of sweet summer flavor in the dead of winter, use the flash-frozen kind. Either way, serve it with ice cream.

MAKES ONE 8 X 8-INCH CRISP;
SERVES 8 TO 10

FOR THE PUMPKIN SEED STREUSEL
1/2 cup (2 ounces) raw pumpkin seeds
3/4 stick (6 tablespoons) unsalted butter
1 cup all-purpose flour
1/4 cup granulated sugar
2 tablespoons plus 2 teaspoons packed dark brown sugar
Finely grated zest of 2 limes
1/4 teaspoon ground cinnamon
1/2 teaspoon salt

FOR THE BERRY CRISP
6 cups mixed berries: blueberries, raspberries, strawberries, blackberries, red currants, mulberries, or any combination of whatever's in season and good

1/3 cup plus 2 tablespoons granulated sugar
1/4 cup tequila
Juice of 1 lime (1 tablespoon)
2 tablespoons all-purpose flour

TO MAKE THE STREUSEL
Preheat the oven to 350°F.

Scatter the pumpkin seeds on a baking sheet and bake them in the oven for about 5 minutes, until they start to pop. They'll round up a little bit and get crunchier and less chewy as they bake.

Cut the butter into cubes (so it melts faster), put it in a small pot, and melt it over medium heat.

In a mixing bowl, combine the flour, granulated sugar, brown sugar, pumpkin seeds, lime zest, cinnamon, and salt. Mix everything together well, and then pour in the melted butter straight from the pot. Stir in the butter with a spoon or a spatula.

Mix the dough together with your hands. Pick up handfuls of the dough and clump it together so you end up with little lumps—in other words, so it looks like streusel.

You can use the dough right away, or you can hold it at this stage by laying it out flat on a baking sheet, chilling it in the fridge, and then putting it in the freezer in a self-seal plastic bag or an airtight container. It will hold for a month, and you can use it straight out of the freezer.

TO MAKE THE BERRY CRISP
Preheat the oven to 350°F.

Wash the berries, pull off the stems, and pile the berries all together in a large mixing bowl.

Add the sugar and tequila, squeeze in the lime juice, and mix everything together well so the fruit is coated and shiny. Add the flour last and mix everything together well with a wooden spoon. (If you add the flour before the liquid, you'll end up with lumps.)

Pour the berries into a deep-dish pie pan or an 8-inch baking dish, and use your fingers to distribute the streusel on top so that all the fruit is thickly covered and there are a lot of little streusel lumps.

Put the pan on a baking sheet (to catch drips) and put it on the middle oven rack. Bake the crisp for 30 minutes.

Then rotate the pan and let it bake for another 10 minutes. When it's ready, the berry filling will be thick and bubbling up, and when you press down on the streusel you should get a little bounce-back, rather than a very liquidy feeling.

Pull the crisp out of the oven and let it cool on the countertop for about an hour, so that everything sets up right and nobody gets burned. (You can also make this ahead of time and reheat it in the oven right before you serve it; store it, covered, on the countertop, not in the fridge, so that it doesn't get mushy.)

RUSTIC PEACH AND CORNMEAL TART WITH LEMON VERBENA CREAM

From the time I was eight years old or so, my dad used to take me to dirt-track races out in the Pennsylvania countryside every year. Just outside of Doylestown, there was this roadside stand with a big sign reading PEACHES AND CREAM. That was all they served: cream custard with fresh peaches and syrup. It was the best food we had on the whole trip. That's the inspiration for this tart. I added the lemon verbena because it just goes really well with peaches.

This tart is a little less intense workwise than making a pie, and a lot more forgiving, since the dough doesn't need to look perfect. The lemon juice in the tart crust helps keep gluten from forming, so the dough is more tender than your average pie crust.

If there's a farmers' market in your neighborhood, you can get your lemon verbena there when it's in season—in New York, that's July and August, which is also fresh peach season. If you can't find fresh verbena, you can always sub out the dried stuff they use for tea. . . . But if you can't find fresh, ripe, beautiful peaches, you should probably make something else for dessert.

MAKES ONE 8-INCH TART;
SERVES 6 TO 8

FOR THE CRUST
1 1/4 cups all-purpose flour
2 tablespoons cornmeal
1 1/2 tablespoons granulated sugar
1 teaspoon kosher salt
1 stick (8 tablespoons) cold unsalted butter,
    cut into 1/2-inch cubes
Juice of 1 lemon (2 tablespoons)
1/4 cup sour cream

FOR THE PEACHES
4 ripe medium-sized peaches, pitted, peeled, and
    sliced thin
1/4 cup plus 2 tablespoons granulated sugar
1 tablespoon all-purpose flour

TO FINISH THE TART
All-purpose flour, for flouring your work surface
1 tablespoon Demerara sugar or other coarse sugar

FOR THE LEMON VERBENA CREAM
2 cups heavy cream
1 cup fresh lemon verbena (leaves, stems, and all),
    or 1/4 cup dried
2 tablespoons powdered sugar

TO MAKE THE DOUGH
Combine the flour, cornmeal, sugar, salt, and butter in a food processor fitted with the metal blade. Pulse until the butter is reduced to small pebbles and coated with the flour and cornmeal.

Scoop the dough into a small mixing bowl, and let it cool down in the fridge, uncovered.

Pour 1/4 cup of water into a small bowl and add 1 ice cube.

Squeeze the lemon juice through a strainer into another small mixing bowl (so the seeds don't end up in the pie dough). Add the sour cream and the cold water, and whisk everything together so you have a smooth, milky liquid.

Take the dough out of the fridge and pour the sour cream mixture into the bowl. Using a rubber spatula, combine the ingredients, turning and mixing gently for 30 seconds or so until you've got a nice moist dough.

Use your hands to shape the dough into a ball. Then flatten it into a disk (so it's pretty close to the shape you'll want to work with—that makes it easier to deal with when it cools and hardens).

Wrap the dough up well in plastic wrap and chill it in the fridge for an hour or so. (It will hold in the fridge for up to 3 days at this point; you can stash it in the freezer for a month.)

TO MAKE THE PEACH FILLING
Pile the peach slices in a medium-sized mixing bowl. Add all the sugar, and stir so the peaches are coated.

Add the flour, mixing everything together well. (If you put the flour in first, it will go all lumpy when it hits the peach juice.)

TO MAKE THE TART
Preheat the oven to 375°F.

Line a baking sheet with parchment paper. (You don't want to use a tart pan here because this tart is rustic and free-form.)

Flour your work surface, and then turn the chilled dough out onto it. Use a rolling pin to roll the dough out into a round, turning the dough every few rolls to keep the circumference even. When the dough is too big to turn, turn the direction of the rolling pin instead, working not only straight up and down and across but on diagonals, too. If the dough starts to stick to the surface as you work with it, use a metal spatula to lift it up, and sprinkle some more flour underneath. Pinch together any frayed edges as you go. When you're done, the dough should be pretty thin—about $1/8$ inch thick and 12 inches or so in diameter (but not so thin that you can see through it).

Pinch the edges together all the way round, so the outside of the circle is pretty smooth and even. If the dough looks lumpy, roll it once more.

Position your parchment-lined baking sheet near your work surface. Then fold an edge of the dough over the rolling pin and roll the dough up, like a window blind, around the rolling pin; lift it onto the baking sheet and unroll it. If pieces break off, pinch them back together. Smooth things out by patting the dough down with your hands. It's OK if the edges of the dough reach up the sides of the baking sheet.

Use a spoon and your hands to lay the peaches thickly on the tart dough, leaving a good 2 inches bare all around the edge. Then grab the edges and fold them up around the peaches, so that the peaches closest to the sides are covered by the dough and the ones in the center are still exposed. Pinch the dough to repair any breaks, and pull off any excess pieces.

Sprinkle the coarse sugar generously over the top of the tart—on the dough and on the exposed peaches.

Put the tart in the oven on the middle rack. Let it bake for about 1 hour, until the filling is bubbling and the crust is golden brown.

TO MAKE THE LEMON VERBENA CREAM
While the tart is in the oven, bring the cream to a boil in a small pot over medium-high heat.

Rinse off the lemon verbena, and put it in a bowl—stems, leaves, everything.

Pour the hot cream over the verbena.

Chill the mixture in the fridge for 30 minutes, uncovered, so you get a nice verbena flavor. (Don't let the

>>>

mix sit in the fridge for longer than that: if you steep fresh herbs for too long, they start to taste grassy.)

Take the bowl out of the fridge and strain the cream through a fine-mesh strainer into the bowl of a table-top mixer; throw out the stems and leaves.

Add the powdered sugar and, using the whisk attachment, whisk the cream and sugar together until you have soft peaks. (You can do this by hand if you don't have a mixer, but you'll need a really strong wrist.)

TO FINISH THE DISH

Let the tart cool to room temperature, and then cut it into individual pieces. (If you cut into it when it's still hot from the oven, it will fall apart.)

Top each piece with a big scoop of the verbena cream, and put some more on the side.

DIRT TRACK EATS

My dad's a big race fan—he likes old-school, down-home, dirt-track racing. In the summers, when we were kids, he would get home from work on a Friday, load me and my brother into the car, and head out to one of the great dirt tracks: Sharon Speedway in Ohio or Mercer Raceway in Pennsylvania; Ransomville Speedway in upstate New York, all the way up by the Canadian border; Winchester Speedway; Silver Spring; Williams Grove . . . If a bunch of guys drove crazy-fast in stylized cars on a track made of dirt and rocks, we were there.

The crowd at the races was mostly good ol' boys, wherever we went; but there were definitely regional differences in style. If you got out toward the real farmland—not the industrial farms, but the old-fashioned family places—you got farmers in overalls and Carhartts; over toward the East Coast, it was a lot of truck drivers and the kind of folks my dad calls "citybillies." But no matter where we went, there were racetrack queens, cheerleader types in skimpy outfits posing on trucks in the midfield—so I was always pretty happy.

Dirt tracks are pretty hard-core: there aren't a lot of rules or barriers separating you from the action. My dad liked to stand right at the curve in the track, where you got maximum tire-grinding and blowouts and accidents. To protect us from flying car parts and rocks, he made a shield out of Plexiglas, with handles attached to the back. It was the kind of thing a medieval knight would carry into battle, if he was doing battle with a monster with a V-8 engine. You would stand behind this thing, and pieces of metal and rubber and parts of the track would come right at you at a couple hundred miles an hour. The finer stuff—ground-up window glass, for example—sprayed over the top, like automotive rain. It was the best.

You could go down to the pits in the middle of the track, too—right there with the cars speeding all around you—and stand behind the guys working on the cars. A race car would zoom off the track, and all these guys would swarm over the car, doing this crazy hard-core work at high speed—hoods up, wheels up, engines red-hot. That's what I wanted to be when I grew up: a pit guy.

Everything happened right there in the middle of the track: people camped out, drove their RVs right up and lived on the track while the races were on. And the food was served up down there, too. People lived on the stuff from the concession stand, which was usually a cinder-block shed painted green with a big sign that said Nachos! and Jumbo Pepsis! Everything was jumbo: burgers, dogs, fries, sodas, beers.

Off the track, though, the food was pretty good. I ate my first Reuben sandwich in Silver Spring, Pennsylvania—culinary gateway to the East Coast. And I was a big fan of a little custard shop between Doylestown and Williams Grove called Peaches & Cream. That's pretty much what they served: custard with fresh peaches, and nothing else. At the end of a long day at the racetrack—heading home with ground-up glass in your hair, pieces of the dirt track in your eye, and a little bit of deafness in both ears—peaches and cream really hit the spot. That's what America's all about, right?

SOUR CHERRY PIE

My mom's side of the family is from Manistee, Michigan, just south of where most of the sour cherries in the States are grown. My mom loves sour cherries, but they were really hard to find in Cleveland, so when we were kids, she used to buy the frozen pre-pitted ones and bake them into pies. In New York, there are lots of small local growers, so you can find them at the Greenmarket when they're in season, but they're only around for a few weeks in early summer. Fresh sour cherries are really something special, and they makes great pies, but if you can't get your hands on them, don't worry about it: the frozen ones work just fine. This pie is great with vanilla ice cream.

MAKES ONE 9-INCH PIE; SERVES 6 TO 8

FOR THE FILLING
1 $\frac{1}{2}$ quarts (6 cups) sour cherries (preferably fresh)
1 $\frac{1}{4}$ cups granulated sugar
3 tablespoons all-purpose flour

FOR THE CRUST
All-purpose flour, for rolling the dough
1 recipe pie dough (see page 266), chilled

TO FINISH THE PIE
1 egg
$\frac{1}{4}$ teaspoon kosher salt
$\frac{1}{2}$ teaspoon granulated sugar
1 tablespoon Demerara sugar or other coarse sugar

TO MAKE THE FILLING
Wash the sour cherries and pit them, dropping them into a large bowl and keeping any juice that lands in the bowl along with them. (Know what's cool about sour cherries? You can pit them with your thumbs.) Save the pits! (See Note.)

Drain any cherry liquid from the pits and pull out any stems that might have ended up in the bowl. Add the liquid to the cherries.

Crush the cherry pits: Lay an old towel on a thick cutting board, put the pits in the middle of the towel, and fold the towel over. Then, with a meat tenderizer or the bottom of a small, heavy saucepot, crush the cherry pits, using the tenderizer or saucepot, as a hammer. It's loud and a little hard to do, but it's worth it, because it lets you get at the amaretto flavor inside the cherry pits. (If you lean in, you'll be able to smell the amaretto as soon as the pits are crushed.)

Wrap the crushed cherry pits in cheesecloth. (You can also put the pits inside a tea ball.)

Pour the cherries into a large pot, add the sugar and the bundle or tea ball of cherry pits, and mix everything together with a wooden spoon.

Add the flour and mix again, so the cherries are coated in the flour.

Cook the cherries over medium heat for about 6 minutes, until the juice—released by the sugar—comes up to a bubble. Then turn the heat to low and let the cherries simmer slowly for about 25 minutes, until the juice thickens up, the cherries cook, and the amaretto flavor from the pits is really released.

Let the cherries cool in the fridge for at least 8 hours, covered, so that they're infused with the cherry pit flavor.

TO MAKE THE PIE CRUST
Flour your work surface. Then take the pie dough out of the fridge. Flour one piece of dough on both sides, and lay it out on the floured surface.

>>>

Using a rolling pin, roll the dough out flat, until it's big enough to lay over your pie pan with some left over for folding under the edge of the pan.

Once the dough is rolled out, roll it over the rolling pin (like you're rolling up a window blind), and then lift it over your pie pan and unroll it. Pat it down into the pan and make sure all the important parts are covered. If you've got too much dough on one part and not enough on another, pull off the overage and reattach it where it's needed, like you're working with clay.

Crimp the edges up above the edge of the pie pan, so you have a thicker edge all the way around above the height of the pan. To make it pretty, lay the index finger of one hand flat on the edge of the dough and then, with the thumb and index finger of your other hand, pinch the edge up right beside it (so you have sort of a wave pattern going, up and down). Repeat, turning the pie pan, around the edge of the pie.

Let the crust chill in the fridge for at least 30 minutes before you go on.

While the crust is in the fridge (and your tabletop is already floury), flour and roll out the second disk of dough in the same way.

Use a pizza cutter or a sharp knife to cut long ½-inch-wide strips of dough for the lattice top; as you cut them, lay them on a baking sheet. You'll need some shorter pieces, too, so don't worry if the rolled-out dough is uneven in length or width. (But be careful not to kill your table or countertop with your blade.) If you have too many pieces for your baking sheet, layer them carefully on top of one another.

Put the baking sheet in the fridge to cool for at least half an hour.

Preheat the oven to 375°F.

When the bottom crust has chilled, lay a piece of parchment paper (or tin foil) over the top of the pie pan and push it down with your fingers so it lines the crust. Fill the crust with pie weights or dried beans.

"Blind bake" the crust—bake it without the actual pie filling inside—for about 25 minutes, until the top edges are just golden and the shape is set (the bottom will still be a little bit soft). This lets you firm up the bottom of the crust before you put the cherries in—otherwise, the crust will go soggy underneath the fruit.

Take the parchment paper and weights out, and put the crust back in the oven for 10 minutes, so it turns golden and firms up. Then pull the crust out of the oven, but leave the oven on. Let the crust cool for 15 minutes or so.

Take the lattice dough out of the fridge.

TO FINISH THE PIE

Whisk together the egg, salt, and granulated sugar in a small bowl.

Take the cherry-pit bundle out of the bowl of filling, and then pour the cherry filling into the pie crust. Use a spatula to spread the cherries and juice evenly across the crust.

Top the pie with the lattice: Lay 5 evenly spaced strips across the width of the pie, and then take 2 of the 5 strips—numbers 2 and 4 if you're counting across—and fold them back over themselves in half. Then lay 1 strip in the other direction across the pie, and fold the 2 folded-back strips down again over that strip. Fold the other 3 original strips back, put down another strip across crosswise, and fold the 3 strips down again, and so forth until you've finished half the pie. Then turn the pie and repeat with the other half. Basically, you're weaving. Pinch the ends of the strips to the rim of the pie.

Using a pastry brush (or a small spoon), brush the egg wash over the lattice; then sprinkle the coarse sugar on top.

Put the pie pan on a rimmed baking sheet (to catch any spillage), and put the pie on the middle oven rack (still at 375°F). Keep an eye on your pie. You don't want the top to burn while the rest of the pie bakes, so if the top edge starts to really darken up, use a pie shield, or lay a piece of foil loosely on top.

When the cherry filling is bubbling and thick and the lattice is golden brown (about 1 1/4 hours, depending on your oven), take the pie out of the oven and let it cool before you cut into it (otherwise, it will fall apart).

NOTE

This recipe calls for crushing up the cherry pits to bring out the amaretto flavor inside. This is actually a very old technique: I found it in a Fannie Farmer cookbook published a hundred years ago. If you really want to skip that step (or you're working with frozen cherries without pits), you can always add a teaspoon of almond extract—but it's pretty amazing how the crushed cherry pits really do give the pie a very cool almond flavor.

SOUR ORANGE PIE

Sour orange juice is a big ingredient in Caribbean cooking; I think it's delicious. It's tough to find sour oranges up north, and there's no real commercial sour orange juice, but down south, where the sour orange trees actually grow, it's pretty popular. My grandma had a sour orange tree in her yard, and she used to make sour orange pie instead of Key lime pie. You can top this pie with a Key lime-style meringue if you want, or you can just serve it up with a scoop of sweetened whipped cream on top.

MAKES ONE 10-INCH PIE; SERVES 8

FOR THE CRUST
$1/2$ stick (4 tablespoons) unsalted butter
9 graham crackers (1 sleeve)
$1/4$ cup dark brown sugar
1 tablespoon all-purpose flour
$1/2$ teaspoon kosher salt
2 ounces white chocolate ($1/2$ cup)

FOR THE FILLING
Very finely grated zest of 2 oranges
Very finely grated zest of 1 lemon
Juice of 1 orange ($1/4$ cup), or $1/4$ cup good-quality store-bought orange juice (see Note)
Juice of 3 to 5 lemons ($3/4$ cup)
$1 1/2$ cups granulated sugar
$1 1/2$ sticks (12 tablespoons) unsalted butter
4 large eggs
4 large egg yolks
1 teaspoon kosher salt

TO MAKE THE CRUST
Preheat the oven to 350°F.

Melt the butter in a small pot over medium heat.

Meanwhile, break the graham crackers up into large pieces, and grind them to a powder in a food processor; you should have $1 1/2$ cups.

In a large mixing bowl, combine the graham cracker powder, brown sugar, flour, salt, and melted butter. Mix everything together with your fingers until you end up with small pebbles.

Add 1 tablespoon of warm water, and mix everything together with your hands. You want to end up with dough the consistency of wet sand, so that it sticks together when you squeeze a handful.

Pour the dough into a pie pan, and spread it over the entire surface, pressing it down on the bottom and against the sides. Make an even outside edge by pressing with your fingers all the way around. (What you see is what you get here: if you put a smooth, even crust in the oven, that's what you'll end up with, so you want to get rid of any bumps or lumps now.)

Put the pie pan on the middle oven rack and bake the dough, uncovered, for 10 minutes. Then rotate the pan (to make sure everything bakes evenly) and let the crust bake for another 10 minutes, until it's golden brown and firm and smells yummy.

While the crust is baking, melt the white chocolate in a double boiler—or in a bowl set over a pot of hot water, or in a microwave on a low setting (checking it every few seconds). White chocolate burns really easily, so you need to melt it super-gently.

When the crust comes out of the oven, use a spoon to spread the white chocolate over the surface, smoothing it out with your fingers. Make sure you leave a gap at the top edge—you don't want the white chocolate to show over the filling. You want to do this while the white chocolate and the crust are both still warm, so the white chocolate spreads easily and doesn't set up and harden too fast. The chocolate will act as a sealant, to stop the crust from going soggy when you pour in the filling (it keeps the crust really crisp even after it's finished baking, so when you take the pie out of the fridge the day after you make it, you don't have sogginess). Set aside the crust to cool.

TO MAKE THE FILLING AND BAKE THE PIE

Preheat the oven to 325°F.

Zest the oranges and lemons, using a microplane grater if you've got one—you want the zest to be as fine as possible.

Squeeze the orange through a sieve into a measuring cup to make sure you've got the right amount of juice. Do the same with the lemons.

Combine the orange and lemon zest, the orange and lemon juice, 1 cup of the sugar, and the butter in a medium-sized saucepot. Stir everything together, and cook the mixture over medium heat for about 4 minutes, until the butter melts.

Whisk everything together again, and keep cooking, whisking frequently, for about 6 minutes, until the mixture boils up and the white-yellow layer that forms on the top has mostly boiled away (it's just like you're clarifying butter). The liquid will turn caramel-colored.

While the citrus mixture is cooking, whisk together the eggs, yolks, the remaining $1/2$ cup sugar, and the salt in a large mixing bowl.

When the citrus mixture is ready, pour it slowly into the egg mixture. Whisk everything together well.

Strain the mixture through a fine-mesh sieve into a large mixing bowl, using a spoon to push the liquid through but leaving most of the zest in the sieve. The liquid will be bright egg-yellow.

Pour the liquid filling into the pie crust (but don't overfill it). Put the pie pan on a baking sheet, and set it on the middle oven rack. (Be careful when you transfer it to the oven!)

Let the pie bake for about 35 minutes; it's done when the filling firms up, so it jiggles but isn't liquid anymore, and it bubbles on the outside edge.

Let the pie cool completely before you cut into it. It's good at room temperature, but you can keep it in the fridge and serve it cold, too—it holds pretty well for a day or so.

NOTE

Here I've faked the flavor by combining orange juice and lemon juice. (If you happen to have a sour orange tree growing in *your* yard, squeeze in 1 cup of the juice instead.)

PIE DOUGH

....

People think that pie dough is hard to make right, but it's really all about two things: cold water and mixing. My mom taught me that in one of my very first cooking lessons, when I was about eight years old. Mom's trick was to pour some cold water from the tap into in a bowl, and then to add one ice cube to chill the water down. And when it comes to mixing, the answer is: Don't have the fear. Do it more. Really well-mixed dough is easier to work with, and it bakes up nice and flaky.

MAKES ENOUGH FOR ONE 8- TO 10-INCH DOUBLE-CRUST PIE

3 cups unbleached all-purpose flour
1 tablespoon granulated sugar
1 1/2 teaspoons kosher salt
2 sticks (1 cup) cold unsalted butter, cut into small pieces
1/2 cup cold lard (or vegetable shortening)

Pour 1/2 cup of cold water into a bowl and add 1 ice cube.

Combine the flour, sugar, and salt in a large mixing bowl. Add the butter and lard, and break them down with a pastry cutter or a fork, pressing and cutting and working hard, until the flour begins to look wet. You'll still be able to see some separate pieces of butter and lard.

Add the ice water, pouring the water evenly across the dough.

Keep working the dough, using your hands to knead it: push it together, turn it, fold it, push it together, and so on. If the dough isn't coming together, add a bit more water, a teaspoon at a time. But if you're finding a nice dough is forming under your hands, don't add more water—especially since once you put it in the fridge, the moisture in the dough will disperse and the dough will get a bit wetter. (Dough is really weather-sensitive. If it's a humid day, you may need a little less water; if it's superdry out, you may need a little more.) The dough is ready when it's come together well and forms a smooth ball or mass.

Divide the dough in half. Flatten each piece out into a disk; then wrap each dough disk in plastic wrap, pressing down to flatten it more and to get the plastic wrap to adhere. (If the dough is chilled flat instead of in a ball, you'll have less hard work to do later—rolling out cold dough is much harder than working with warm dough.) One of these disks will be the top crust and one will be the bottom crust.

Chill the dough down in the fridge for at least 1 hour—if you can let it cool overnight (8 hours or so), that's ideal. (The dough can be frozen for up to 1 month. Thaw it out in the fridge overnight before you use it.)

ON THE ROAD WITH DAD AND VINCE

In 1995, my brother and my dad and I decided we were going to drive cross-country. We plotted it out on the map when I was home for Christmas: Cleveland to Cali, four weeks to make it across and back in my dad's brown '87 Beauville van with 197,000 miles on it. It was going to be great. Epic. Unparalleled.

Our very first food stop set the tone for the way things were going to go. My dad is a big fan of speed: once he's on the road, all he can think about is getting to where we're getting to. None of this "the journey is the destination" crap for him, even when the journey is really supposed to be the destination, as in: when you decide to drive cross-country with your kids for no particular reason. Not me. I am a wanderin' man. I wanted to explore, to get out of the car and be with the people. Basically, I wanted to eat. I was all about getting off the highway to find the local restaurant of my dreams: a place serving the best burgers and homemade ice cream and hot-out-of-the-oven biscuits in the whole wide world. I wanted Midwestern manna.

When I spotted a little worn-out joint with an old-school sign off the highway in Morris, Illinois, between Chicago and the Iowa border, I was sure I'd found the real thing. My dad and my brother were not interested. They wanted to go to Cracker Barrel, right off the highway, where you get two country vegetables with your pork chop or sugar-cured ham, plus Homemade Buttermilk Biscuits or Corn Muffins with real butter!

I told them no. I told them we were going to have an authentic experience. Because that's what we were here to do. That was *the whole point.*

My brother said, throwing up his hands, "Okay, dude, it's all you." My dad said something unprintable and threw the van into park. We headed into the cafe.

Inside, it was more truck stop than local cafe: Formica tabletops, wood paneling, impatient waitresses. The place was full, crowded with locals and truckers. That was a good omen, I thought: they say truckers know where the best food is, right?

And anyway, it had that old-school sign. No place with a sign like that could be anything but authentic.

The menu was definitely old-school roadside. My dad and my brother went straight for the burgers and fries, but I wanted to show them what culinary authenticity was all about. So I ordered chipped beef on toast. I'd never had it before, but it sounded very American to me: wheat and beef, the Midwest in a dish. I imagined thick slices of toast, topped with brown and glistening beef wedges and dripping with gravy, real elemental American comfort food.

My dad and my brother got preformed formerly frozen beef patties on formerly frozen white-bread buns, with formerly frozen fries on the side and a bottle of Heinz for decoration. I got a sticky cornstarch-based brownish stew poured over a couple of pieces of toasted Wonder bread, with instant potatoes on the side.

For the next hundred miles or so, I learned all the different ways two guys can say, "I told you, dude!"

Then, as we crossed the Mississippi into Davenport, Iowa, and just when I was thinking about poking a sharp pencil in my ears to make it stop: sweet vindication. Right there, by the side of the road, there was a car, trunk open, and a sign that looked like it might have been written by a third-grader. On the sign, two words. HOMEMADE PIES. I twisted the wheel hard and got us off the freeway before my dad or my brother could hand up any kind of opinion.

The Pie Lady of Davenport was a cheerful blond housewife-type, wholesome and vaguely Amish-looking, standing tall beside the trunk of her brown '76 Cutlass Ciera, under a pink picnic umbrella she'd rigged up for herself. She wore a dress with puffy white sleeves and a high neck and a flower print, and over it she wore an apron reading IOWA GROWN FOR GOODNESS. Inside that trunk was pure America: rhubarb-strawberry pies, sour cherry pies, sweet berry pies . . . She had a cash box and a folding chair and a sweet Midwestern accent, and I was so happy I wanted to cry. I wanted to tell her I loved her.

Those pies got us through the next five hundred miles of driving. My dad said they weren't as good as my mom's pies, and he was probably right—but since my mom wasn't standing beside a '76 Cutlass Ciera on a secondary road outside Davenport, Iowa, the Pie Lady was fine with me.

STRAWBERRY-RHUBARB FOOL

Fool is a great meet-the-parents dessert: it looks really impressive and beautiful when you present it in those individual glasses, but it's actually super-easy to put together. You can make fool with any kind of seasonal fruit combo, but my favorite is the classic sweet-sour mix of strawberry and rhubarb. It's grown-up and yummy at the same time: you just can't go wrong with this one.

I use white balsamic vinegar here. That's pastry princess extraordinaire Karen DeMasco's idea: she says it's a little softer than regular balsamic. If you can't find it, you can sub out ordinary balsamic vinegar, though it might change the color and sharpen up the flavor a little bit. If you can't get your hands on any gingersnaps, you can use any kind of sweet crunchy cookie, like Italian amaretti or even Nilla Wafers.

SERVES 6

FOR THE CREAM MIXTURE

$1/2$ pound rhubarb (about 3 to 4 medium-sized stalks), washed, ends removed, and cut into 2-inch pieces

$1/2$ pint ($1/4$ pound) strawberries, washed, stems removed, and halved

$1/4$ cup plus 2 tablespoons sugar

1 cup heavy cream

$1/4$ cup buttermilk

FOR THE STRAWBERRY COMPOTE

2 pints (1 pound) strawberries, washed, stems removed, and halved

2 $1/4$ teaspoons sugar

$3/4$ teaspoon white balsamic vinegar

FOR FINISHING THE DISH

About 1 dozen gingersnap cookies, crumbled

TO MAKE THE CREAM

Combine the rhubarb and strawberries in a medium-sized mixing bowl. Pour the sugar over the fruit and toss everything together with a wooden spoon and your hands, so the fruit is coated with sugar. (You want the sugar to draw the juices out of the fruit.)

Let the fruit sit in a warm place, covered with plastic wrap, for at least an hour, so it begins to macerate. (You can also cover it and leave it overnight in the fridge.) You should end up with at least $1/2$ cup of liquid in the bowl.

Scrape the strawberries, rhubarb, and juice into a medium-sized pot. Cook the fruit over medium heat, stirring regularly to keep everything from sticking, for about 7 minutes, until it softens up, cooks down, and gives off a lot more liquid. The strawberries should be very soft but not falling apart, and the rhubarb should be tender.

Pour the fruit mixture into a blender. Blend for about 45 seconds, starting on low and working up to a high speed, until everything is smooth and well combined (the fruit mix should look like warm sorbet).

Open the blender, scrape down the sides to make sure all the stringy rhubarb bits are in the mix, and then blend again for 15 seconds or so.

Pour the fruit puree into a bowl and cool it down in the freezer for about 45 minutes, until it's completely chilled. Open the freezer and stir the fruit mix every so often to make sure it cools evenly.

Meanwhile, whip the cream and buttermilk in the bowl of a tabletop mixer fitted with the whisk attachment on medium speed (#4 on a KitchenAid). Whip the cream for about 8 minutes, until it's thick and holds a soft peak. (You can do this by hand, but it will take at least 15 minutes and a really strong wrist.)

TO MAKE THE STRAWBERRY COMPOTE

In a large mixing bowl, mix the strawberries, sugar, and vinegar so that the fruit is coated in the sugar-vinegar mix.

Cover the bowl with plastic wrap and leave it on the countertop for at least 10 minutes, until the sugar dissolves.

TO FINISH THE DISH

When the strawberry-rhubarb puree has cooled, take it out of the freezer and fold about one third of the whipped cream into it with a rubber spatula, so that the mixture looks like swirled ice cream.

Mix in the rest of the whipped cream, so that what you've got looks like marbled ice cream.

Set out 6 highball glasses (or small bowls). Scoop a couple of spoonfuls of the cream-fruit mixture into each glass; layer a couple of spoonfuls of the strawberry compote on top; and then add a layer of crumbled gingersnaps. Repeat the layers until you reach the top of the glass.

Chill the fool in the fridge until you're ready to serve it.

FYI

I call rhubarb a fruit here, and that is not a mistake. It's true that in the rest of the world, the long red stalk is considered a vegetable, but here in the U.S. of A., we actually had a court case on this important question. Vegetables lost: rhubarb is officially an American fruit.

MEXICAN BAKED APPLES WITH ANCHO CARAMEL

This recipe has got kind of a North-South thing going on. Baked apples are seriously old-school American, and apples are so good with spices and raisins. Know what else is good with apples? Chile powder. So I figured, why not put it all together? You get the fruity sweetness from the baked apple, plus some spice and bite and savoriness (and a little crunchiness) from the filling. The ancho chile is the unexpected taste here—you get just a flash of heat to kick things up. If you want to hit every flavor contrast going, serve this with vanilla ice cream or whipped cream. But remember to peel the apples: you don't want to end up with that leathery baked-apple skin.

SERVES 6

FOR THE CARAMEL
1/2 cup sugar
1 tablespoon unsalted butter
1 teaspoon ancho chile powder

FOR THE FILLING
1/2 cup pine nuts
1/2 cup golden raisins
2 teaspoons ancho chile powder
2 teaspoons ground cinnamon
1/2 teaspoon ground allspice
1/2 teaspoon kosher salt
1 teaspoon vanilla extract
1/4 cup dark brown sugar

FOR THE APPLES
6 baking apples (I like Crispin, Pink Lady, or Granny Smith)

TO MAKE THE CARAMEL
Pour the sugar into a small saucepan and add just enough water to dampen it—about 1/3 cup—so you've got a sandy consistency. (If any of the sugar is completely dry, it will burn before it melts.)

Cook the sugar over medium-high heat, letting it bubble, for about 10 minutes, until it turns a golden caramel color. It will bubble less as the water boils off and the caramel starts to color. You don't want the sugar in one part of the pan to get dark before the rest, so keep a careful eye as the color starts to change. If the sugar in one area of the pan starts to change color before the rest, whisk that part in so that the caramel cooks evenly. To see if the sugar is ready, stir the whisk in the pot and then hold it up and let a little caramelizing sugar drip off. The color should be gold; in the pot, it may look more golden brown.

Pull the pan from the heat and whisk in the butter and chile powder. (The butter will stop the sugar's cooking process.)

Pour the caramel into the cups of a 6-cup muffin tin.

TO MAKE THE FILLING
Toast the pine nuts in a dry sauté pan over low heat until they've just turned golden brown, keeping a close eye on them and shaking them around every few seconds so they don't burn.

Combine the pine nuts and all the other filling ingredients in a food processor fitted with the steel blade. Pulse until you have a coarse crumb (about 15 seconds).

Preheat the oven to 400°F.

Peel and core the apples.

Put the apples, top side down, over the caramel in the cups of the muffin tin.

Cover the bottom of a roasting pan with tin foil (there's a lot of sticky splatter here and you don't want to wreck your pan). Put the muffin tin in the roasting pan and cover the pan tightly with tin foil. Put the roasting pan on the middle oven rack, and bake the apples for 25 minutes.

Use a pair of tongs and a soup spoon to turn each apple in the muffin cup, spinning and lifting so that the top of the apple is now facing up.

Fill each apple core with 2 to 3 tablespoons of the filling, tamping it down a little—but not too firmly—as you go. The filling should spill over the top a little bit. Then put the roasting pan back in the oven, uncovered this time, and bake for another 15 minutes, or until the apples are soft on the outside when you poke them (they shouldn't be soft all the way through—you don't want them turning to mush) and they've turned golden brown wherever there's caramel.

Pull the roasting pan out of the oven and let it sit for about 5 minutes, so the apples cool and set up a little. Then pull the apples out of the muffin tin, using a spoon and your fingers, and put them on a plate.

Scoop out a little bit of the liquid and filling left in the bottom of each muffin cup, and pour it over the apples. Serve them warm.

CHEF'S TIP

. . . .

The caramel pot will be really tough to clean. Fill it with water, put it back on the stove, bring the water up to a boil, and let the caramel cook off the sides before you try to wash it.

PINEAPPLE-GINGER ICE

Shaved ice is an old-school New York thing. In my neighborhood, when the weather gets hot, you still see the guys with the carts, handing out little paper cups of shaved ice topped with syrup in crazy-bright colors. But the mecca of shaved ice, in my opinion, is actually nowhere near New York (sorry, Corona Ice King): it's in Hawaii. The north shore of the island of Oahu is legendary surf country, and the town of Haleiwa is right in the middle of the action. The heart of the action *off* the beach? That would be Matsumoto Shave Ice, an olden-days general store that just happens to have what Hawaiians call a "shave ice" machine in the back. The machine runs all day long, shaving ice off huge blocks; when you get to the front of the line, you pick your flavor, and the guy behind the counter pours it over some ice and hands you a cup of icy deliciousness. You can get all the regular flavors (lemon, vanilla), plus Asian-fusion stuff (red beans, *li hing mui*—salty red plum), and some Island flavors, like coconut cream and "Hawaiian special." The place is almost as big an attraction as the beach; there's always a long line of people snaking through the store, surfers and locals and tourists, all waiting patiently, jammed in between the racks of sunglasses and the potato chips. No surprise: shave ice is the perfect snack on a hot Hawaiian afternoon. So I figured: what's good for Oahu must be good for a sticky-hot New York City summer, right? It's fast and easy, and it's got the kind of bright, intense flavors that cool you down fast: it's a real flavor bomb of a frozen dessert.

SERVES 6

½ medium-sized pineapple, trimmed, peeled, and cubed
¼ cup sugar
One 12-ounce bottle very gingery ginger beer (I like Fentimans)

Put the pineapple cubes in a blender. Starting on low and working your way up to high speed, blend for 30 seconds or so, until you have a thick puree.

Spoon the pineapple puree into a medium-sized mixing bowl. Whisk in the sugar; then slowly pour in the ginger beer. Whisk everything together.

Put the pineapple mixture in the freezer and let it freeze for at least 2 hours, until it's pretty solid. If you want to speed up the freezing process, you can pour the puree into a pie pan or a rimmed baking sheet, but be careful: it will slosh around and things can get messy.

When the puree is frozen, use a bench scraper or a knife to break it into ice-cube-sized pieces. Put these in a food processor fitted with the steel blade, and puree until there are no big chunks left.

You can serve the ice right away or store it in an airtight container in the freezer. Scoop it out like ice cream. You can even serve it in little paper cups, if you're feeling it.

TOASTED COCONUT CAKE

On our drives to Florida, we used to stop at a place in DeLand called Holiday House—a standard Southern meat-and-three kind of cafeteria. You chose your meat at the top of the cafeteria line—roast beef, fried chicken, pork chops—and then you walked down the line with your tray to pick out your sides. They had all the Southern standards: green beans, mashed potatoes, sweet potatoes, biscuits, collard greens, coleslaw, potato salad. The savory food was OK, but the real good stuff was at the end of the line. Holiday House is where I fell hard for coconut cake.

The stuff they served up on those little chilled cafeteria plates was the traditional Southern-style coconut cake, with lots of thin layers of frosting. Here we do something a little bit different: just two thick layers of meringue-style frosting, with some toasted coconut on the outside layer. It's just the way I like it.

MAKES A TWO-LAYER 8-INCH CAKE;
SERVES 8 TO 10

FOR THE TOASTED COCONUT
$^3/_4$ cup sweetened flaked coconut

FOR THE CAKE LAYERS
1 stick (8 tablespoons) unsalted butter, at room temperature, cut into $^1/_2$-inch pieces; plus 1 tablespoon unsalted butter, at room temperature, for greasing the cake pans
4 tablespoons all-purpose flour
$^3/_4$ cup plus 2 tablespoons sugar
Half of a 15-ounce can of sweetened cream of coconut (I like Coco Lopez)
2 eggs, separated
1 $^1/_4$ cups plus 2 tablespoons cake flour
$^1/_2$ teaspoon baking powder
$^1/_4$ teaspoon baking soda
$^3/_4$ teaspoon kosher salt

$^1/_2$ cup buttermilk
$^1/_2$ teaspoon vanilla extract
$^1/_2$ cup Malibu rum

FOR THE FROSTING
2 cups sugar
$^1/_4$ cup light corn syrup
3 large egg whites
1 teaspoon vanilla extract
2 teaspoons coconut extract
1 $^1/_2$ teaspoons kosher salt

TO FINISH THE CAKE
$^1/_4$ cup sweetened flaked coconut

TO TOAST THE COCONUT
Preheat the oven to 350°F.

Line a baking sheet with a piece of parchment paper.

Shake the coconut onto the parchment paper, and spread it out evenly with your hands.

Toast the coconut on the middle oven rack for about 8 minutes, until it turns golden. Once the coconut starts to brown on the edges, move it around with your fingers every couple of minutes, so the outside pieces don't burn before the stuff in the middle is done. Keep an eye on the coconut—once it starts to color, it goes fast.

Pull the baking sheet out of the oven and set it on the counter to cool. You'll want to let the coconut cool to room temperature before you work with it.

TO MAKE THE CAKE LAYERS
Preheat the oven to 350°F.

Butter the bottom and sides of two 8-inch cake pans (preferably springform). Then dust the pans with the flour: Put 2 tablespoons of the flour into one buttered pan and shake it around. Hold the pan on its side over the sink, and tap it so the excess flour shakes out. Do the same with the second pan.

Combine the butter pieces, sugar, and cream of coconut in the bowl of a tabletop mixer fitted with the paddle attachment, and mix starting on low speed (#2 on a KitchenAid) and moving up to medium (#4 on a KitchenAid). After 30 seconds to a minute, when the mix is light and fluffy, stop the mixer and scrape down the sides of the bowl.

Turn the mixer back on, and with the mixer running, add the yolks of the 2 eggs (hold on to the egg whites for now). Keep mixing for 5 to 7 minutes, until everything is well combined and light and fluffy.

Meanwhile, in a medium-sized bowl, whisk together the cake flour, baking powder, baking soda, and salt. (You can also sift them, but that takes more time and equipment, and whisking accomplishes the same thing.)

Measure the buttermilk into a liquid measuring cup, and add the vanilla extract. (It will be much easier to pour this way.)

Turn the mixer speed down to low, and pour in one-third of the flour mixture, then one-third of the buttermilk, then another one-third of the flour, and so on until all the flour and buttermilk has been mixed in.

Stop the mixer, scrape down the sides, and then mix everything again until the batter is well mixed and emulsified.

Pour the batter into a clean bowl. Then wash the mixer bowl really well (if there's any fat left in the bowl at all, the egg whites won't whip up in the next step).

Put the egg whites in the mixing bowl, and using the whisk attachment, whip the eggs for about 8 minutes, until they form a meringue. You want to start the mixer on low (#2 on a KitchenAid), and then, once

the eggs start to bubble, move it to medium (#4 on a KitchenAid): meringues are better when you build them slowly, because they have a more stable structure. When the meringue is almost formed—when the egg whites have turned translucent and have begun to have some structure—turn the mixer up to high for the last few seconds. The meringue is done when it holds a soft peak: when you scoop out a little bit, it won't stand straight up, but instead slumps over a bit without breaking.

Fold the meringue gently into the batter, using a spatula. (This lightens up the batter a little bit.)

Using the spatula, pour the batter into the 2 cake pans, dividing it evenly. Smooth the batter out with the spatula. Then put the cake pans on a baking sheet (this makes it easier to turn the cakes and stops bits from dropping and burning on the bottom of the oven). Put the sheet on the middle oven rack, and bake the cake layers for 25 minutes.

Rotate the cakes and bake them for about 20 minutes more, until the tops are golden brown and the cake is a little bit springy to the touch.

While the cake layers are still warm, release them from the springform pans if you used them, or turn them out of your cake pans onto a baking sheet, and use a pastry brush (or a spoon) to brush and pat the tops of the layers with the Malibu rum. You want the cakes to soak up as much of the rum as possible.

Let the cake layers cool to room temperature for an hour or so before you frost and finish them.

TO MAKE THE FROSTING
When the cake layers have almost completely cooled, preheat the oven to 375°F.

>>>

Pour the sugar and corn syrup into a small saucepot. Add 1/2 cup of water (enough to make sure that there are no dry pockets of sugar—those will burn before everything else cooks), and gently mix and scrape everything together with a spatula, making sure you've left no dry sugar in the mix or sugar crystals on the sides of the pot above the water level.

If you have a candy thermometer, attach it to the side of the pot now. Then cook the sugar mix over medium-high heat for about 10 minutes. The mixture will steam, bubble low, and then start to bubble up high as the water boils off (about 5 minutes in). It's ready when the water reduces, the volume of the bubbling slows down a little, and the bubbles get bigger. The temperature should read 242°F on a candy thermometer. (If you let the sugar get too hot, it will color, and it will harden into a ball when you add it to the egg whites.)

Meanwhile, as soon as you put the sugar on, put the egg whites in the bowl of a tabletop mixer fitted with the whisk attachment. Whisk the egg whites on low speed throughout the time that the sugar's cooking. (The whisk attachment doesn't reach the egg whites on my KitchenAid, so I don't screw it in all the way; since the mixer's on low, the attachment works fine.)

When the sugar is ready, turn the speed on the mixer up to medium (#4 on a KitchenAid), and pour the sugar mixture slowly down the side of the mixing bowl as the whisk runs. (If you loosened your whisk, screw it in tightly now!)

Add the vanilla, coconut extract, and salt. Turn the speed up to medium-high (#6 on a KitchenAid) and keep mixing for 5 minutes or so, until you have a thick, glossy white mixture. You want to get the frosting on the cake while it's still warm.

TO FINISH THE CAKE

Frost the cake as soon as the frosting is ready—if you leave the frosting sitting around, it will thicken up and you won't be able to work with it. With the cake layers still on the baking sheet, put about half of the frosting onto the middle of one layer with a spatula (an offset spatula's great if you have one). Spread the frosting out so the cake is thickly covered.

Sprinkle the toasted coconut over the top of the frosted layer.

Flip the second cake layer on top of the first layer, using the springform pan bottom to lift it (if you aren't using a springform, lift the cake carefully, using the largest lifting implement you've got). Then put the rest of the frosting on the top layer and spread it out evenly. Use the spatula to make the top ridged and pretty.

Sprinkle the 1/4 cup unbaked coconut over the top of the layer cake.

Put the cake back in the oven on the middle oven rack and let it bake for about 10 to 12 minutes. You want to just toast the top, so the coconut browns up and the frosting colors a little, but you don't want the frosting—or the coconut—to burn, so keep an eye on things.

Pull the cake out of the oven. You can serve it as soon as it's cool enough to handle; you can let it cool down to room temperature; it's even great the next day, if you store it in the fridge under a cake cover.

CHEF'S TIP

....

Don't make the frosting until the cakes are ready for it. The frosting sets up as soon as it cools, and you want to be able to spread it nice and thick while it's still warm.

POTICA

Potica, an Eastern European coffee cake, is a classic in my family. Every Christmas and Easter, my mom makes five or six poticas and gives them out to relatives; then, if I'm coming home, she makes a whole other batch. I have a pretty intense relationship with potica: I have to have it every December or it's just not Christmas. I eat it for breakfast with a cup of coffee, at lunch with whipped cream, after dinner with ice cream from Honey Hut, Cleveland's finest . . . there's basically no time of day or night when potica isn't a good idea.

There are about a thousand potica recipes around; my mom's been tweaking hers for years. Some versions bake the potica in squares or in long flat rolls, but my mom's is baked in a Bundt pan. It's really good when it's fresh-baked, but some people think it's even better a day later; it keeps pretty well stored in a cake keeper on the countertop.

MAKES ONE IO-INCH BUNDT CAKE;
SERVES I6 IF NOBODY STEALS EXTRA PIECES

FOR THE DOUGH
2 sticks (1 cup) unsalted butter, plus a little extra for
   greasing the resting bowl
1/2 cup cold whole milk
4 1/2 teaspoons active dry yeast
3 tablespoons sugar
3 egg yolks
3 cups all-purpose flour
1 teaspoon kosher salt

FOR THE FILLING
1 1/2 cups walnuts
3/4 cup dried pitted dates
3 egg whites
1 cup plus 3 tablespoons sugar
1/4 cup whole milk
1 teaspoon ground cinnamon

TO FINISH THE POTICA
1/2 cup all-purpose flour, for working the dough
1 tablespoon unsalted butter, at room temperature,
   for the pan

TO MAKE THE DOUGH
Cut the 2 sticks of butter into cubes (so it melts faster) and melt it in a small saucepan over medium heat (about 3 minutes).

Remove the pan from the heat and whisk in the cold milk, so that the butter cools down a little. Pour the mixture into a large mixing bowl.

Put the yeast in a medium-sized mixing bowl, and add 1/4 cup of warm water and 1 tablespoon of the sugar to activate the yeast. Whisk everything together until there are no lumps.

Separate the eggs and put the whites aside—you'll need them for the filling. Add the yolks to the butter mixture and whisk everything together.

Pour the butter-egg mixture into the yeast mixture, and whisk everything together.

Pour the flour, the remaining 2 tablespoons sugar, and the salt into a large mixing bowl (if the one the eggs and butter were in is your largest bowl, wash it before you start!). Mix everything together gently with a rubber spatula. Then use the spatula to make a well—an open space—in the center of the bowl.

Pour the egg-butter-yeast mixture into the well. The well is a good way of incorporating the wet into the dry: pull in a little bit of flour, mix, then add a bit more, until everything is incorporated.

When everything comes together, knead the dough with your hands inside the bowl until it forms a thick, flattish disk.

>>>

4

5

6

10

14

15

Grease another bowl with the extra butter, put the dough in it, cover the bowl with plastic wrap, and let it chill in the fridge for at least 3 hours. (You can do this a day ahead, but don't let the dough sit for longer than 24 hours—after that, your yeast will start to die.)

TO MAKE THE FILLING
Preheat the oven to 350°F.

Spread the walnuts out on a baking sheet so that they aren't overlapping, and bake them in the oven until they release a toasty aroma (about 10 minutes, depending on your oven). Then pull them out of the oven and let them cool on the countertop till you're able to handle them.

Pour the dates and walnuts into a food processor fitted with the steel blade, and pulse until they're reduced to pebble-sized pieces (about 10 seconds). Keep an eye on things: walnuts have a bad habit of turning into butter if you overgrind them, especially when they're warm. Set the date-nut mixture aside.

Put the reserved egg whites in the bowl of a tabletop mixer, and whip them with the whisk attachment on a low setting (#2 on a KitchenAid) until you can't see the bottom of the bowl anymore and the eggs are white and bubbly but still liquid (about 1 minute).

Turn the speed up to medium (#4 on a KitchenAid), add 1 cup of the sugar, and then turn the speed up to medium-high (#8 on a KitchenAid). Let the egg whites and sugar whip together for about 6 minutes, until the whites have formed a meringue and are very white and thick and sticky-looking: when you pull some out with a spoon, it should hold its shape. Don't worry about overwhipping: meringues with this much sugar cannot be whipped too much.

Meanwhile, combine the milk, cinnamon, and the remaining 3 tablespoons sugar in a medium-sized pot. Stir everything together gently with a rubber spatula, making sure no cinnamon is left on the sides of the pot (it will burn and flavor everything). Then set the pot over low heat, add the date-walnut mixture, and mix everything together gently. Let it cook for about 1 minute, until the mixture forms a thick, nutty paste.

Spoon the date-nut-milk paste into a large mixing bowl.

Using a rubber spatula, fold about one third of the meringue into the date-walnut mixture so it lightens up a bit. Then spoon in the rest of the meringue and mix everything together well.

TO FINISH THE POTICA
Flour a work surface.

Take the dough out of the fridge, unwrap it, and cut it in half. Put one half back in the fridge. (You want to work with the dough right out of the fridge; it's easier when it's cold.) Sprinkle flour over the top of the other half and use a rolling pin to roll it out into a big rectangle (about 20 x 15 inches), flouring the work surface and the dough as you go so it doesn't stick. You want the dough to be as thin as possible without tearing. This dough is pretty durable, so you can really work it.

Grease the inside of a Bundt pan, using your hands to spread the butter around evenly and make sure everything is covered.

Pour half of the filling onto the middle of the dough. Spread it across the dough with an offset spatula or a rubber spatula, leaving about an inch bare on the top and bottom but working all the way out to the edges on the long sides. The filling should be nice and smooth.

Starting at the bottom, roll the dough—with the filling inside—as tightly as you can, keeping the roll even across its width. Patch any holes that appear with little bits from the other half of the dough.

Fit the rolled dough into the bottom of the Bundt pan, wrapping it around the center with the seam side up (so that when you flip the potica out of the pan later, the seam isn't on top).

Repeat the rolling-out, filling, and rolling-up process with the second half of the dough. Lay the rolled-up dough over the first roll in the Bundt pan, with the seam side down (to prevent leaks). Then cover the Bundt pan tightly with plastic wrap.

Turn the oven on to 350°F to preheat, then put the potica on top of the stove (away from the vent, so it doesn't crust up and cook) or in another warm place,

and leave it to rise for about 45 minutes, until the dough is higher than the rim of the pan.

Preheat the oven to 350°F.

Pull the plastic wrap off the Bundt pan, put the pan on a baking sheet (to protect the cake from scorching on the bottom), and put it on the middle oven rack. Bake the potica for 30 minutes.

Rotate the baking sheet and bake the potica for another 30 minutes, until the top is a deep golden brown and, when you tap it with flat fingers, it's firm and sounds almost hollow, like a drum.

Pull the potica out of the oven and set it aside to cool for about 10 minutes, until you can handle it. Then invert a big plate over the Bundt pan, and flip the pan and plate together so the potica slides out onto the plate. You can serve this while it's still warm; it's great with coffee.

ROOT BEER CAKE

My life is all about banging things out, getting things done, moving fast—but sometimes a detour from the fast lane can be a good thing, even for me. Years ago, Gwen and I were on our way home from a road trip to the Canadian Maritimes when we were forced off the highway by some epic construction. We ended up on a wandering road that took us through a charming series of dying industrial towns. There was not much to see . . . and definitely nothing to eat. But then, in Fall River, Massachusetts, right at the border of Rhode Island, we stumbled across culinary gold: an old gas station converted into a root beer stand. The owner, a retired A&W root beer guy, was behind the counter; all he served was root beer in frosted glasses. Our root beer came with a long lecture about chilling the glass, not the root beer itself (that kills the taste). We sat at a broken-down old picnic table and sipped. I'm all about root beer, and that roadside glassful was the best I ever tasted. This recipe is my stab at bringing that taste to cake—because the only thing better than root beer is root beer plus cake.

There's a mad-scientist component to this recipe: when you whisk the baking soda into the molasses and root beer, there's going to be some crazy bubbling up going on, straight out of sci-fi. Don't worry: it's completely normal.

MAKES ONE 10-INCH CAKE; SERVES 8

FOR THE CAKE

1 tablespoon unsalted butter, at room temperature, for the pan
1 1/2 cups plus 1 tablespoon all-purpose flour
One 12-ounce bottle (1 1/4 cups) root beer
1/2 cup molasses
1/2 teaspoon plus 1/8 teaspoon baking soda
3/4 cup dark brown sugar

1/4 cup plus 2 tablespoons vegetable oil
3 tablespoons plus 1 teaspoon granulated sugar
One 1-inch piece of fresh ginger, peeled and grated on a microplane or on the finest side of a box grater (1 teaspoon)
2 teaspoons vanilla extract
1 large egg
1 3/4 teaspoons baking powder
1 1/4 teaspoons ground star anise
1 1/2 teaspoons ground cardamom
1/2 whole nutmeg, grated (or 2 teaspoons ground nutmeg)
Finely grated zest of 2 lemons
1 teaspoon kosher salt
1/2 teaspoon fresh-ground black pepper

FOR THE ROOT BEER GLAZE

3/4 cup heavy cream
1 tablespoon sassafras bark (or 1/2 teaspoon sassafras extract; see Note)
2 cups powdered sugar
Pinch of ground star anise
Pinch of ground cardamom
1/4 teaspoon kosher salt
1/4 whole nutmeg, grated (or about 1 teaspoon ground nutmeg)
Finely grated zest of 1/2 lemon

TO MAKE THE CAKE

Preheat the oven to 350°F.

Grease the bottom and sides of a 10-inch cake pan well with some of the butter.

Cut out a piece of parchment paper so it fits closely into the bottom of the cake pan. Line the bottom of the pan with the parchment, and then grease the parchment with more butter.

>>>

Shake 1 tablespoon of the flour into the cake pan, and shake it around so it sticks to the butter. Tap out any excess flour that doesn't stick to the parchment or to the sides of the pan.

Pour the root beer and molasses into a deep medium-sized pot, and bring the mixture to a boil over high heat. (You need those high sides because the baking soda will froth up very high, and you don't want it to spill over! So make sure there's some meaningful space between the liquid and the top of the pot.)

Pull the pot off the heat and whisk in all the baking soda, so it froths up. Then put the pot right in the fridge to cool down a little.

While the root beer mix is cooling down, whisk the brown sugar, vegetable oil, granulated sugar, ginger, and vanilla extract together in a mixing bowl. The mixture will be a little chunky at this point.

Crack the egg into the bowl and whisk well. The egg is what makes everything come together smoothly: you should have a thick paste. Set this aside.

In another mixing bowl, combine rest of the flour with the baking powder, star anise, and cardamom. Grate in the nutmeg and lemon zest, and add the salt and pepper. Whisk everything together so it's well combined.

Take the root beer mixture out of the fridge. Pour a third of the flour mixture into a large mixing bowl; pour in one-third of the root beer mixture, then one-third of the sugar paste. Whisk everything together slowly (so it doesn't splash everywhere), and then add another one-third of the flour, another one-third of the root beer, and so forth, until everything is combined in the bowl. (The mix doesn't need to be completely and smoothly combined until the last of the wet and dry mixtures are in the bowl.) You should have a very wet, almost liquid batter.

Pour the batter into the cake pan, put the pan on a cookie sheet (to catch drips and splashes), and put it on the middle oven rack.

Bake the cake for 45 minutes without opening the oven at all (this cake will sink if you shake it up while it's baking). Check it: the cake should be high and dark brown, with a little bit of spring-back when you touch it (but not too much—it's a very moist cake). If it's not quite ready, rotate the pan and put it back in the oven for another 5 minutes before checking it again. The whole baking process shouldn't take longer than 55 minutes, even in a slow oven.

WHILE THE CAKE IS BAKING, MAKE THE GLAZE
Whisk the cream and sassafras together in a small pot, and bring it up to a boil over medium-high heat.

As soon as it boils, pull the mixture off the heat, pour it into a glass or ceramic container (something that won't crack from the heat), and put it in the fridge. Let the mixture cool for about 30 minutes while the sassafras steeps into the cream, so you have a nice root beer flavor.

In a mixing bowl, combine the powdered sugar, star anise, cardamon, and salt. Grate in the nutmeg and lemon zest, and whisk everything together.

Strain the cooled cream through a fine-mesh strainer into a small mixing bowl (so the sassafras pieces don't end up in the glaze).

Gently whisk 1/2 cup of the cream into the powdered sugar mixture, holding back the last 2 tablespoons to see if you need it. If the mixture is dry and not coming together as a glaze, add more cream. Whisk the mixture well, until you have a shiny, thick liquid.

TO FINISH THE CAKE
When the cake is ready, pull it out of the oven and let it rest for about 5 minutes.

Flip the cake out of the pan onto a serving plate.

Spread the glaze thickly on top of the warm cake with a spoon. The glaze will melt and drip down the sides as you slather it on.

You can serve the cake as soon as it's cooled to room temperature—but like all spice cakes, it's even better the day after you make it. Store it covered at room temperature.

NOTE

···

Sassafras is key in the glaze. I buy it at Kalustyan's, the mind-blowingly-good spice shop on lower Lexington Avenue in New York. If your local specialty store doesn't stock it, you'll be able to get it online—I found it on Amazon. You can substitute extract if you can't get your hands on the bark. I also give a substitute for fresh nutmeg here—but if you can find it, the fresh-grated stuff is way better than the powdered kind.

PEANUT-BUTTER-OATMEAL-CHOCOLATE-CHIP COOKIES

Karen DeMasco, the pastry chef at Locanda Verde, is a genius big-deal award-winning New York pastry queen—but she's also a Midwestern girl at heart, and a Clevelander just like me. That means she loves really old-school American desserts—and nobody, but nobody, makes a better cookie than Karen. This is her version of the classic after-school recipe—only much, much better.

MAKES 30 COOKIES

FOR THE TOASTED OATS
1/2 stick (4 tablespoons) unsalted butter
1 cup rolled oats

FOR THE COOKIES
1 1/2 sticks (12 tablespoons) unsalted butter,
    at room temperature
1/2 cup dark brown sugar
1/2 cup granulated sugar
3/4 cup creamy peanut butter
1 1/2 cups all-purpose flour
2 teaspoons baking soda
2 teaspoons kosher salt
12 ounces (2 cups) chocolate chips

TO MAKE THE TOASTED OATS
Melt the butter in a large sauté pan over medium heat.

Pour the oats into the melted butter and cook, stirring frequently, for about 3 minutes, so that they absorb the butter and toast up. When they're ready, they'll smell toasty—a little bit like popcorn—when you lean in close.

Set the oats aside, off the heat.

TO MAKE THE COOKIES
Preheat the oven to 350°F.

Line 3 baking sheets with parchment paper and set them aside.

Combine the butter, brown sugar, granulated sugar, and peanut butter in the bowl of a tabletop mixer fitted with the whisk attachment. Mix everything together on medium-low speed (#2 on a KitchenAid) for about 3 to 4 minutes, until the mixture is well combined and creamy. Scrape down the sides of the bowl every 30 seconds or so as things mix, so that everything ends up in the bowl.

Meanwhile, in a separate bowl, whisk together the flour, baking soda, and salt.

Add about half of the flour mixture to the peanut butter mixture, and mix on low speed (#1 on a KitchenAid) for about 10 seconds, until the dry stuff is mixed into the wet stuff.

Scrape down the sides of the bowl, add the remaining flour mixture, and mix everything together until you've got a thick doughlike mixture.

Add the toasted oats and chocolate chips, and mix on low speed for another 20 seconds or so, until the dough really comes together. It should be pretty dry.

Use a tablespoon to scoop up rounds of cookie dough, and pop each round onto an ungreased baking sheet.

Use the bottom of a measuring cup to flatten the cookies a little, so they measure 1 1/2 to 2 inches across. (This dough doesn't relax much, so if you don't flatten them out, you'll end up with ball-shaped cookies.)

Bake the cookies for about 8 minutes. Then rotate the baking sheets so that everything will bake evenly, and bake for another 8 minutes or so, until they're a little bit golden around the edges but still soft. (They'll harden more as they cool.)

You can serve these cookies as soon as they've cooled down, or you can store them in an airtight container for 2 or 3 days.

JASMINE RICE PUDDING

Rice pudding is old-school comfort food, eaten, in some form, all over the world. The inspiration for this one, which is dressed up with Thai flavors—cardamom, lemongrass, coriander, mango—comes from the version of a dessert called Sticky Rice with Mango served at Lotus of Siam, a great Thai restaurant in a strip mall in Vegas. The "comfort" in that dish comes from the fact that it cools you down after you set your mouth on fire eating the super-hot Thai food the place serves up.

SERVES 6 TO 8

$1/4$ vanilla bean
3 large strips orange peel, white pith removed
4 cardamom pods
1 cup jasmine rice
One 4-inch piece of lemongrass, cut into 8 pieces
1 quart whole milk (plus extra for thinning
    at the end if necessary)
$1/2$ cup plus 2 tablespoons sugar
$1/2$ teaspoon kosher salt
1 cup sour cream
About $1/4$ teaspoon ground coriander (a pinch for
    each serving)
1 mango, peeled, cut away from the pit, and
    cut into small cubes

Slice the vanilla bean down the middle, scrape the seeds out, and put the pod and seeds in a large pot set over low heat. Add the orange zest, cardamom pods, rice, and lemongrass. Let everything toast for 4 minutes or so, until you can smell the fragrance coming up.

Add $1^1/2$ cups of water to the pot, turn the heat up to medium-low, and let the rice cook at a simmer for about 5 minutes, until most of the water has been absorbed.

Add the milk, cover the pot, turn the heat down to low, and let the rice cook for about 30 minutes, until most of the milk has been absorbed and you can see individual grains of rice at the top of the mixture. Stir every so often to make sure the rice doesn't stick to the bottom of the pot.

Pull the pot off the flame, add the sugar and salt, and stir.

Pour the rice mixture into a metal bowl and put it in the fridge to cool, uncovered, for 30 minutes or so.

When the rice is cool enough to handle, take it out of the fridge and pull out the cardamom pods, vanilla pod, orange zest, and lemongrass pieces. Stir the rice around so it cools evenly, and put it back in the fridge.

When the rice pudding has cooled completely (about 1 hour), take it out of the fridge and mix in the sour cream with a spatula. If the pudding is very thick, you can thin it out with some more milk—$1/2$ cup or so. (The rice pudding will keep for a couple of days in the fridge.)

When you're ready to serve the rice pudding, spoon it into small bowls or shot glasses. Sprinkle a pinch of coriander and a spoonful of mango over each serving.

MOCHA PUDDING

Bill Cosby was right: kids love chocolate pudding. But why should children have all the fun? This pudding is definitely not for the kiddie table: it's all grown up, a dark, coffee-infused adult treat. I love coffee in any form. It's in my blood: my great-grandparents on my dad's side were in the coffee business back in Livorno, Italy. But coffee desserts? Like caffe mocha, the inspiration for this pudding, that's a totally American concept. Whatever: everybody will finish their broccoli when this pudding is dessert.

These puddings are great served very cold, with a big scoop of crème fraîche (which cuts the fat a little) or whipped cream (which just amps up the whole fat thing in a pretty amazing way).

SERVES 6, WITH A LITTLE BIT LEFT OVER

FOR THE COFFEE CREAM
2 cups whole milk
2 cups heavy cream
$1/2$ Bourbon vanilla bean, split lengthwise, seeds scraped out
$1/2$ cup whole coffee beans
$1/4$ cup sugar

FOR THE PUDDING
8 egg yolks
$1/4$ cup sugar
4 ounces bittersweet chocolate
2 ounces unsweetened chocolate
$1/2$ teaspoon kosher salt

TO MAKE THE COFFEE CREAM
Combine the milk, cream, vanilla bean, coffee beans, and sugar in a medium-sized pot, and bring to a boil over medium-high heat.

Pull the pot off the stove, pour the mixture into a bowl, and let it steep in the fridge, uncovered, for at least 30 minutes. (It can hold in the fridge at this point for up to a couple of days. The longer it steeps, the stronger the flavor will be, though if it's going to be in the fridge for a while, you should probably cover it up when it's cooled.)

TO MAKE THE PUDDING
Preheat the oven to 300°F.

Strain the coffee cream mixture through a sieve into a medium-sized saucepan; throw away the coffee beans and the vanilla bean.

Bring the coffee cream up to a boil over medium-high heat (about 8 minutes). Make sure you keep an eye on the pot so the cream doesn't boil over.

Meanwhile, whisk the egg yolks and sugar together in a medium-sized mixing bowl.

Put the bittersweet and unsweetened chocolate into another medium-sized mixing bowl. When the coffee cream comes up to a boil, pour about one third of it over the chocolate and whisk well, so you have a shiny liquid mixture and the chocolate is completely melted. Then whisk in the rest of the coffee cream. (If you add all the cream at the same time, the chocolate will get grainy.)

Whisk about one third of the chocolate mixture into the egg mixture, and then add the egg-and-chocolate mix back to the chocolate bowl and whisk everything together well, so it's a little bit frothy. (The back-and-forth here lets you temper the eggs without cooking them.)

Whisk in the salt.

Strain the mixture through a sieve into another bowl, to make sure there are no egg chunks or unmelted chocolate pieces.

Put 6 coffee cups (or 6-ounce ramekins) inside a large pot, a deep baking pan, or a roasting pan—anything you can cover with tin foil without the foil touching the tops of the cups.

Fill a liquid measuring cup with some of the pudding mixture, and pour 3/4 cup (6 ounces) into each coffee cup. Refill the measuring cup and repeat until there's pudding in every cup.

Add warm water to the pot so it reaches halfway up the sides of the cups. Then cover the pot with foil, leaving it a bit open so you can see what's going on as you move it into the oven (just in case water sloshes or something spills). When you get the puddings into the oven, seal the tin foil up tight, making sure there are no holes, rips, or tears. You want the pudding to steam beneath the foil.

At the half-hour mark, unseal the tin foil to let some of the steam out (so the puddings don't oversteam).

Reseal the tin foil and keep baking the puddings for another 15 minutes. Release some of the steam again, reseal, and keep baking for another 15 minutes.

Check the puddings. If they've firmed up, take them out of the oven; if not, let them go for another 10 minutes. They're done when they jiggle like Jell-o but aren't liquid anymore and a dark ring has formed around the outer edge of each pudding.

Take the pot out of the oven, uncover it, and let the puddings cool down a little, still resting in the water bath. When you're able to handle them, move them out of the pot and into the fridge so they can cool down completely (about 2 hours). Serve 'em with crème fraîche or whipped cream.

SAUCES, DRESSINGS, AND EXTRAS

APPLESAUCE WITH ROSE WATER

You know how when you bring a bag of ripe apples home from the farmers' market, and you open up the bag, and that sweet-tart aroma drifts out and fills your kitchen? Well, to me, the scent of roses is a big part of that delicious smell. So when I make recipes with fresh apples, I like to add a splash of rose water at the end, to reintroduce that kitchen-filling aroma. This applesauce is great with the Cider-Glazed Rack of Pork (page 149); it's also my favorite side for homemade pierogies (page 202).

MAKES ABOUT 4 CUPS

3 pounds apples (Winesaps are my favorite; Gala and McIntosh are good here, too), cored, peeled, and chopped into $1/2$-inch chunks
3 cups apple cider
Pinch of ground cinnamon
Pinch of ground nutmeg
Juice of 3 lemons (about $1/4$ cup)
$1/2$ teaspoon rose water

Mix the apples, cider, cinnamon, and nutmeg together in a large pot, and cook over medium-high heat.

At about the 3-minute mark, as the apples and spices begin to cook, squeeze the lemons through a strainer into a bowl (so the seeds don't end up in the apple sauce) and add the lemon juice to the pot. Mix everything together and keep cooking, uncovered, until the apple mixture comes up to a simmer.

Turn the heat down to medium and keep cooking for about 45 minutes, until all the liquid has been soaked up and the apples are soft and glistening.

Pull the pot off the heat, add the rose water, and mix well. You can serve the applesauce as soon as it cools down; it will keep, covered, for a couple of weeks in the fridge.

FIG CHUTNEY

At the end of the fig season in late August, the Mission figs from California are supersoft and full of sugar. That's the best time to make this chutney. You want figs that are actually overripe, so they're soft and mushy inside, a little more brown than pink in color. I love this chutney with good cheese; you can serve it with grilled meats; or you can just spread it on toast to have with your morning coffee.

MAKES 2 QUARTS

2 pounds black Mission figs
1/2 cup white wine vinegar
1 cup red wine vinegar
1 cup light brown sugar
1/2 teaspoon salt
2 teaspoons sweet paprika
1 tablespoon mustard seed
1/4 teaspoon crushed red pepper flakes
1 small onion, diced superfine (3/4 cup)
One 2-inch piece of fresh ginger, peeled and
    minced fine (about 2 tablespoons)

Cut off the stem of each fig, shave off the base of the fig, and then cut the fig into eighths.

Combine both vinegars with the brown sugar, salt, paprika, mustard seed, and red pepper flakes in a large, deep saucepan and bring the mixture up to a boil, stirring so that the sugar dissolves.

Add the figs, onions, and ginger to the pot, and stir everything together. Keep the mixture simmering on a low bubble for about 45 minutes, until the liquid is reduced by about three fourths and everything is coated in a shiny glaze. The chutney will taste pretty strong, but don't worry: it's going to mellow as it cools. By the time you serve it cold, the flavors will be perfect.

Let the chutney cool to room temperature on the countertop; then scoop it into an airtight container and let it cool in the fridge overnight. It's good to go the next day. You can store it in a plastic bag in the freezer or in a mason jar in the fridge for up to a month.

GRECO'S BARBECUE SAUCE

Matt Greco and I started working together at Café Boulud when he was a hardcore kid straight out of Fredericksburg, Texas; now he's got his own place, a restaurant in Brooklyn called Char No. 4, serving some of the best American food in New York. Matt comes from a serious barbecue family—his dad's pit is the stuff of legends—and his barbecue sauce is the best I've ever had, an unbelievable combo of sweetness, spice, and smoke. It's great on grilled chicken, roast pork, ribs . . . I even put it on baked potatoes.

This isn't a sauce you want to throw together the day you're serving it: you want to make it at least a day in advance, so there's time for the flavors to meld. You can keep the sauce in the fridge for up to 2 weeks, or in the freezer for up to 6 months. It's great with my Mac-'n-Cheese-Stuffed Meatloaf (page 143).

MAKES ABOUT 1 QUART

2 tablespoons corn oil
1 large Vidalia or other sweet onion, sliced
    (about 2 cups)
Two 28-ounce cans crushed tomatoes
One 12-ounce bottle of beer (Matt likes Shiner Bock,
    but you can use any amber beer)
One 12-ounce can of Dr Pepper
1 cup ketchup
1/4 cup Worcestershire sauce
1/2 cup apple cider vinegar
1/4 cup molasses
1/2 cup dark brown sugar
1 tablespoon ground cumin
1 tablespoon chili powder
5 canned chipotle peppers in adobo
8 cloves garlic, peeled and crushed
Juice of 2 lemons (5 tablespoons)

Heat the oil in a large saucepan over medium-high heat. Add the onions and slowly caramelize them for about 10 to 15 minutes, stirring occasionally to keep them from sticking to the pan. Turn the heat down to medium as the onions cook, to avoid burning.

In a large saucepot, stir together all of the other ingredients except the lemon juice.

When the onions are caramelized, add them to the mixture in the saucepot. Turn the heat to medium-high and allow the mixture to come to a boil.

Turn the heat down to a low boil, and let the sauce simmer for about an hour, until it reduces and the flavors come together. Stir the sauce every so often and scrape the sides of the pot down with a spatula every 15 minutes or so, to make sure that anything that splashes onto the sides doesn't burn, drop into the pot, and flavor the sauce.

When the sauce has thickened up, pull it off the heat and use a hand blender to blend it up right in the pot. You want to really break down the chipotle peppers, onions, and garlic, bringing everything together so you have a thick, smooth paste. (You can also puree the sauce in a blender.)

Stir in the lemon juice. Blend everything together with the hand blender once more, to make sure the sauce is smooth and well combined. The sauce should be brick-red, rich, tangy, sweet and spicy, with just a little kick of citrus for balance.

GREEK DRESSING

In New York City, every single diner has a Greek salad on the menu. I love a big Greek salad, and I've eaten them in a million diners, but I've never found a joint where the dressing is as good as the feta, the vegetables, and the anchovies. So when I decided, one summer afternoon, to make a Greek salad at home with some really juicy tomatoes and super-fresh vegetables from the farmers' market, I wanted to fix that problem. I turned to this old recipe of mine from back in the day. It's great as a dressing for Greek salad, but it also makes a really delicious dip for raw vegetables or topping for sandwiches: I like to pour it on my Sunday afternoon roast-turkey-and-tomato.

MAKES I CUP, ENOUGH FOR 4 SALADS

1/4 cup extra-virgin olive oil
3 shallots, diced small (about 1/4 cup)
1/8 teaspoon crushed red pepper flakes
1 clove garlic, diced small (about 1/2 teaspoon)
1/2 teaspoon ground coriander
1/4 teaspoon ground fennel seed
1/4 teaspoon ground cumin
1 teaspoon dried oregano (preferably dried
    on the branch)
2 teaspoons Dijon mustard
Juice of 2 limes (about 1/4 cup)
1/2 cup Greek yogurt (I like Fage brand; you can
    use nonfat if you want, as long as it's thick)

Heat the olive oil in a small saucepan over low heat.

Add the shallots and let them cook for a minute or so, until they just start to soften.

Meanwhile, use a heavy knife to chop the red pepper flakes, or crush them up with the side of the knife.

Add the garlic to the saucepan and cook the mixture for another minute, until the garlic softens up and releases its aroma. The garlic will burn pretty fast if you don't keep an eye on it, and if that happens you'll need to start again, so keep stirring!

Pull the pan off the heat and stir in the coriander, fennel, cumin, crushed chile flakes, and dried oregano. Then add the mustard and stir everything together well so you have a thick, pastelike mixture.

Scrape the mixture into a small mixing bowl. It should smell good—a mustardy, spicy, garlicky mix.

Add the lime juice, yogurt, and 1/4 cup of water, and whisk everything together well. Put the dressing in the fridge to cool it down before you serve it. The dressing will keep in the fridge for a couple of days.

MUSTARD SAUCE

You know how really delicious French sauces are always full of cream and butter? Well, this is a French sauce on a diet. It's still delicious, but it's thickened up with good old American cornstarch, so you don't need all that dairy. Don't worry: I'm not going all health-foody on you—I'm just balancing out the pecan-crusted codfish, which has a ton of butter in it. (Nice, right? The sauce is light; it's the fish you've got to watch out for.) It's great with chicken and steak, too.

MAKES 1 CUP

³/₄ cup chicken broth or water
2 teaspoons cornstarch
2 tablespoons Dijon mustard
2 tablespoons stone-ground mustard
1 tablespoon honey
Pinch of salt
Pinch of fresh-ground black pepper

Heat the chicken broth in a small saucepan over medium-high heat.

Meanwhile, in a small bowl, stir the cornstarch together with 3 tablespoons of cold water. (You're making a slurry, because if you just dump the cornstarch into the hot broth, you'll end up with cornstarch lumps, which is no good.)

When the broth comes up to a boil, drizzle in the cornstarch slurry while whisking the broth.

When you've added all the slurry, lower the heat to a simmer and whisk for another few seconds, until everything is combined.

Let the mixture cook for 2 minutes, so that the starch cooks out and the liquid thickens up.

Pull the saucepan off the heat and add both mustards and the honey, whisking them in well. Season the sauce with the salt and pepper. Serve it up while it's warm.

NOTE

You can make this sauce ahead of time and hold it in the fridge, but the cornstarch will really thicken up as it cools, so make sure you warm the sauce up slowly on the stove to get it back to the right consistency. You might have to add a little bit of water to get it to come back together.

NEW ORLEANS RÉMOULADE

Your standard-issue rémoulade is a French sauce, a lot like an American tartar sauce; it's usually white and made with eggs and mayonnaise. But in New Orleans, people love their red rémoulade, which is tomato-based and egg-free and goes great with the shrimp and crab people eat by the pound down there. This is a variation on my favorite New Orleans rémoulade: the version they used to serve at the long-lost Uglesich's restaurant (see Anthony's Slaw, page 170, for more on this New Orleans institution). This is a great side for my shrimp recipe on page 102: it's sweet, spicy, smoky, and fresh-tasting, all at once. It's also stupid-easy.

MAKES 4 CUPS

2 celery stalks, diced fine (1 cup)
4 green onions, diced fine (1 cup)
1/4 cup fresh parsley leaves, chopped fine
1/2 onion, diced fine (1/2 cup)
2 cups canned tomato puree (I like Jersey Fresh)
1 cup ketchup
1/2 cup Creole mustard or other grainy mustard
3 tablespoons prepared horseradish
3 tablespoons Worcestershire sauce
1 tablespoon Tabasco sauce
1/3 cup red wine vinegar
1 tablespoon sugar
2 teaspoons sweet paprika
1/2 cup corn oil or grapeseed oil
Juice of 2 lemons (5 tablespoons)

Combine all the ingredients in a large bowl, and stir well.

Serve this right away, with shrimp (or you can hold it in the fridge for up to 4 days).

PICKLED CHERRIES

Pickled cherries may sound kind of strange, but they're pretty great: the contrast between the rich, sweet cherries and the tang of the vinegar is what makes this recipe go. You can use either sweet or sour cherries–both are delicious. The cherries make a great condiment for meat dishes; they're good with terrines or pâtés, tossed in a salad, or just on their own, for snacking.

MAKES ABOUT 2 QUARTS

2 pounds cherries (sweet or sour), pitted, stems
  removed
2 cups white vinegar
$^1/_2$ cup sugar
1 cinnamon stick
5 black peppercorns
1 bay leaf
1 whole piece star anise
2 allspice berries (or a pinch of ground allspice)
Pinch of crushed red pepper flakes
$^1/_2$ teaspoon fennel seeds
10 coriander seeds (or a pinch of ground coriander)

Pour the cherries into a large heatproof mixing bowl.

In a large pot, combine the vinegar, sugar, and $^1/_2$ cup water. Whisk everything together well, and bring the mixture to a boil over high heat.

Add all the spices to the pot, and whisk to make sure there's no sugar left on the bottom.

Pull the pot off the heat and pour the hot liquid over the cherries.

Pour the cherries into a storage container. I like to pickle the cherries in a glass mason jar, but you can really use any kind of jar with a good top. Whatever you're using, cool the cherries in the fridge without the lid on.

When the cherries have completely cooled, close the jar. You don't need to worry about making the jar seal airtight as long as you store the cherries in the fridge, because there's so much acidity in the pickling liquid that it kills any bacteria. The cherries will keep in the fridge for up to 6 months.

PICKLED JALAPEÑOS

There's a lot you can do with pickled jalapeños. They're a kick-ass accompaniment to fish dishes; the pickling liquid is really good for salad dressings; the onions are delicious chopped up in sauces; and they're the secret ingredient in Anthony's Slaw (page 170). It's a great condiment to have around.

MAKES 2 QUARTS

3 cups rice vinegar

1 cup sugar

1 medium onion, quartered

3 cloves garlic, peeled and crushed

1 1/2 pounds fresh jalapeño peppers (about 20 jalapeños)

In a large pot, combine the rice vinegar, sugar, onions, garlic cloves, and 1 cup of water. Bring the mixture to a boil over high heat and let it cook, uncovered, for about 10 minutes, until the flavors meld and the onions and garlic have softened up. The garlic might turn blue while it cooks. Don't worry about it: that just means you bruised it when you crushed it.

While the liquid cooks, prick each jalapeño all over, 8 times or so, with the tip of a sharp knife, deep enough to pierce the skin. This way, some of the pickling juice will actually get inside the pepper. (Make sure to wash your hands after you do this—and trust me, you don't want to rub your eyes.)

Put the jalapeños in a glass jar or other noncorrosible container, and ladle the hot vinegar mix (including the onions and garlic) over the peppers. You're going to be crying for sure as you do this, so get ready (and remember to wash your hands again).

Let the mixture cool until the jar is just warm to the touch, and then put it in the fridge with the lid on. The jalapeños should sit overnight—at least 8 hours—before you use them. They'll keep in the fridge for up to 2 months.

PICKLED RAMPS

You don't see crocuses coming up or baby birds hatching in New York City, but there are still some pretty reliable signs that spring has finally arrived. The one I look for is when the ramps show up in the Greenmarket. They're pretty much the first edible thing that comes up in the Northeast, so when you see them piled on the tables at the farmers' market, winter is officially over. Ramps are a wild leek in the allium family (their relatives include garlic, onions, leeks, and green onions, and they look like tough-guy green onions). They grow wild all over the East Coast and the Southeast, in wet forested areas. I first learned about ramps when I worked in a resort up in the Virginia mountains for the summer season when I was nineteen: the local guys used to pick them and sell them to the resort kitchen. Once I got to know them, they took me out and showed me some of their spots; I learned how to pick ramps, and in the resort kitchen, I learned how to pickle them and how to sauté them. In 1993, I was cooking at Lespinasse when a farmer walked into our four-star, super-fancy New York kitchen with some of those fresh, delicious hillbilly ramps—and a jar of the pickled stuff. I've made them in the spring ever since then.

You can use pickled ramps in dressings and sauces; they're great with terrines, wild game, and seafood. I use these in my skate recipe (page 86).

MAKES 2 QUARTS

2 pounds fresh ramps
5 cups rice vinegar
1 1/2 cups sugar
1 1/2 teaspoons fennel seeds
1 tablespoon coriander seeds (or 1/2 teaspoon ground coriander)
1 cinnamon stick (or 1/8 teaspoon ground cinnamon)
1/4 teaspoon crushed red pepper flakes
3 allspice berries
1 teaspoon whole black peppercorns (or 1/2 teaspoon ground black pepper)
2 bay leaves

Put a large pot of salted water on to boil. Fill a large bowl with ice and cold water, and set it aside.

With a small paring knife, cut the roots off the bottoms of the ramps.

Peel the outside layer of skin back, as you would with a green onion, and then wash the ramps really well. It might take two or three washes to get them clean, since they grow wild in the dirt.

Trim the ramps right where the green leaves start. Hang on to the leaves—you can use them for other dishes, like Baked Eggs with Asparagus and Ramps (page 248).

When the water comes to a boil, drop the ramp stems in, pressing them down with a wooden spoon to make sure they're all covered by the water.

Allow the ramps to cook on high heat, uncovered, until their color starts to fade and they soften up a little bit (1 1/2 to 2 minutes or so). Your cooking time here will depend on the size of your ramps, which depends on when they're picked—so keep an eye on them. You don't want them supersoft.

Pull the ramps out of the water with a strainer or spider, and put them in the ice water bath, so they stop cooking.

Pour the water out of the cooking pot, and pour the rice vinegar in its place. Add the sugar, whisk to combine, and bring the mixture up to a boil.

Pull the pot off the heat and add all of the spices and the bay leaves.

I like to pickle the ramps in a glass mason jar, but you don't have to: any kind of jar will do. Put the ramps in the jar and pour the hot liquid right and seasonings over them; then let them cool in the fridge with the lid off.

When the ramps have cooled completely, close the jar. You don't need to worry about making the jar seal airtight because there's so much acidity in the pickling liquid that it kills any bacteria, as long as they're stored in the fridge. They'll keep there for up to 6 months.

PICKLED RED CABBAGE

This is an old dish of mine that I like to have around in the wintertime. The cabbage tastes sweet, savory, and a little bit like licorice (that's from the star anise). It's good with wild game, chopped up and put into slaws, or as an accompaniment for roasted beets.

MAKES ABOUT 2 QUARTS

1 head red cabbage
2 teaspoons salt
4 cups white vinegar
1 1/2 cups sugar
1 cinnamon stick
1 teaspoon fennel seeds
2 whole pieces star anise
1/4 teaspoon crushed red pepper flakes
2 tablespoons coriander seeds
1 teaspoon whole black peppercorns
2 bay leaves

Quarter the cabbage, cut off the stem and the core from each quarter, and pull off any brown or soft leaves. Slice each quarter so that you end up with thin slices that will fall apart into ribbons.

Pile the cut cabbage into a big bowl. Add the salt and mix it in with your hands, so that the salt coats the cabbage.

Put a plate that's slightly smaller than the bowl on top of the cabbage, and then cover the whole thing with plastic wrap. Let the cabbage sit in the fridge overnight (or at least 8 hours). The salt will draw the water out of the cabbage, and the plate will weight the cabbage down and help press the water out. This takes out some of the overly cabbagy, strong flavor.

The next day, move the cabbage from the salting bowl to a mason jar or an earthenware pot, squeezing the water out with your hands as you go (like you're squeezing a sponge). You should end up with about 1/2 cup of water on the bottom of the bowl. Toss the water down the sink, and set the cabbage aside in the jar or pot.

In a medium-sized saucepot, combine the vinegar, sugar, and 2 cups of water. Bring the mixture to a boil over medium-high heat.

Meanwhile, lay a piece of cheesecloth out flat and pile all of the spices and the bay leaves in the middle. Tie the cheesecloth closed in a bundle and add it to the cabbage jar. (If you don't have any cheesecloth, you can just put the spices directly in with the cabbage, but you'll need to warn people about biting down on spice pieces.)

When the vinegar mixture boils, pour it right over the cabbage and spices. Let it cool in the fridge with the lid off.

When the cabbage has cooled completely, close the jar and put it back in the fridge. It will pickle overnight (about 12 hours). You don't need to worry about making the jar seal airtight because the acidity in the pickling liquid kills any bacteria, as long as it's stored in the fridge. It will keep there for up to 6 months.

THANKSGIVING FIG AND HAZELNUT STUFFING

People think of stuffing as the ultimate American dish—something you can't do Thanksgiving without, probably invented by a pioneer with a Cuisinart. But it's interesting: if you research the historical roots of stuffing, it turns out that the earliest records come up in cookbooks from back in Roman times—so you could say that stuffing was invented by the Italians. I've been doing this stuffing on Thanksgiving in my Italian restaurants for the last few years. It's Thanksgiving fusion food, I guess. (Think about all the possibilities: Thai stuffing! Chinese stuffing! Argentinian stuffing! You could really get creative here.)

My recipe is based on the idea that there will also be a turkey somewhere in your kitchen, waiting to be stuffed; since turkeys vary so much in size, you can fill the cavity and then bake the rest of the stuffing on the side. If you don't have a turkey lying around, you can always just bake the stuffing without stuffing it into anything at all.

MAKES ENOUGH FOR 1 TURKEY,
PLUS SOME ON THE SIDE

2 cups dried figs, stems cut off, cut into roughly
    8 pieces each
1 cup Frangelico (amaretto, whiskey, or bourbon will
    also do the trick)
One 2-pound loaf ciabiatta or other rustic Italian
    bread, crust left on, cut into 1 1/2-inch chunks
    (about 12 cups)
1/3 cup extra-virgin olive oil
1 pound sweet Italian sausage, casings removed
3/4 stick (6 tablespoons) unsalted butter
2 medium onions, diced (about 2 cups)
2 celery stalks, chopped (about 1 cup)
3/4 cup hazelnuts, chopped
2 tablespoons fresh thyme leaves
2 teaspoons dried sage
5 cups chicken broth

1/2 teaspoon salt
1/4 teaspoon coarse-ground black pepper
1/4 cup fresh celery leaves, chopped

Preheat the oven to 400°F.

Put the figs in a bowl and pour the Frangelico over them. Add 1 cup of hot water, and set the figs aside to hydrate on the countertop, uncovered.

Spread the bread chunks on a baking sheet and toast them on the middle oven rack for about 10 minutes, just until they start to crisp up. Then pull them out of the oven and hold them on the countertop.

Heat the olive oil in a large saucepan over medium-high heat. Add the sausage and brown the sausage for about 3 minutes, breaking it up with a wooden spoon as it cooks so there aren't any big lumps.

Pull the sausage out of the pan onto a plate using a slotted spoon, then put the pan back on the fire on medium-low.

Add the butter, onions, and celery to the pan, and let them cook for 2 minutes or so, until the onions start to soften.

Add the sausage back to the pan, then add the toasted bread, the figs and their liquid, the hazelnuts, thyme, sage, chicken broth, salt, and pepper. Stir everything together until the bread absorbs the liquid.

Stuff your turkey cavity with as much stuffing as it will hold, and proceed to cook the turkey.

Spoon the rest of the stuffing into a greased baking pan, and bake it at 325°F for 1 hour, until the top is a little bit crispy and the inside is delicious. Garnish the stuffing with the celery leaves, and serve it alongside your turkey.

INDEX

Note: Page references in *italics* indicate recipe photographs.